A CULTURAL HISTORY OF PEACE

VOLUME 1

A Cultural History of Peace
General Editor: Ronald Edsforth

Volume 1
A Cultural History of Peace in Antiquity
Edited by Sheila L. Ager

Volume 2
A Cultural History of Peace in the Medieval Age
Edited by Walter Simons

Volume 3
A Cultural History of Peace in the Renaissance
Edited by Isabella Lazzarini

Volume 4
A Cultural History of Peace in the Age of Enlightenment
Edited by Stella Ghervas and David Armitage

Volume 5
A Cultural History of Peace in the Age of Empire
Edited by Ingrid Sharp

Volume 6
A Cultural History of Peace in the Modern Age
Edited by Ronald Edsforth

A CULTURAL HISTORY
OF PEACE

IN ANTIQUITY

Edited by Sheila L. Ager

BLOOMSBURY ACADEMIC
LONDON · NEW YORK · OXFORD · NEW DELHI · SYDNEY

BLOOMSBURY ACADEMIC
Bloomsbury Publishing Plc
50 Bedford Square, London, WC1B 3DP, UK
1385 Broadway, New York, NY 10018, USA
29 Earlsfort Terrace, Dublin 2, Ireland

BLOOMSBURY, BLOOMSBURY ACADEMIC and the Diana logo are trademarks of
Bloomsbury Publishing Plc

First published in Great Britain 2020
This edition published in Great Britain, 2024

Copyright © Bloomsbury Publishing, 2020

Sheila L. Ager has asserted her right under the Copyright, Designs and Patents Act, 1988,
to be identified as Editor of this work.

Cover image © Paolo Cordelli / Getty Images

All rights reserved. No part of this publication may be reproduced or transmitted i
n any form or by any means, electronic or mechanical, including photocopying,
recording, or any information storage or retrieval system, without prior permission
in writing from the publishers.

Bloomsbury Publishing Plc does not have any control over, or responsibility for, any
third-party websites referred to or in this book. All internet addresses given in this
book were correct at the time of going to press. The author and publisher regret
any inconvenience caused if addresses have changed or sites have ceased to
exist, but can accept no responsibility for any such changes.

A catalogue record for this book is available from the British Library.

A catalog record for this book is available from the Library of Congress.

ISBN: HB: 978-1-4742-3846-5
PB: 978-1-3503-8572-6
Set: 978-1-3503-8603-7

Series: The Cultural Histories Series

Typeset by RefineCatch Limited, Bungay, Suffolk
Printed and bound in Great Britain

To find out more about our authors and books visit www.bloomsbury.com
and sign up for our newsletters.

CONTENTS

List of Illustrations		vi
General Editor's Preface		x
	Introduction *Sheila L. Ager*	1
1	Definitions of Peace *Sarah Bolmarcich*	19
2	Human Nature, Peace, and War *Kurt A. Raaflaub*	37
3	Peace, War, and Gender *Lynette Mitchell*	55
4	Peace, Pacifism, and Religion *Julia Wilker*	71
5	Representations of Peace *Judith Fletcher*	89
6	Peace Movements *Craige B. Champion*	107
7	Peace, Security, and Deterrence *Jason Crowley and Cecilia Ricci*	125
8	Peace as Integration *Paul Burton*	143
Notes		161
Abbreviations and Bibliography		173
Contributors		195
Index		197

ILLUSTRATIONS

INTRODUCTION

0.1 The *soros* (burial mound) of the 192 Athenians killed at the Battle of Marathon; Marathon, Attica, Greece.   2

0.2 The coronation of Charlemagne depicted in a medieval French manuscript.   2

0.3 Ramesses III smiting his enemies on the wall of his mortuary temple at Medinet Habu; Luxor, Egypt.   5

0.4 The Battle at the Milvian Bridge between Constantine and Maxentius, by Gianfrancesco Penni (1496–1528); Vatican, Italy.   8

0.5 Relief from the Arch of Titus commemorating the Roman victory in the Jewish War of 66–73 CE; Rome, Italy.   13

CHAPTER 1

1.1 Engraving from *Crabb's Historical Dictionary* (1825) depicting the Athenian rhetorician Isokrates.   24

1.2 Ivory head from the royal tombs of Vergina thought to depict Philip II of Macedon; Archaeological Museum, Thessaloniki, Greece.   25

1.3 Aeneas arrives in Latium, offering an olive branch to King Evander and his son Pallas; detail from the *Stories of Aeneas*, by Pietro da Cortona (1596–1669); Palazzo Doria Pamphili, Rome, Italy.   29

1.4 The first Roman emperor, Augustus, wearing an oak leaf crown; Glyptothek Museum, Munich, Germany.   30

1.5a and 1.5b Aureus of the Emperor Gallienus (r. 253–268 CE); on the obverse, portrait of Gallienus; on the reverse, image of Peace holding branch and sceptre, with legend PAX AVGVSTA. ANS 1944.100.30853.   32

CHAPTER 2

2.1 A Roman coin of the imperial period, with two clasped hands and the legend CONCORDIA AVGG ("Harmony of the Emperors").   41

2.2 Cuneiform copy of the peace treaty signed between the Egyptians and the Hittites after the Battle of Kadesh; Archaeological Museum, Istanbul, Turkey.   48

ILLUSTRATIONS

2.3 Terracotta warriors and horses from the army arranged in large pits near the mausoleum of the first Chinese emperor, Qin Shihuangdi; Xi'an, Shaanxi province, China. 49

2.4 Moche (Mochica) ceramic pot vessel in the form of a warrior clubbing a submissive man over the head; private collection, Lima, Peru. 50

2.5 Greek relief sculpture (fifth century BCE) depicting men rowing a trireme, a Greek warship (the so-called "Lenormant Relief"); National Archaeological Museum, Athens, Greece. 52

CHAPTER 3

3.1 *Andromache intercepting Hector at the Scaean Gate*, by Fernando Castelli, 1811; Pinacoteca di Brera, Milan, Italy. 56

3.2 Attic white-ground lekythos depicting a departing warrior being handed his armour by his wife or mother, fifth century BCE; National Archaeological Museum, Athens, Greece. 58

3.3a Attic white-ground lekythos depicting a woman handing spear and helmet to a dead warrior seated at his tomb, fifth century BCE. 60

3.3b Line drawing of Figure 3.3a; from Ernest Arthur Gardner, *A Catalogue of Greek Vases in the Fitzwilliam Museum*, Cambridge University Press, 1897, plate xxxi. 61

3.4 *Queen Zenobia's Last Look on Palmyra*, by Herbert Schmalz, 1888; Art Gallery of South Australia, Adelaide, Australia. 63

3.5 *The Intervention of the Sabine Women*, by Jacques-Louis David, 1799; Louvre Museum, Paris, France. 67

CHAPTER 4

4.1 Votive relief sculpture of Ares with Aphrodite, fifth century BCE; National Archaeological Museum, Venice, Italy. 74

4.2 Bronze sculpture of Athena wearing a crested war helmet, fourth century BCE; National Archaeological Museum, Athens, Greece. 75

4.3a and 4.3b Gold coin of the emperor Nero, 64/5 CE; portrait of Nero on obverse, depiction of Temple of Janus with doors closed on reverse. BM 1946.1004.43. 79

4.4 Remains of the Temple of Mars Ultor (Mars the Avenger) in the Augustan Forum, Rome, Italy. 80

4.5a and 4.5b Gold coin of the emperor Vespasian, 75 CE; portrait of Vespasian on obverse, figure of Pax, holding branch in right hand and sceptre in left hand, on reverse. 82

viii ILLUSTRATIONS

CHAPTER 5

5.1 The Shield of Achilles (Scuda di Achille), from Giulio Ferrario, *Il Costume Antico e Moderno di tutti i Popoli* ("The Ancient and Modern Costume of All Nations"), 1831. 90

5.2 Roman copy of the fourth-century BCE Greek statue of Eirēnē holding the infant Ploutos, by Kephisodotos; Glyptothek Museum, Munich, Germany. 94

5.3a and 5.3b Cistophoric coin issued in Ephesos, 28–20 BCE. Obverse: portrait of Augustus with legend IMP CAESAR DIVI F COS VI LIBERTATIS P R VINDEX; reverse: figure of Pax holding caduceus in right hand, within wreath. RIC I (2nd edn) Augustus 476, ANS 1944.100.39180. 100

5.4 The "Tellus Panel" from the Ara Pacis Augustae, first century BCE; Rome, Italy. 102

5.5 Sculptural group depicting the members of the tetrarchy, the four emperors, early fourth century CE; now in St. Mark's Basilica, Venice, Italy. 104

CHAPTER 6

6.1 Engraving showing T. Quinctius Flamininus granting the Greeks their freedom (the "Isthmian Proclamation"). 117

6.2 Portrait of a Hellenistic king, often identified as Antiochos III (r. 223–187 BCE); Louvre Museum, Paris, France. 118

6.3 Detail of the breastplate of the Prima Porta statue of Augustus, depicting the return of the legionary standards lost to the Parthians; Vatican Museum, Vatican City, Italy. 121

6.4 Engraving from *The Pictorial History of Scotland* (1859) depicting Calgacus delivering his speech to the Caledonians before the Battle of Mons Graupius. 122

CHAPTER 7

7.1 Relief sculpture of the goddess Athena contemplating a gravestone (?), known as the "Mourning Athena", fifth century BCE; National Archaeological Museum, Athens, Greece. 126

7.2 Vase painting depicting hoplite warriors in phalanx formation, seventh century BCE (the "Chigi Vase"); National Etruscan Museum, Villa Giulia, Rome, Italy. 129

7.3 Athenian grave stele with relief sculpture of a cavalryman, known as the Dexileos Stele, fourth century BCE; Kerameikos Museum, Athens, Greece. 130

ILLUSTRATIONS   ix

7.4 *The Battle of Lake Regillus*, by Tommaso Laureti, 1587–1594; Capitoline
     Museums, Rome, Italy. Google Art Project.   134

7.5 Portrait of Tiberius and Gaius Gracchus, by Jean-Baptiste Guillaume,
     1848–1853; Musée D'Orsay, Paris, France.   135

7.6a and 7.6b Coin of Nero (64–68 CE); obverse: head of Nero and legend
     NERO CLAVD CAESAR AVG GER P M TR P IMP P P; reverse: figure
     of Securitas, seated right, on throne, resting head against right hand and
     holding short sceptre in left; in front, lighted and garlanded altar, legend
     SECVRITAS AVGVSTI S C II. *RIC* 1 (2nd edn) Nero 406, ANS
     1957.172.1548.   139

CHAPTER 8

8.1 The ancient Near East in the Bronze Age. From Wittke et al. (eds.),
     Historical Atlas of the Ancient World, 2009.   145

8.2 Bas-relief of a four-winged guardian figure representing Cyrus the Great;
     Pasargadae, Fars, Iran.   147

8.3 Naophoros statue of Udjahorresnet, showing part also of the
     hieroglyphic record of his deeds; from Ippolito Rosellini, *Monuments of
     Egypt and Nubia*, 1832–1844.   148

8.4 Portrait of Alexander the Great, fourth century BCE; Archaeological
     Museum, Pella, Greece.   150

8.5 The Roman Empire. From Boatwright (2012) *The Romans: From Village
     to Empire* (2nd ed.).   153

GENERAL EDITOR'S PREFACE

RONALD EDSFORTH

When people learn that I study and teach peace history, they often look puzzled and ask me, "Does peace have a history?" *A Cultural History of Peace* is an emphatically positive response to that question. Yes, peace has a history. The original scholarly essays collected in these six volumes clearly show that peace always has been an important human concern. More precisely, these essays demonstrate that what we recognize today as peace thinking and peace imagining, peace seeking and peace making, peace keeping and peace building have long recorded histories that stretch from antiquity to the twenty-first century. All of us who have contributed to *A Cultural History of Peace* believe that present and future generations should have the opportunity to recognize and understand the importance of this peace history.

Very few universities and colleges had a faculty who taught and researched peace history before the end of the Cold War. Even today, most professors who do peace history moved into it from other specializations in History or other academic disciplines. Most contributors to *A Cultural History of Peace* are professional historians, but Anthropology, Sociology, Political Science, Journalism, Art History, Religion, and Classical Studies are also represented. These fifty-six contributors work on four continents in thirteen different countries. Their participation in this project tells us that peace history has earned a global recognition in academia that not so long ago was unimaginable. Their essays build upon prior scholarship, but they are also introducing new research and new interpretations. As a whole *A Cultural History of Peace* highlights our humanity, something that has been for too long overshadowed in history by the inhumanity of war and other forms of violent conflict. Pursuing answers to new and seldom asked questions, these collected essays expand our knowledge of when, how, and why people in the past pursued peace within their own societies and peaceable relations with people from other societies.

The South African novelist Nadine Gordimer wisely observes, "The past is valid only in relation to whether the present recognises it." (2007: 7) In other words, what happened in the past is not necessarily history. History is made when scholars produce meaningful answers to the questions they ask about the past. The past cannot change, but history can and does change when scholars ask new questions, and when they use previously undiscovered or ignored evidence to develop new interpretations of the past. Evidence of what people said or did, or said they did, are basic materials out of which scholars shape answers to questions like "Does peace have a history?" Of course, to answer this particular question about the past, we must have in mind some definition of peace. Like most people we probably immediately think of peace as *not war*, a classic definition that describes peace in negative terms, as an absence of the type of violent conflicts that still loom so large in popular histories and stories about the past. The American psychologist and peace activist William James succinctly summed up this common way of framing of the past, simply stating, "History is a bath of blood." (1910: 1)

James' description of history still plays well in a world that during the last century experienced the massive casualties and devastation of two world wars, genocides, and

GENERAL EDITOR'S PREFACE

numerous civil wars, as well the fears created by transnational terrorism and still-threatening nuclear arsenals. And significantly, a bath of blood framing continues to shape the priorities of most mainstream reporting of the news from around the world—"if it bleeds it leads"—when, in fact, most people today live in zones of peace where their lives are not threatened by violent political conflict. A human being's chances of dying in war have been historically low in this century, and in striking contrast to the peaks of worldwide violence reached during the global conflicts of the twentieth century. (https://ourworldindata.org/war-and[JR1]-peace) Yet so accustomed are we with framing history *and* the present as a bath of blood, most of us have difficulty comprehending these facts. Steven Pinker recently noted this problem in the preface to *The Better Angels of Our Nature: Why Violence Has Declined,* saying, "Believe it or not—and I know that most people do not—violence has declined over long stretches of time, and today we might be living in the most peaceable era in our species' existence." (2011: xvi) It is not just a coincidence that the rapid growth and globalization of peace studies has happened since the end of the Cold War. Undoubtedly, some of questions raised in *A Cultural History of Peace* have been influenced by the extraordinary recent decline of interstate warfare and resolution of many longstanding civil wars.

A Cultural History of Peace demonstrates that for several thousand years peace has been regarded as a highly desirable social condition, perhaps most especially when the violence and cruelty of war have been in the ascendency. Describing this collection of peace history essays as a cultural history—rather than social, political, diplomatic, or international history—is appropriate because throughout history peace has emerged from the cultures of groups, societies, and nations that developed practical ways to peaceably settle serious conflicts. Here I employ the broad environmental definition of culture that psychiatrist and classics scholar Jonathan Shay uses in his brilliant book, *Achilles in Vietnam*: "Our animal nature, our biological nature, is to live in relation to other people. The natural environment of humans is primarily culture, not the "natural world" narrowly defined as other species, climate, etc." (1995: 207) Surely no human culture is ever truly homogeneous or free from conflicts that arise from serious differences between individuals and groups. Murder and warfare are the bloodiest ways that humans have dealt with those with whom they have serious differences. Bath of blood history foregrounds these activities when we peer into the past. Peace history does something very different. It reveals the long unfinished task of making human cultures peaceable environments that encourage the expression of our most humane instincts: respect for all others who are human like us, and sympathy for those humans who are fearful and/or suffering.

In a remarkable book, *Humanity: A Moral History of the Twentieth Century*, philosopher Jonathan Glover describes respect and sympathy as "human responses" that although they are "widespread and deep-rooted" are often blocked. Frequently aggressive and cruel instincts find expression in warfare and encouragement in cultures that reserve the highest honors for warriors and their blood sacrifices. Yet clearly respect and sympathy have been absolutely necessary for the survival of our social species. Respect and sympathy are, in Glover's words, "the core of our humanity which contrasts with inhumanity." However, as Glover recognizes, "humanity is only partly an empirical claim. It remains also partly an aspiration." (1999: 24–25) *A Cultural History of Peace* presents strong evidence for the empirical claim, as well as the aspiration. It focuses on the many people in the past who worked to establish peace within their own societies and peace with other societies by institutionalizing respect and sympathy; people who are unlikely to be highlighted as heroes in bath of blood histories.

As General Editor of this title in the Bloomsbury Publishers' cultural history series, I have had to follow two major guidelines. The first one required six volumes of essays that follow the same chronological order as other titles in the series. Accordingly, *A Cultural History of Peace* is presented in volumes focused on Antiquity, the Medieval Age, the Renaissance, the Enlightenment, Age of Empire, and the Modern Era since 1920. This chronology order is Western-oriented and something of a barrier to producing a truly global history of peace. Nonetheless, some of the essays in the first five volumes of *A Cultural History of Peace*, and all the essays in Volume 6 present peace history in a global perspective. Indeed those essays show that envisioning a more peaceful interconnected world and finding ways of realizing that vision is a crucial component of the complex of historical processes we today call "globalization."

Bloomsbury's other major guideline required the eight topical essays in each volume of *A Cultural History of Peace* to concentrate on identical themes in peace history. My first task as General Editor was developing the eight major themes for these collected essays. Developing the major themes was difficult particularly because I recognized that a kind of "translation" problem arises when applying modern ideas about peace to the study of peace history in earlier eras when those ideas, or at least modern formulations of them, were absent. I only started doing peace history in 1998 after two decades of teaching and writing concentrated almost exclusively on American history. Not surprisingly, I remained focused on the modern era when preparing my first peace history courses and new research projects. That focus on the modern era was reinforced by what I learned in a peace research seminar at the University of Oslo in the summer of 2007. Thus I knew that my initial selection of themes for this collection could be criticized as present-oriented. Many hours of discussion with my colleagues in Dartmouth's History Department convinced me that this "translation" problem was not insuperable, and that after significant revision my original ideas would be viable focal points for *A Cultural History of Peace*.

These six volumes validate this conviction. Each one contains an introductory overview of the historical era written by its editor and eight thematic essays written by specialists. They develop the following themes: Definitions of Peace; Human Nature, Peace, and War; Peace, War, and Gender; Peace, Pacifism, and Religion; Representations of Peace; Peace Movements; Peace, Security, and Deterrence; and Peace as Integration. This structure facilitates long views of key subjects in peace history. Anyone interested, for instance, in putting together a chronologically ordered history of how peace has been defined from antiquity to the modern era can achieve this goal by reading in order each of the first chapters in the six volumes of *A Cultural History of Peace*. When they do so, they will discover the distinction between "negative" and "positive" definitions of peace that are commonly used in peace research today is useful when formulating questions about pre-modern definitions of peace. But they will also see that the modern distinction between negative peace and positive peace is a simple model that may hinder understanding the variety and richness of what people since antiquity actually meant when they spoke and wrote about peace.

How people in different times and places have understood what we usually call "human nature" has deeply influenced what they said and did about making peace and war. Human nature is, of course, a tricky term. Does it even exist? If it does, is it an endowment of fixed characteristics, or malleable and evolving? And if by human nature, we mean "instinctual," does this mean "inevitable," or are instincts better understood as potential behaviors that have been repressed or expressed depending on environmental

GENERAL EDITOR'S PREFACE

influences produced by particular cultures at particular times in the past? The essays in this collection that develop the theme "Human Nature, Peace, and War" make clear that prevailing beliefs about human nature, whether faith-based or secular, have always played an essential role in how people understand what kinds of peace are possible in their imperfect material world.

Peace and war are among the most clearly gendered historical categories, as Chapter 3 in *A Cultural History of Peace* makes abundantly clear. It has been common all over the world for women to be regarded as "life-givers" and men as "life-takers." Of course there are deviations from this global historical pattern. The Truong sisters of Vietnam and Joan of Arc are among the most famous transgressors of the male monopoly of military power. However, women like them have been exceptional. More commonly, women have provided material and psychological support to male warriors. And perhaps most significantly, some of them have been peace thinkers and peacemakers. Indeed, the widespread idea that peace is feminine has been a source of political legitimacy for women, not just a barrier to achieving political power.

Although pacifism in Western democracies is now usually understood as a principled and often religiously inspired refusal to engage in violence, in other historical settings people who could justify certain violent actions and some wars were still considered "pacifists" whenever they opposed militarism or an ongoing war. On such occasions the deeply subversive cultural implications of nonviolence—its resistance to the idea that history must be written in blood—have been manifest. The essays herein that develop the theme "Peace, Pacifism, and Religion" enable readers to better understand the ambiguous role of religious faith in peace history. They describe religious traditions that link faith and peace, but also ancient and enduring traditions that link religion to the promotion of war.

Since antiquity countless artists, sculptors, composers, poets, playwrights, and writers have produced representations that reflected, but also shaped, understandings of peace in their cultures. Ancient symbols of peace like the olive branch and the dove that were incorporated into religious iconography have never lost their currency, even when used by secular peace activists. Many other representations of peace created during the last two millennia have also survived. Chapter 5 in this collection presents a long history of these representations of peace. These representations have often been of peace imagined because their creators could not find real peace in contemporary political cultures. The accumulated representations of peace now form a vast and priceless cultural reservoir, much is easily accessed via the internet. Currently, new representations of peace are being produced and deposited in this cultural reservoir everyday, while old ones are revived and reconfigured by peace activists around the world.

Peace and anti-war movements have always produced and deployed representations of peace, but they have not been a constant presence in the past. Chapter 8 describes collective efforts to prevent wars, or to stop them from continuing, as well as organized opposition to militarism. Throughout history peace movements have been condemned as subversive, especially when they resisted ongoing wars authorized by political authorities. And even when they have failed to achieve peace, as they have frequently done in the past, peace movements extended the contemporary cultural bases for challenging militarism and the glorification of warfare. Peace movements have over the long run produced traditions of anti-militarist thinking that in this century are mobilized by peace activists whenever interstate warfare threatens global peace.

Today most global peace activists regard the achievement of security via the threat of force as itself a problem, partly because this kind of negative peace has so frequently broken down in the past. The six essays in this collection that explore the theme "Peace, Security, and Deterrence" nonetheless demonstrate the strong and enduring appeal of this approach to peace. Although the perception problem modern political scientists call "the security dilemma" has been recognized since antiquity, the political practicality and immediately recognizable results of deterrence has almost always prevailed in the face of building threats made by military rivals. Enshrined in the modern era as a form of political realism, deterrence policy shaped the nuclear arms that saw rival superpowers each deploy tens of thousands of nuclear weapons that if used would have certainly destroyed civilization. Yet today, most national governments still equate peace with security and produce deterrence policies that create military alliances and threaten adversaries with war.

The last chapters of each volume address a theme that many people mistakenly identify as a modern phenomenon: peace through integration, as if it must be something resembling the European Union. These chapters show that the social order imposed by expanding empires, kingdoms, and nation-states has long been proclaimed as a form of peace, even when peace was not the reason for the warfare that preceded it. Moreover, its principal beneficiaries have often identified their empires as an expanding civilization, most famously Pax Romana and more recently Pax Americana. Yet since the medieval age another kind of peace achieved by nonviolent agreements built upon shared characteristics of identity has been imagined, and occasionally implemented.

Christianity's claim to be a universal church that could bring all people together in a brotherhood of Christ opened the door for identifying "humanity," a word first used during the Renaissance. Then science, especially eighteenth century taxonomy, provided a secular path to a similar end: the recognition that all humans are in very important ways, a single unique species of life. In the modern era, threats to the continued existence of this humanity in the form of global catastrophes such as nuclear warfare and climate change have contributed to an unprecedented "species consciousness" and the claim that all humans have rights that must be respected. Unprecedented communications technologies that today allow us to see and hear people from all over the world in real time have facilitated the expansion of global peace and human rights networks. Although during the five years that *A Cultural History of Peace* has been in the making, politics that divide people into hostile groups have gathered strength in many countries, the long history presented in this collection suggests the cultural foundations for peace, so long in the making, will weather the present storm, and humanity will continue to make itself a global reality.

Introduction

SHEILA L. AGER

The isles of Greece, the isles of Greece
Where burning Sappho loved and sung,
Where grew the arts of war and peace,
Where Delos rose, and Phoebus sprung!

—George Gordon, Lord Byron
(*Don Juan*, Third Canto lxxxvi 1)

The year 500/499 BCE conventionally marks the opening of what is known as the Classical Age, the great age of Greek antiquity, a century long thought to have been the zenith of classical culture in terms of political development, artistic achievement, and literary genius. That year saw also the beginnings of a local dispute that would spark a perfect storm of war. Miletos, a Greek polis ("city-state"; pl. poleis) on the coast of Asia Minor, rebelled against its Persian overlord and instigated other rebellions up and down the Aegean coast, in a movement known as the Ionian Revolt. Well aware that they could not hope to battle the enormous Persian Empire on their own, the Milesian leader Aristagoras appealed to the leading Greek city-states, Sparta and Athens, for assistance. The Spartans rejected this appeal, but the Athenians embraced it. They sent a small fleet to the aid of the Ionians, a fleet that marked what the ancient historian Herodotos, quoting the epic poet Homer, called "the beginning of evils" (5.97). The Athenian ships did very little in the end, but the simple fact of their involvement—and the fact that the Athenian crews were involved in the accidental burning of Sardis, a local Persian seat of government— drew them to the attention of the Persian king, Darius the Great:

> The story goes that when Darius learnt of the disaster, he did not give a thought to the Ionians, knowing perfectly well that the punishment for their revolt would come; but he asked who the Athenians were, and then, on being told, called for his bow. He took it, set an arrow on the string, shot it up into the air and cried: "Grant, O God, that I may punish the Athenians." Then he commanded one of his servants to repeat to him the words, "Master, remember the Athenians", three times, whenever he sat down to dinner.
>
> —Hdt. 5.105

While the details of the story may not be accurate, Darius did indeed remember the Athenians, and in 490 BCE sent an expedition across the Aegean to punish them. Contrary to the Persian expectations, the outnumbered Athenians defeated their forces at Marathon in a hard-fought battle that is still commemorated today.

This blow to Persian prestige resulted in a much larger expedition a decade later, led by Darius' son Xerxes, now with the intent to absorb all the Greek states into the Persian Empire. Some of the most famous battles of history—Thermopylai, Salamis, Plataei— ultimately resulted in a Greek victory.

FIGURE 0.1: The *soros* (burial mound) of the 192 Athenians killed at the Battle of Marathon; Marathon, Attica, Greece. Photo by DeAgostini, courtesy of Getty Images.

FIGURE 0.2: The coronation of Charlemagne depicted in a medieval French manuscript. Photo by Leemage/UIG, courtesy of Getty Images.

INTRODUCTION 3

Our other terminus is the time of Charlemagne: on Christmas Day in 800 CE, the Carolingian ruler was crowned as "Emperor of the Romans" in St. Peter's Basilica by Pope Leo III. The Frankish courtier Einhard's description of the decades leading up to the coronation tells a tale of constant fighting, such as Charlemagne's war against the Saxons:

> No war taken up by the Frankish people was ever longer, or more savage, or cost so much labour, because the Saxons, like almost all the peoples inhabiting Germany, were by nature fierce and given over to the worship of demons and were opposed to our religion and did not think it shameful to violate or transgress either human or divine laws.
>
> —*VKM* 7

Einhard goes on to celebrate both the extension of Charlemagne's Frankish empire and his benevolent relations with kings beyond its borders, such as Alfonso II of Asturias, the eastern Caliph Harun al-Rashid, and various Byzantine emperors (in spite of the fact that Charlemagne's coronation as Emperor was an implicit challenge to the imperial rule in Byzantium; *VKM* 16, 28).

Between the world of the Greek city-states and the competing empires of Charlemagne's day lies a vast gulf of social, cultural, religious, and political transformation. Nevertheless, threads of continuity are woven into this tapestry of change, and prominent among them is the human propensity for war. Our view may be somewhat distorted by the fact that from the fifth century BCE until the twentieth century the proper subject of "history" was largely defined by historians themselves as politics and war. Yet the effect of war on states and populations has been so devastating throughout history that it is fair to say that whatever distortion might lie in historians' accounts cannot exaggerate the impact of war on all aspects of the human experience.[1] Teasing out ancient concepts surrounding peace inevitably involves extensive discussion of the ancient experience of war, and if this volume often seems to privilege the latter, it is only because it throws a sharper light on the ancient ideas around peace that it explores.

CHALLENGES

There are numerous challenges in talking about the concept of peace in antiquity, as the chapters in this volume demonstrate. First is the reality that, while conflict and amity are both constants of the human condition, "peace" *per se* is a concept that has fluctuated throughout history and across cultures. "War" is at first glance an easier concept to define, though the plethora of terminology employed today—"militarized conflict", "counterterrorism operation", "active hostilities"—all demonstrate the ways in which words can be employed to define and shape reality. Fighting a "war" without actually declaring it is in today's world a way of evading responsibility in the face of modern ideas around international law; in antiquity, to make war without a formal declaration could be a serious breach of international custom.[2] Modern definitions tend to require a minimum number of casualties in order to define a conflict as a war, something that would have made little sense to the citizens of an ancient Greek city-state: "limited wars may be limited for a major power but devastating for a minor one" (Weigall 2003: 237).[3] Singer and Small set the threshold of casualties at a thousand battle-related deaths in order for a conflict to be defined as a "war"; many of the smaller Greek city-states had fewer than a thousand citizens to put in the battlefield in the first place.

As for "peace", it lies along a spectrum that stretches from negative peace to positive peace; it is, as Kurt Raaflaub says, "a polyvalent notion" (Raaflaub 2007b: 1). In the ancient world, this spectrum of circumstances and behaviors consisted of "not war", neutrality, non-engagement, treaties, bilateral and multilateral alliances, positive diplomatic relations, friendship, and kinship (putative or real) between states. Nevertheless, few ancient societies explicitly engaged with the question of the meaning of peace (Raaflaub 2016b: 2; but cf. van Wees 2016: 158–9).

A further challenge in talking about peace in antiquity is that throughout human history war has not necessarily been regarded as an unmitigated evil, nor peace at any cost as a desirable goal. Ideas and ideals of global peace are a relatively recent phenomenon. Moreover, specific cultural values have a significant impact on a society's views of war and peace. Both the Greeks and the Romans had militarized cultures that applauded militaristic values (Harris 1991; Eckstein 2006a, 2008). Military prowess was regularly seen as the pinnacle of masculine achievements and a measure of a man's worth for other pursuits, including political office. The leading politicians of the Athenian democracy were the elected *strategoi*, the generals. The powerful kings of the Hellenistic age emphasized their masculinity through their military might (Austin 1986; Roy 1998). Members of the Roman senatorial class regularly climbed the ladder of political influence and office—the *cursus honorum*—on the basis of their successful military experience. "No one is eligible for any political office before he has completed ten years' service," says Polybios (6.19.4), though in fact this requirement seems to have become attenuated by the first century BCE (Harris 1991: 12; Eckstein 2006b: 574–5).

To relinquish this identification of militarism with manliness, to substitute instead a universally pacifist value system, would have made little sense to the Greeks and Romans. Their beliefs were encased in myth and memory. Achilles is the "best of the Achaians" because he kills the most men, Agamemnon the lord commander because he commands the most men. In the *Iliad*, the gods fight alongside the humans. No traditional god of any significance embodied the concept of peace, though Greek Ares and Roman Mars embodied war.[4] Ares in particular represented the brutality and savagery of war, but even the gods of civilized behavior had their own weapons: Zeus his lightning bolt, Athena her spear, and Apollo his bow. In 421 BCE, the Athenian comic playwright Aristophanes gave voice to the weariness the Athenians (and other Greeks) felt with the last decade of fighting in his play *Peace* (*Eirēnē*). Peace herself is (perhaps appropriately) a passive character, no more than a mute statue, who has been bound and imprisoned in a cave by the brutal character War; Aristophanes' comic hero, the Athenian farmer Trygaios, flies up to heaven on a giant dung beetle in order to free her. The gods themselves, immortal as they are, care nothing for peace among humankind (Ager 2005).

Cultural beliefs and values in antiquity—as in every era—thus had a powerful impact on ancient attitudes towards war and peace, and the Greeks and Romans were not alone in their espousal of manly martial virtues. Persian youths were taught above all else to ride, to use the bow, and to tell the truth (Hdt. 1.136). The most important role of the Egyptian Pharaoh was to stand as a warrior against the forces of chaos and the adversaries of Egypt, both human and cosmic; Pharaohs were repeatedly depicted on temple walls in the pose of smiting enemies (Bickel 2016).

In the twelfth century BCE, Ramesses III of Egypt turned back an invasion of the so-called Sea Peoples, and had the following inscription placed on his mortuary temple to celebrate that fact:

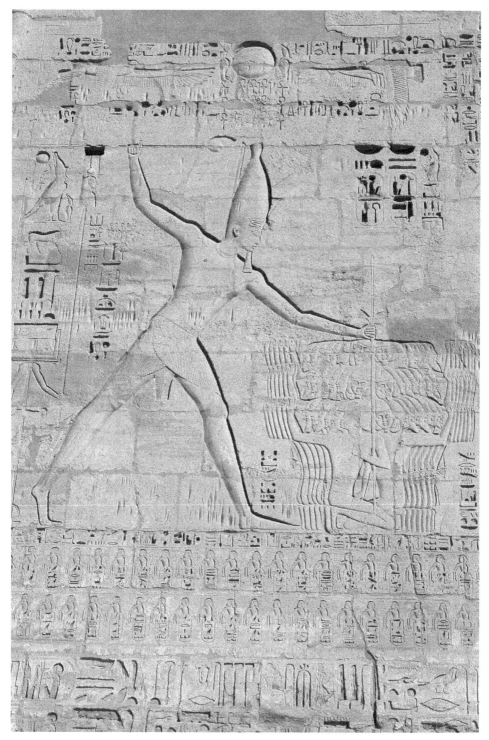

FIGURE 0.3: Ramesses III smiting his enemies on the wall of his mortuary temple at Medinet Habu; Luxor, Egypt. Photo by Werner Forman Archive/Heritage Images, courtesy of Getty Images.

I organized my frontier in Djahi, prepared before them: princes, commanders of garrisons, and *maryanu* (warriors). I have the river-mouths prepared like a strong wall, with warships, galleys and coasters, (fully) equipped, for they were manned completely from bow to stern, with valiant warriors carrying their weapons. The troops consisted of every picked man of Egypt. They were like lions roaring upon the mountain tops. The chariotry consisted of runners, of picked men, of every good and capable chariot-warrior. The horses were quivering in every part of their bodies, prepared the crush the foreign countries under their hoofs. I was the valiant Montu [war god], standing fast at their head, so that they might gaze upon the capturing of my hands . . . Those who reached my frontier, their seed is not, their heart and their soul are finished forever and ever. Those who came forward together on the sea, the full flame was in front of them at the river-mouths, while a stockade of lances surrounded them on the shore. They were dragged in, enclosed, and prostrated on the beach, killed, and made into heaps from tail to head. Their ships and their goods were as if fallen into the water.

—*ANET* 262–3

The Assyrians were legendary for the terror they inspired in other peoples, as were the later Parthians, Huns, and Mongols, though allowance needs to be made here for the propaganda of their enemies (and victims). As for the Far East, during the period of the Warring States in China (*c.* 500–221 BCE), different dynasties struggled for control of the whole in a rivalry that was only ended with the establishment of the Qin unified empire: "China was never a pacifist culture and Confucianism was never a pacifist ideology".[5]

The moral and/or cultural justification of war was and is an extremely important concept in most human societies, and is certainly relevant to ancient views on the subject of peace (Bederman 2001: 207–66; Hunt 2012; cf. Moses 2018). Philosophies of war and peace in antiquity, from the Mediterranean through to the Far East, tended to hold that defensive wars were justified, while offensive were not. Naturally, that stance begs the question of what is meant by "defensive" and "offensive": for instance, honorable vengeance was a perfectly acceptable reason for going to war, even if the avenging party employed a sledgehammer to take down a fly. The aggressive campaign of Xerxes in 480–479 BCE, with its goal of absorbing all of Greece into the Persian Empire, had at its core the motive of punishing the insult that the Athenians had delivered to the Persians at the time of the Ionian Revolt and again at the Battle of Marathon, or so Herodotos says (7.5.2; 7.8b–c). In turn, when Alexander the Great launched his invasion of the Persian Empire in 334 BCE, the propaganda aimed at the Greek troops who accompanied him was that the campaign was vengeance for the destruction wrought by Xerxes' invasion of Greece a century and a half earlier. But Alexander's own reasons for invading Persia were inextricably linked to the concept of personal military glory: the Macedonian king kept a copy of the *Iliad* with him throughout his campaign and deliberately assimilated himself to such great warriors of the Greek heroic past as Herakles and Achilles.

Thucydides, in his history of the great Peloponnesian War between Athens and Sparta and their respective allies, provides a detailed analysis of the proximate causes of conflict in contradistinction to ultimate underlying causes. Such proximate causes may truly spark a war in situations of enhanced international tension—much as the Cuban missile crisis in 1962 led the US and the USSR closer to war—but they may also function as pretexts for vindication of conflict that would otherwise be difficult to justify. Thucydides' famous statement on the truest cause of the Peloponnesian War—Spartan fear of growing Athenian power—should be read in conjunction with his later statement that years later the Spartans

INTRODUCTION 7

felt a sense of guilt in beginning the war, in that they had rejected Athenian offers to settle their differences peacefully through arbitration (1.23.6; 7.18.2). They had initially tried to justify themselves on the basis of alleged injuries the Athenians had caused to others, but ultimately the Spartans evidently recognized that their pretexts for a just war rang hollow.

Although most ancient societies justified aggression and conflict in ways that conformed to their own ethical, cultural, and religious principles—and their own security and self-interest—it was the Romans who explicitly articulated an overarching concept of just war (*bellum iustum*) (Wiedemann 1986; Watson 1993; Ager 2009; Berchman 2013).[6] According to the historians Livy and Dionysios of Halikarnassos, Rome had developed a formulaic ritual at a very early date in its history to confirm that all its wars were just (Livy 1.24, 1.32; Dion. Hal. *Ant. Rom.* 2.72). The gods were called upon to witness that Rome, not its enemy, was the injured party, and a college of priests, the *fetiales*, were charged with ensuring that all the appropriate ritual was carried out. There is some debate over whether fetial procedures in the early Republic were as they are described in our sources, but certainly the Romans maintained a strong conviction throughout the centuries that their wars had to be just and the Roman cause approved by the gods. Military defeat was generally interpreted as the result of a failure to have ensured these prerequisites.

The Roman attachment to the concept of just war provided an avenue for the somewhat paradoxical integration of the (initially) peace-centered religion of Christianity into the command structure of a militant society.[7] The emperor Constantine (306–337 CE) favored Christianity and ultimately became a convert, but most of his early career was spent in dismantling by force of arms the structurally cooperative system of the tetrarchy established by his predecessor Diocletian and establishing himself as sole ruler. Hagiographic accounts of Constantine, both Christian and pagan, sublimate Constantine's personal ambition and emphasize instead his selfless dedication to coming to the aid of others (all his rivals are portrayed as tyrannical monsters) and his devotion to the Christian god. The famous story of his vision prior to the Battle of the Milvian Bridge against his enemy Maxentius in 312 CE—a cross of light in the heavens with the sign "In this, conquer"—illustrates the blending of the Roman idea of just war and the beliefs of Christianity into the figure of the soldier of Christ (Euseb. *Vit. Const.* 28–9; cf. Lactant. *De mort. pers.* 44).[8]

In the next century, St. Augustine took up the idea and elaborated philosophically on the idea of just war: in the *City of God*, he advises Christians that, while the necessity to fight just wars is regrettable, to fail to engage in such a war could itself be a sin. By the time of Charlemagne, all Christian rulers could be represented as just kings fighting just wars against the forces of chaos. "They found so much gold and silver in the palace," says Einhard of Charlemagne's campaign against the Huns, "and so much valuable booty was taken in the battles that the Franks might be thought to have justly taken from the Avars what the Avars had unjustly taken from other peoples." (*VKM* 13).

Prior to the arrival of Christianity on the scene, the ancient world did not for the most part experience religious conflict (at the same time, as we have seen, the gods of the Greeks and Romans were not gods of peace). Wars might be fought for the prestige of control over religious sanctuaries, and sanctuaries themselves were not infrequently subjected to damage or pillaging in times of warfare. The so-called "sacred truce" declared at the time of the Olympic Games was not intended to bring lasting peace to the Greek world; it was simply a hiatus in hostilities to allow all Greeks to attend the sacred ceremony of the Games. Even so, war between Elis and Arkadia disrupted the Games of 364 BCE when the fighting between the opposing forces spilled over into the sacred precinct itself (Xen. *Hell.* 7.4.28–32). As time went on, many religious sanctuaries became

FIGURE 0.4: The Battle at the Milvian Bridge between Constantine and Maxentius, by Gianfrancesco Penni (1496–1528); Vatican, Italy. Photo by Fine Art Images/Heritage Images, courtesy of Getty Images.

pro-active in protecting themselves by seeking grants of inviolability (*asylia*) from various states (Rigsby 1996).

Nevertheless, despite the fact that sanctuaries might become objects of conflict, neither Greeks nor Romans (nor Persians, for that matter) fought wars over religious dogma. The polytheistic cultures of Greece, Rome, and much of the Near East provided flexible space for the co-existence of many gods and many beliefs, even mutually contradictory ones. Although the Achaimenid rulers of Persia themselves adopted Zoroastrianism, a semi-monotheistic religion, their policy towards their imperial subjects was religious tolerance and respect for the gods of different peoples. Naturally, this does not mean that they tolerated uprisings instigated by religious leaders, any more than the Romans did (Wiesehöfer 2007: 124–7). Tensions between the Romans and the Jews were not, from a Roman viewpoint, religious, though of course religion was a significant part of the Jewish perspective. Monotheistic beliefs by definition cannot admit rival gods, but the Jewish refusal to conform was seen by the Romans as an inexplicable and antagonistic political statement. Once monotheism, with the adoption of Christianity, became the dominant religious framework of the Roman Empire, the door was open for conflict over religious dogma. Finally, with the rise of Islam in the seventh century CE, the porous polytheism of Greek and Roman culture vanished and the Mediterranean and Near East became the battleground of competing monotheistic beliefs.

Glorification of war and justification of war were thus distinctive features of the ancient paradigm: "peace at any cost" was not a motto for antiquity. Moreover, the ancients had a share in the common characteristics that have created challenges to lasting peace throughout human history. Their world, like the modern one, was politically anarchic: there was no overarching authority to establish and maintain peace (with the exception of

INTRODUCTION

imperial rule, as we shall see later). A Realist perspective, such as that taken by Arthur Eckstein in his examinations of the Hellenistic and Roman worlds, emphasizes the security-consciousness of states existing in such a system (Eckstein 2006a, 2008). With no effective collective security, states cannot afford to let down their guard or put away their suspicions of others. "What most men call peace (*eirēnē*) is really only a fiction," says Plato, "and in cold fact all states are by nature fighting an undeclared war (*polemos akēryktos*) against every other state" (Pl. *Leg.* 626a).[9]

BLESSINGS

In spite of these challenges in exploring the concept of peace in antiquity, and in spite of the arguably eternal human propensity for violence, yearning for peace too is a human constant. None of what was stated earlier should be taken to mean that the blessings of peace were unappreciated in antiquity, or that the agonies of war went unrecognized. Indeed, the degree of philosophical and rhetorical energy expended on developing principles of justified conflict is a clear indication that peace was considered the more desirable state of affairs. "No one is fool enough to choose war instead of peace (*eirēnē*)," says the Lydian ruler Kroisos, "in peace sons bury fathers, but in war fathers bury sons." (Hdt. 1.87.4). But it is typical of the ancient paradigm that learning comes too late. In Herodotos, Kroisos is blinded by his own imperialist fervor and invades the realm of Cyrus of Persia; it is only after his defeat by Cyrus that Kroisos' eyes are opened to the benefits of choosing to live in peace.

Yearning for peace in poetry and drama and philosophy was always played out against a backdrop of war; perhaps the only way to appreciate peace is to experience its opposite. Sympathy for the defeated is plentiful in Greek literature, though rarely is it conjoined with a call to end all aggression and conflict. The Trojans were a compelling exemplar. The *Iliad* is a poem of conflict, but Homer celebrates peace by shining a light on the heartrending consequences of war (Tritle 2007). Andromache's words to her husband, the Trojan prince Hektor, speak to the agony of the survivors of conflict (6.407–13):

> Your own great strength will be your death, and you have no pity
> on your little son, nor on me, ill-starred, who soon must be your widow;
> for presently the Achaians, gathering together,
> will set upon you and kill you; and for me it would be far better
> to sink into the earth when I have lost you, for there is no other
> consolation for me after you have gone to your destiny—
> only grief.

Yet the truth is that Hektor must die: he feels fear and grief at the thought of his impending death, both for himself and his family, but it is neither in his fate nor in his inclination to turn his back on his masculine duty to defend his people.

The fate of the Trojan survivors is explored in the Athenian playwright Euripides' *Trojan Women*, in which the royal women of Troy lament the loss of their men and their own inevitable fate as slaves of the Greek conquerors. The play was staged in early 415 BCE, and it is next to impossible to think that Euripides was not pointing a finger at his compatriots: only a few months before, the Athenians had attacked the small island of Melos, killing all its men and enslaving its women and children. But was the play a call to action or was it simply—like much of Greek drama—a statement on the tragic reality of the world?

On the comic side, Aristophanes' peace plays—*Acharnians*, *Peace*, and *Lysistrata*—are sheer fantasy, and were meant to amuse, not to provide a roadmap to peace. Nevertheless, the themes he explored in these plays demonstrate that thoughts of peace were in the air and people were longing for it in their minds: peace is always better than war in Aristophanes. He typically revels in the simple joys of food and drink and sex, and mocks the bellicose among his fellow citizens, such as Kleon and Lamachos, whose war-mongering actions rob the ordinary citizenry of these pleasures (Giovannini 2007: 147–8; Tritle 2007: 183–5; Ruffell 2017). Like Aristophanes, though in a very different vein, the Roman Vergil celebrates the simple joys of a peaceful country life in his poetic collections *The Eclogues* and *The Georgics*. These poems were written during the final decades of the Roman civil wars, a context in which the delights of peace was a particularly poignant subject, and Vergil's poetry reflects the contrast between war and peace much as Aristophanes' comedies did.

Greek and Roman writers such as Aeneas Tacticus, Polyainos, and Frontinus wrote technical treatises on warfare and strategy, but the ancients have left us little in the way of textbooks on peace. The Greek speechwriter and political pamphleteer Isokrates famously urged the leading states of Greece to make peace with one another, but both the mechanism and the ultimate aim of such a peace was to be a military expedition against the Persian Empire. In the flawless worlds devised by the philosopher Plato in *The Republic* and *The Laws*, a perfectly run state governed by philosopher rulers will *ipso facto* be harmonious, at least within its own borders. But only in a world where *all* states are governed in the same fashion will interstate war be eliminated. That such a state of affairs would be desirable might be implicitly understood, and the Athenian speaker in Plato's Laws certainly seems to represent that viewpoint. Nevertheless, his two companions, the more militant Cretan and Spartan speakers, who expect war to be a commonplace reality, no doubt reflected real contemporary perspectives. Similarly, the fifth century BCE Chinese philosopher Sunzi (Sun Wu), author of *The Art of War*, argued that peace would ensue under a ruler who applied himself to the perfect (just and benevolent) methods of rule, and who applied methods of peace to bring about the end of war; but just war (defensive rather than offensive) would continue to be a reality (Yates 2016).

Peace within the state was to be sought after at least as much as peace abroad, and both Greek and Roman history attest to the devastating consequences of civil war. The civil wars of the last decades of the Roman Republic tore the state apart and culminated in the foundation of autocratic rule. During the struggles of the late fifth century BCE, the war between democratic Athens and oligarchic Sparta and their respective allies was made even more bitter by the political divides within states. Thucydides preserves a stark and terrible account of *stasis* (civil strife) in the city-state of Corcyra in 427 BCE (3.70–85). The democrats of Corcyra favored Athens, the oligarchs Sparta; it is worth quoting Thucydides at length for his thoughts on the interaction of internal and external war and peace:

> So savage was the progress of this revolution (*stasis*), and it seemed all the more so because it was one of the first which had broken out. Later, of course, practically the whole of the Hellenic world was convulsed, with rival parties in every state— democratic leaders trying to bring in the Athenians, and oligarchs trying to bring in the Spartans. In peacetime (*eirēnē*) there would have been no excuse and no desire for calling them in, but in time of war, when each party could always count upon an alliance which would do harm to its opponents and at the same time strengthen its own position, it became a natural thing for anyone who wanted a change of government

INTRODUCTION

to call in help from outside. In the various cities, these revolutions were the cause of many calamities—as happens and always will happen while human nature is what it is, though there may be different degrees of savagery, and, as different circumstances arise, the general rules will admit of some variety. In times of peace and prosperity, cities and individuals alike follow higher standards, because they are not forced into a situation where they have to do what they do not want to do. But war is a stern teacher (*biaios didaskalos*); in depriving them of the power of easily satisfying their daily wants, it brings most people's minds down to the level of their actual circumstances.

—3.82.1–2

Then, as now, civil war and foreign war may go hand in hand: so many of the terrible conflicts that have ravaged the world over the last century had (and have) their basis in internal divisions along ethnic, religious, or political lines. These divisions can extend beyond the borders of the state as parties on all sides appeal to sympathizers from outside. In ancient Greece, as we see in Thucydides, the divide often fell along the line of political disagreement between democrat and oligarch.[10] Plato spoke to the need to address conflict within the community as a prerequisite to establishing a successful polity:

The highest good, however, is neither war (*polemos*) nor civil war (*stasis*) (God forbid we should ever need to resort to either of them), but peace (*eirēnē*) and goodwill among men . . . [anyone who] adopts foreign warfare as his first and only concern will never make a true statesman in the true sense; he'll become a *genuine* lawgiver only if he designs his legislation about war as a tool for peace, rather than his legislation for peace as an instrument of war.

—*Leg.* 628c–e; Saunders translation, adapted

Civil war harrowed up the most devastating of emotions and impulses: grief, hatred, rage, betrayal, vengeance. Reconciliation and communal unity—what the Greeks called *homonoia* and the Romans *concordia*—could be desperately difficult to achieve.[11] It remains the case today that one of the most salient factors in conflict is whether there has been previous conflict. The phrase "yearning for the blessings of peace" often conjures up the emotions of grief and pity, and aligns the emotions with an anti-war stance: but such a notion ignores the more aggressive emotions of anger and hate and bitter memories, which are enormously resistant to peace-making and reconciliation.

MECHANISMS

The smaller players on the landscape of the ancient world had a particular appreciation of the blessings of peace. It was a world without security, and safety and prosperity usually lay in having a protector, whether through a system of collective security (often fragile), or through having a big powerful friend. The propaganda of the Hellenistic kings, for example, was that they exercised their military might chiefly as defenders of the weak (Roy 1998: 113; Koehn 2007). Ideally, the king was not supposed to be a ravening wolf slaughtering all his sheep, but rather a militant shepherd guarding them from the other wolves. Numerous inscriptions survive recording the gratitude of Greek city-states for the protection and favor afforded to them by a powerful benefactor. The following example, part of an honorary decree voted by the people of Teos for the king Antiochos III around the end of the third century BCE, is typical (the Teians here describe Antiochos' various benefactions):

When he stayed in our city he saw that we were exhausted both in our public and our private affairs because of the continuous wars and the great burden of contributions we were bearing. Wishing to display piety towards the god to whom he consecrated our city and territory, and wanting to do a favour to the people and the association of Dionysiac artists, he came forward in person in the assembly and granted to our city and territory to be holy, inviolate and free from tribute, and undertook to free us himself from the other contributions we pay to King Attalos (I), so that by bringing about an improvement in the city's fortunes he would receive the title not only of benefactor of the people, but of its saviour.

—Hermann 1965: 34–36; translation: Austin 2006 no. 191, slightly adapted

The relationship between city and king was pragmatic and mutually satisfactory: the king could provide peace, security, and assistance with provisions if necessary, not to mention less tangible benefactions such as assurances that there would be no interference with a city's traditional laws and constitution. In return, the city could provide loyalty (even worship), military recruits, local quarters for royal troops, and—often with the assistance of those troops—some degree of local stability. Unfortunately, the city was often the vehicle through which Hellenistic kings fought with each other; in the third century BCE in particular, the Greek and indigenous communities of Asia Minor were passed back and forth, often violently, through the hands of rival rulers.

The concept that peace and stability can be imposed from without by a superior power comes as no surprise. Yet it may seem ironic that widespread systemic peace was most successfully achieved in antiquity under the aegis of complete imperial control. The *pax Romana*, also known as the *pax Augusta*, is conventionally defined as the period of peace throughout the Mediterranean established with Octavian's defeat of Cleopatra and Antony at Actium in 31 BCE and lasting until the crisis that overtook the Roman Empire in the third century CE.[12] Octavian's victory marked both the end of the Roman civil wars and the absorption of Egypt, the last great Hellenistic kingdom, into the empire. Most of the Mediterranean littoral was now Roman provincial territory, and a network of friendly alliances with kings beyond the borders of the provinces assisted in maintaining peace at the frontiers. There were significant exceptions to frontier peace, however: in Europe, the Germanic tribes, and in Asia, the Arsakid Parthians and their successors the Sassanid Persians. Peace within the empire should therefore not be construed as peace with parties outside it, and peace within the empire itself disintegrated badly in the third century CE.

The Roman Empire was the most enduring and successful of imperialist peacemakers in the ancient world, but there are other examples. After the failure of the Ionian Revolt, Herodotos tells us that the Persian satrap Artaphernes compelled the Ionian city-states to swear an oath committing all future disputes among themselves to arbitration rather than taking violent action against each other. These and other measures taken at the same time are described by Herodotos as "conducive to peace" (Hdt. 6.43.1; Piccirilli 1973 no. 11; Brosius 2012). Empires do not in general tolerate conflict among their subjects, and the Persians, like the Romans, took action to keep the peace within their borders.

Imperial peace of course served the needs of the imperial power enforcing it, but that does not mean that the needs of the subject members of the empire were completely ignored or that the Persians or the Romans relied solely on force of arms to impose peace (de Souza 2008; Brosius 2012). On more than one occasion, Darius the Great intervened in the actions of his own satraps and officials on behalf of subject peoples such as the Jews and the Greeks of Asia Minor (*Ezra* 5–6; *Syll*[3] 22; Cook 1983: 61, 71–72; Briant 1996:

FIGURE 0.5: Relief from the Arch of Titus commemorating the Roman victory in the Jewish War of 66–73 CE; Rome, Italy. Photo by MyLoupe/UIG, courtesy of Getty Images.

503–9). The Jewish writer Josephus speaks with distaste and contempt of the depredations carried out by the Jewish Sicarii against their fellow Jews who refused to join in the first-century CE revolt (*BJ* 7.254–8); when the Romans took action against the Sicarii they re-established not only Roman domination but also the benefits of Roman peace.[13]

Some Roman governors were indeed venal and corrupt, but their behavior as individuals should not be seen as imperial policy. It is probably dangerous to take the hyper-conscientious Pliny the Younger as an exemplar of the typical Roman provincial governor, but the correspondence between him and the emperor Trajan shows the degree of hard work that at least some of these men put into governing their provinces in the best interests of the provincials as well as the empire as a whole.

Imperial rule, then, could function to build and maintain peace, and was of particular importance to the multitude of smaller polities incapable of arming or protecting themselves against larger predatory neighbors. Nevertheless, the entire construct did entail surrender to conquest by a single power, and whether that power subsequently behaved in a predatory or a merciful fashion was entirely its own choice. Peace through dominance was still peace, but it was conditional on the whim of the dominant authority. The peculiarly Roman practice of *deditio*—the enemy's unconditional surrender into the good faith (*fides*) of Rome—underlines the nature of Roman ideas about peace (Barton 2007; Rosenstein 2007). So too do Vergil's famous lines in the *Aeneid*: granted a vision of the future glory of Rome, Aeneas is advised by the spirit of his father Anchises that the burden and duty of Rome will be to "to set the force of habit upon peace, to spare those who submit and crush in war the haughty".[14] The downside of this exalted vision appears in the work of Vergil's later compatriot Tacitus: "To robbery, butchery, and rapine, they give the lying name of 'empire' (*imperium*)," says the Briton war leader Calgacus, exhorting his men to fight the Romans, "they create a desolation and they call it peace."[15]

In the absence of absolute imperial rule, we also find multilateral attempts to establish and maintain peace among ancient polities, most significantly among the Greek city-states. It was noted earlier that a Realist perspective tends to view war as an inevitable concomitant to human societies. An Institutionalist approach, on the other hand, emphasizes the role that interstate organizations, such as the United Nations, can play in maintaining peace. Although it is commonplace to characterize the ancient world—relative to today—as lacking in diplomatic structures, institutions, and practices conducive to making and keeping peace, the ancient Greeks in particular did develop and experiment with innovative means of doing so. Their limited degree of success in maintaining lasting peace notwithstanding, the instruments developed by the Greeks provided some inspiration to peace seekers constructing the Hague peace institutions and the League of Nations in the nineteenth and early twentieth centuries.

After the defeat of the Persians in 480/479 BCE, the Greek states of the Aegean banded together in an anti-Persian alliance led by Athens, a structure that during the Cold War was frequently likened to the North Atlantic Treaty Organization (NATO). Known today as the Delian League, this alliance did operate to maintain security (not the same as establishing peace) throughout the Aegean. But unlike Rome, the Athenians were not dominant enough to secure a thorough or lasting peace. The alliance itself was fundamentally a military one, though that in itself does not mean it could not be an instrument of peace. When one ally after another sought to leave the compact, they were forced back in, their ships were confiscated, and they were obliged to pay tribute. What started out as a free alliance was converted into what the Athenians themselves acknowledged was an *archē*, an empire (Thuc. 2.62–3); but, lacking the overwhelming power of Rome, Athenian imperialism, far from securing lasting peace, ended up sparking the Peloponnesian War.

In the next century, the Greek city-states experimented with a different type of treaty organization. The fourth century BCE was a time of chronic warfare: the bipolar world of the fifth century, dominated by Athens and Sparta, had dissolved into a series of shifting alliances and unstable multipolarities. It is all the more remarkable—though perhaps unsurprising—that in this atmosphere the Greeks began to develop a type of peace treaty known as a "common peace" (*koinē eirēnē*); Kurt Raaflaub demonstrates that "exceptionally harsh war experiences" were a factor that could trigger a society to actively develop "concepts and theories of peace" (2016b: 4). The first of these treaties was sealed in 387 BCE and is often known as the "King's Peace", since (ironically enough) it was underwritten by the king of Persia (Rung 2008). Over the next several decades, the concept of the common peace was refined further, culminating in the establishment of the Hellenic League of Antigonos I and Demetrios I in 302 BCE (Ryder 1965; Jehne 1994).[16] The innovative basis of a common peace treaty was that it was held to embrace all Greek states, not just those that had been involved in the immediately preceding conflict. It also stated explicitly that all Greek states were to be autonomous, and common peace treaties eventually included a collective security guarantee clause that was supposed to protect the peace by engaging all states to come to the aid of a state under attack.

The common peace treaties of the fourth century were a striking phenomenon (Alonso 2007: 221; Low 2012; Wilker 2012b; Raaflaub 2016d). Striking also is the rapidity with which every one of them failed. The autonomy clause of the very first common peace was exploited by Sparta, which cynically interpreted it to mean that even voluntary inter-state

INTRODUCTION

agreements, such as the recent union between Corinth and Argos, were breaches of the autonomy enshrined in the peace terms: Corinth and Argos were forced by Sparta to forgo their arrangement. It may be tempting to view such failures as rising from inherent problems with the concept and structure of the common peace, but very similar principles underpin modern IGOs such as the United Nations. The mere existence of peace-building institutions that rely on collective security is insufficient in the absence of a widespread will to peace and/or a willingness to employ the paradoxical means of military action to establish peace.[17]

Most notable among other instruments employed by the Greeks to secure peace was the use of third-party conflict resolution (Piccirilli 1973; Ager 1996; Magnetto 1997, 2016). The earliest records we have of this mechanism go back to the cities of ancient Sumer, and it seems highly likely that arbitration and mediation of conflict by third parties arose concurrently with the organization of the first human societies: peace within the group is vital to social survival, and it would have been in the interests of all to have disputes resolved peacefully. If we may judge from the extensive epigraphic record, it seems that third-party resolution became a favored method of dealing with boundary disputes in particular. This was especially so in the case of small states that lacked the resources or the will to employ military means to reach their objectives.

Commitments to resolve future quarrels through third-party arbitration appeared in many peace treaties, most notably perhaps in the Thirty Years' Peace treaty entered into by Athens and Sparta in 446/445 BCE. This commitment failed rather spectacularly with the outbreak of the Peloponnesian War: Spartan fear of Athenian power was simply not a concern that could have been alleviated through arbitration (Ager 1993). Arbitration is in general much better suited to tangible issues than to symbolic ones, where emotions tend to run high and compromise becomes impossible. Even when third parties do manage to minimize violence, they often delay an actual political solution, simply because they do not resolve the underlying tensions (Crocker et al. 2005: 11). It is not at all unlikely that even if the precipitating incidents of the Peloponnesian War had successfully been arbitrated, the war itself would still have occurred.

The Romans were content to adopt Greek practices of arbitration and mediation: as their empire extended into the eastern Mediterranean, they increasingly found themselves called upon to settle local disputes. What Rome did not do, however, was accept the good offices of a third party to settle one of its own disputes. The Greeks, familiar with this method of peaceful conflict resolution, occasionally offered their services, but the idea of mediation between Rome and its enemy was anathema to the Romans. Convinced as they were that their own conflicts were virtually always just and that they were in the right, the Romans were not apt to agree to a peace process that did not promise to privilege the justice of their cause (Ager 2009).

The relative lack of peace-building/peace-maintaining mechanisms and institutions in antiquity might have been somewhat offset by the emphasis on the personal in diplomatic relations, though the framework of personal relations was no guarantee of peace between nations. Among the Near Eastern kingdoms of the Sumerians, the Egyptians, the Babylonians, and the Hittites, friendly kings habitually addressed each other as "brother" (Podany 2010). The kinship was fictive and diplomatic, though royal political marriages might indeed result in real kinship among rulers. In the Hellenistic age as well, such marriages flourished: by the mid-third century BCE, the rulers of the three great kingdoms of Macedon, Egypt, and western Asia were multiply related to each other. Claims of kinship and friendship—as if the international system was an organic macrocosm of the human—can soften the harsh edges of reality in international relations. But putative or real blood relationships rarely interfered with Realpolitik and imperial ambitions: the Ptolemaic and Seleukid rulers of the Hellenistic age regularly fought wars with each other.

In the Classical and Hellenistic periods, Greek city-states often declared formal states of friendship (*philia*) and kinship (*syngeneia*) with one another, even when such kinship was in fact non-existent. Such agreements enabled the citizens of both states to hold certain rights in the territory of the other, such as the right of intermarriage or the right to own real property. The Romans also placed considerable emphasis on the concept of international friendship (*amicitia*): the status of *socius et amicus populi Romani*, "ally and friend of the Roman people", was much sought after, especially by those who had reason to fear Roman power and possible intervention. Ptolemy XII allegedly gave Julius Caesar and Pompey a staggering bribe of 6000 talents in order to induce them to give him the designation of *socius et amicus* (Suet. *Iul.* 54). As we have seen, the existence of a buffer zone of "friendly kings" around much of the periphery of their empire was one of the Roman strategies for maintaining the peace and security of their empire (Burton 2011).

The diplomatic language of friendship and kinship is evident also in late antiquity, where it appears in correspondence between the eastern Byzantine emperors and the Sassanid rulers of Persia. Kavadh I wrote to Justinian I in 529 CE, shortly after Justinian's accession: "We have found it written in our ancient records that we are brothers of one another, and that if one of us should stand in need of men or money, the other should provide them" (Malalas 449.20–50.3, cited by Whitby 2008: 128). But warfare between Persia and the Byzantine Empire remained a regular phenomenon, and far from the two rulers actually being blood kin, diplomatic conventions generally saw to it that they never met: in order to preserve the (superior) dignity of each side, all negotiation was carried out by intermediaries (Wiesehöfer 2007; Lee 2008). As Michael Whitby remarks, the rhetoric of brotherhood did not "imply the existence of significant trust between the states; indeed its repeated manipulation suggests that both sides adopted a cynical approach, with self-interest pre-eminent and few altruistic concessions likely" (Whitby 2008: 129).

As for Charlemagne in the west, he too adopted the terminology of kinship to calm potentially troubled waters:

> He bore the animosity that the assumption of this title [Roman emperor] caused with great patience, for the Roman [i.e., Byzantine] emperors were angry about it. He overcame their opposition through his greatness of spirit, which was without doubt far greater than theirs, by often sending ambassadors to them and by calling them brothers in his letters.
>
> —*VKM* 28

Charlemagne evidently also employed the concept of diplomatic friendship in order to account for what were in fact limitations to his imperial power:

> These are the wars which the most powerful king (*rex potentissimus*) waged with such prudence and success in various lands for forty-seven years, for he reigned that long. In those wars he so nobly increased the Frankish kingdom, which he had received from his father Pippin in a great and strong condition, that he nearly doubled its size . . . He added all of Italy which stretches for more than a thousand miles from Aosta to lower Calabria, which is the border between the Beneventans and the Greeks; then Saxony, which is no small part of Germany and is thought to be twice as wide as the land

occupied by the Franks but similar to it in length; then he added both provinces of Pannonia and Dacia beyond the further bank of the Danube, and also Istria, Liburnia and Dalmatia *save for its maritime cities, which he allowed the emperor of Constantinople to keep, because of the friendship (amicitia) and the pact (foedus) between them.*

—*VKM* 15; my emphasis

CONCLUSION

As we have seen, to speak about peace in the ancient world is impossible without reference to war, in spite of recent efforts to make it so (Moloney and Williams 2017a, 2017b). The subsequent chapters in this volume address various aspects of peace—and war—and flesh out concepts of "positive peace" in antiquity. This introduction has offered a very broad view of antiquity and has no doubt at times indulged in some over-generalization. It should be kept in mind that the parameters of this volume—thirteen centuries of history and multiple different societies, many of them with distinctly different ethnic and cultural backgrounds—mean that we cannot always generalize or extrapolate with accuracy. It is no doubt obvious to the reader that the vast breadth of the subject has demanded a very selective approach. The following chapters, however, provide more nuance, delving into these matters in greater depth and detail.

CHAPTER ONE

Definitions of Peace

SARAH BOLMARCICH

"Peace" is a word slippery with meaning. This is no less true in English than it is in Latin and Greek.[1] During the holiday season, Christians speak or sing of "peace on the earth, goodwill to men," where peace means living in mutual harmony, either between individuals or between groups, including countries. When someone is arrested for "disturbing the peace," the charge refers to their causing a commotion within their community and violating citizens' sense of public order and safety. If your therapist tells you to be "at peace with yourself" or to "make your peace" with an issue, it means to let it go, to accept yourself, to achieve an internal state of tranquility and serenity. Those who die are exhorted to "rest in peace" and let their death be the end of any conflicts they experienced, rather than haunt the living.

Even within the field of international relations, "peace" has varied meanings. When the British Prime Minister Neville Chamberlain returned from Germany after negotiating with Chancellor Adolf Hitler first the Munich Agreement (essentially an attempt at appeasement of Germany by allowing it to annex German-speaking portions of Czechoslovakia, the Sudetenland), and then the Anglo-German Agreement, he boldly stated, "I believe it is peace for our time ... Go home and get a nice quiet sleep." Subsequent events—the Second World War and the Blitz on London—made of Chamberlain a supreme ironist. What he meant by peace was "no future war": he did not sign an official treaty of peace, ending a war, merely a vague statement of future peace between England and Germany. The Treaty of Versailles, by contrast, was an official peace treaty ending the state of war in Europe from 1914–1918; that it also sowed the seeds for future war does not change this.

Here, peace is either the absence of war or conflict and the presence of a passive harmony or tranquility (negative peace), as the examples in the first paragraph attest, or it is, as in the second paragraph, a state that must be striven for, that has to be actively achieved by the fulfillment of certain conditions, either stated or unstated (positive peace), such as the payment of war reparations or the laying down of arms or the giving of hostages. There is a tendency today to believe that peace is the "natural" state in which humans would live, were it not for social tensions, war, or other conflicts. This is not a point of view either the Greeks or the Romans would have recognized, although a few of their philosophers might have dreamt of it. Rather, those who claim peace is a natural state are really referencing a state of passivity, negative peace; successful, positive peace, just like the conduct of war, requires effort and planning.[2] It is in this context that the Greek and Roman attitudes—and their use of this extremely elastic word—must be read.

THE GREEKS

The Greeks had several words that could be equivalent to the English meanings of "peace" outlined above. Libations to the gods, known as *spondai*, are often mentioned in the context of making peace, and so are sometimes taken to mean a peace treaty or truce.[3] *Eirēnē* is an extremely flexible word that covers both legal peace and informal peace, as well as peace in interpersonal relationships. *Hēsychia* refers to peace within oneself, a state of tranquility or serenity; other words like *galēnē* sometimes had a similar meaning. This section takes a closer look at *spondai* and *eirēnē*, considering what they meant to the Greeks, and finally asking whether the Greeks had any notion of positive peace at all.

Spondai

The term *spondai* is used as early as the Homeric poems to indicate "an agreement ratified by libations" (Cunliffe 1977, *s.v.* σπονδαί). It is used only twice in Homer, as a formula, referring to the shaking of right hands (later called *dexiosis*) and the pouring of unwatered wine to seal a compact. The first instance occurs after the near-revolt of the Achaian army in the *Iliad*: Nestor sarcastically comments that the leaders toss into the fire all their compacts and oaths (2.341). This must be a reference to the Oath of Tyndareus, intended to ensure peace in Greece between the princes who were the suitors of Helen by guaranteeing that all would abide by her choice of a husband and all would come to her husband's aid if she were abducted. In this instance, a *spondai* would be trying to build a lasting foundation for peace, but on the basis of deterrence—negative peace. The other instance refers to a violation of a temporary truce in order to allow Menelaos and Paris to fight in single combat over Helen (*Il.* 4.159). Here the intent of the libations has been violated, but peace was not the goal of the libations; rather, it was the settlement of a conflict with the least harm done to the masses of men fighting on each side at Troy. The truce only guaranteed that no one would participate in the conflict except for Menelaos and Paris.

The Iliadic references leave a slightly confused picture, describing as they do two distinct agreements with different goals. The word does not recur in the sense of "truce" or "peace treaty" until the fifth and fourth centuries BCE, when Greece was torn by a number of successive wars, internal and external.[4] Herodotos uses the word in a general sense of "truce" with a temporary or finite purpose (1.21; 7.149). Aischines uses it to describe a five-year truce around 450 BCE (2.172). There was of course the Olympic truce (Thuc. 5.49) and a truce during the celebration of the Eleusinian Mysteries (Aeschin. 2.133; *IG* I³ 6; *IEleus.* 138.150), both of which lasted no more than a few weeks.

Spondai is used by Thucydides to refer to the Thirty Years' Peace (1.35, 44, 78, 87, 146), to the Peace of Nikias (5.18, 21, 30; 6.7), and to a peace between the Spartans and the Argives (5.76). These three peace treaties all brought some form of hostilities to an end: the Thirty Years' Peace, the so-called undeclared "First Peloponnesian War," and the Peace of Nikias, which was to last for fifty years, the Archidamian War; the agreement between the Spartans and the Argives, which countered an earlier hundred-year Athenian treaty with Argos, Elis, and Mantinea, was to last for fifty years as well (Thuc. 5.47, 79).

The Peace of Nikias and the Thirty Years' Peace were notable failures when viewed as instruments of diplomacy seeking a lasting peace. The latter lasted fifteen years, half of its term, and the former—depending on whether you were an Athenian or a Spartan—a mere three to six years (Thuc. 5.56). Both treaties were vitiated by their focus on either preserving or returning to the *status quo* that had existed in Greece prior to the hostilities

DEFINITIONS OF PEACE

they sought to end; they did not address the pressing questions behind those hostilities, such as Athenian imperialism. Additionally, the Peace of Nikias was an essentially toothless document because Sparta's allies did not sign it, and the fulfillment of several key provisions was dependent on those allies' cooperation (Thuc. 5.3, 18, 39, 40).

All three of these treaties—the Thirty Years' Peace, the Peace of Nikias, and the Spartan peace with the Argives—had gain in mind: not tangible gain but the gain of time. The duration of each was to be at least a generation, a long enough period for circumstances to change, either peaceably or with an eye to military gain, as each side husbanded its resources for the next round of conflict. Herodotos makes exactly this point, as the Argives consider medizing and making a thirty-years' truce with the Persians: "it was important to them to secure the thirty-years' truce (*spondai*), to give their sons the chance of growing up during the period of peace" (7.149.1). Although their set durations might seem to indicate that these treaties were meant to establish a long-lasting positive peace, in fact they were merely truces measured in decades.

Spondai vs. eirēnē

Spondai is a word very much belonging to the fifth century BCE; its use in literature and epigraphy declines drastically thereafter. In epigraphy, *eirēnē* begins to be used much more frequently in the fourth century BCE, although its use too dates back to Homer; a similar phenomenon occurs in surviving literary evidence. Why this chronological shift should happen can only be speculated upon; it may parallel a more legalistic tone to Greek diplomacy in the fourth century, such as the use of more detailed oaths. But the Greeks also recognized other differences between the two, and fourth-century authors appeared to be at special pains to distinguish them. For instance, Andokides in *On the Peace with Sparta* observes:

> There is a wide difference between a peace (*eirēnē*) and a truce (*spondai*). A peace is a settlement of differences between equals; a truce is the dictation of terms to the conquered by the conquerors after victory in war, exactly as the Spartans laid down after their victory over us that we should demolish our walls, surrender our fleet, and restore our exiles. The agreement made then was a forced truce (*spondai*) upon dictated terms; whereas today you are considering a peace (*eirēnē*).
>
> —11; trans. Maidment

Another preoccupation of fourth-century diplomacy was at least the *pretense* of equality between allies or signatories to a treaty. Oaths were mutually exchanged when making treaties, for instance, and they were almost always the same oath, with the names of the states involved reversed. The fifth century, by contrast, had practiced equivalency of exchange—protection by Athens in exchange for tribute payments, for example—or straightforward domination. Andokides' distinction also brings to mind the distinction between positive and negative peace mentioned at the beginning of this chapter. As he describes *eirēnē*, it would function as a basis for the kind of lasting peace and growth of community between different groups or nations that positive peace envisions; *spondai* simply serve to eliminate conflict, a negative kind of peace.

However, the two cannot be unrelated in the Greek mind; *eirēnē* is the concept of peace as well as Andokides' suggested peace between equals, while *spondai* is one of the forms of executing it. Xenophon makes this clear: "so Derkylidas [a Spartan general campaigning in Asia Minor] sent to Pharnabazos [the Persian satrap of Phrygia] and asked which he preferred, peace (*eirēnē*) or war. Pharnabazos chose to make a truce (*spondai*), since it seemed to him that Aiolis was now a formidable base directed against Phrygia" (*Hell.* 3.2.1). The *spondai* are the instrument of peace here; Pharnabazos has not been conquered, although he fears he will be. But to get *eirēnē*, which may be the basis for a lasting peace, he must sign a truce (*spondai*), which is a very flawed and temporary means of achieving peace.

Eirēnē

The increasing prominence of *eirēnē* in the fourth century BCE was largely due to the creation of a concept known as *koinē eirēnē*, a common peace to which all Greeks were a party. The first instance was in 387/6 BCE with a multilateral peace treaty, perhaps the first ever (Quass 1991: 40), best known as the King's Peace or the Peace of Antalkidas after the chief enforcer and the chief negotiator. However, the idea of a common peace preceded this first instance of it (Andokides 3.17, 34). The terms of the Peace of Antalkidas, according to Xenophon, were quite straightforward:

'I, King Artaxerxes, regard the following as just: 1. The cities (*poleis*) in Asia and, among the islands, Klazomenai and Cyprus should belong to me. 2. The other Greek cities, big and small, should be left to govern themselves, except for Lemnos, Imbros, and Skyros, which should belong to Athens, as in the past. And if either of the two parties refuses to accept peace on these terms, I, together with those who will accept this peace, will make war on that party both by land and by sea, with ships and with money.'

—*Hell.* 5.1.31

Regarded in the light of previous Greek peace treaties, this peace exhibits a number of peculiarities. It is both multilateral (applying to all Greek states; Wilcken 1942) and unilateral (imposed and enforced by the authority of the Great King; von Scala *SVA* I 1898: 110; Ryder 1965: 2; Jehne 1994: 37). To achieve such an idea without Persian interference, the Greeks would have had to have a centralized authority of their own with the power to enforce treaty terms. None such existed; no Greek city had sufficient status or popularity or trustworthiness in the fourth century BCE to be such an authority. The Panhellenic sanctuaries such as Delphi and Olympia, where treaty-texts were often posted or erected, and which were occasionally used as instruments of arbitration between Greek cities, were themselves too much at the mercy of their fellow Greeks to be the truly neutral parties such enforcement would have required. While the idea of a common peace suggests a dream of common security, that vision on its own does not appear to have been a serious encouragement to self-enforcement for the Greeks. The only true solution would have been an outside state like Persia, possessed of the respect and the authority that enforcement of such an agreement required.

The Peace of Antalkidas was ineffective; it ultimately became a means for city-states, particularly Sparta—who benefited the most from the Peace and was also the first to violate it (Xen. *Hell.* 5.1.36, 5.2.1–7)—to attack cities that they deemed were not adhering to the Peace by allowing their fellow Greeks to be free and autonomous. Over the next quarter of a century, several *koinai eirēnai* were implemented, each of them failing almost as soon as the ink was dry. While this series of common peace agreements in the twenty-five years from 387 to 362 BCE suggests that the Greeks had an interest in pursuing an active, positive peace in their country, it is the opposite that is true. Just like *spondai*, common peace agreements served to end an armed conflict. Unlike *spondai*, however, they were not stated to exist for a fixed term. Instead, the presumption appears to have been that all states would abide by them, and that they could theoretically exist in perpetuity if states continued to observe their provisions. What common peaces did not do was lay down the kind of federal infrastructure that would preserve such a peace; they depended on an "enforcer" such as the Great King. The idea of "positive peace" today rests on exactly that kind of federal infrastructure that the Greeks lacked and that, say, the European Union has. Federal organizations alone do not guarantee continued peace, of course; the Boiotian League, the Achaian League, and the Arkadian League, all Greek federal states, each occasionally suffered internal conflict themselves; the advantage of a federal system is that it offers a way to resolve conflict before hostilities erupt (Beck and Funke 2015a).

The idea of a common peace, although obviously attractive to the Greeks, was ultimately ineffective. As with the Peace of Nikias and the Thirty Years' Peace, the underlying issues that caused warfare between the Greek cities at the time, such as Spartan imperialism, were not solved by any of these agreements. Rather these peaces attempted to inculcate from the top down a respect for and a non-aggressive attitude towards other Greek cities that did not in fact exist except perhaps in the few minutes it took a state's ambassadors to swear oaths upholding the agreement. In the end, these common peaces were a negative example of peace.[5]

There were some significant differences between international relations in the Archaic and Classical periods and in the Hellenistic period. First, the presence of powerful Hellenistic monarchs often at war with their royal brethren changed diplomatic behaviors. Second, the Hellenistic period saw the rise of federal states, particularly in Greece, to combat that royal power; these states ideally offered peace among their own members if not with Macedonia or Sparta. And third, states in the Hellenistic period appear to have been much more eager to utilize interstate arbitration than they had been previously. Yet despite all this, peace was maintained with the threat of war, however theoretical: from the king, from an arbitrator (or as an alternative to arbitration if it failed), and from the strong centralized apparatus of the federal states.

Philip's Ambition, Isokrates' Dream

A far more idealistic vision of a common peace existed in the fourth century BCE; this was the idea of a Panhellenic peace articulated by the orator Isokrates, who laid forth an argument for peace among the Greeks—*all* Greeks.

Noting the traditional hostility of his audience to those who counseled peace because peace flew in the face of human nature (*On the Peace*: Or. 8.5–6), Isokrates indicates that he knew how hard a row he had to hoe against the traditional Greek mindset of the ineluctability of warfare. Isokrates' proposal is really quite simple:

> I maintain, then, that we should make peace (*eirēnē*), not only with the Chians, the Rhodians, the Byzantines, and the Koans, but with all mankind, and that we should adopt, not the covenants of peace (*synthēkai*) which certain parties have recently drawn up, but those which we have entered into with the king of Persia and with the Spartans, which ordain that the Greeks be independent, that the alien garrisons be removed from the several states, and that each people retain its own territory. For we shall not find terms of peace more just than these nor more expedient for our city.

—Or. 8.16

FIGURE 1.1: Engraving from *Crabb's Historical Dictionary* (1825) depicting the Athenian rhetorician Isokrates. Photo by Ken Welsh/*/Design Pics/Corbis, courtesy of Getty Images.

Isokrates fully supports the practice of the common peaces outlined in the previous section, of whose failures he must have been fully aware. To convince his audience, he takes the tack that such peaces are advantageous, a resuscitation of Thucydides' *to sympheron*, which was usually used to justify brutality in war.[6] He lists these advantages: security, no war, no danger, freedom from civil war, and prosperity as citizens are freed from taxes and allowed to pursue their occupations, such as farming and trading, once again. He also dangles the possibility of the Athenians reclaiming their hegemony over Greece, as leaders in peace, not in war.

Isokrates realizes that what his scheme requires is a leader and a cause behind which the Greeks could become united, abandoning any petty warfare among themselves, much as their ancestors had done during the Persian Wars. Ultimately, he settled on Philip of Macedon (*To Philip*: Or. 5; *Letters* 2, 3). To some degree, Philip fulfilled Isokrates' dream, uniting the Greek states, except Sparta, under his leadership in the League of Corinth, with the intention of marching against Persia (Diod. Sic. 16.89, Just. *Epit*. 9.5.4–7). But first he made "peace" by subduing Greece. Even the best-articulated vision of peace from an ancient Greek thinker turned out to be predicated on the assumption of continued war.[7]

Famously, ancient Athenians held the idea that a citizen who was not involved in politics, who was passive, was an *apragmōn* (actionless) man guilty of *apragmosynē* (failure to act). But *apragmosynē* was a fault of cities as well: the Corcyraians beg Athenian forgiveness for their *apragmosynē* when they request an alliance with Athens against Corinth (Thuc. 1.32). Another type of inaction in foreign affairs was *hēsychia*,[8] a crime of

FIGURE 1.2: Ivory head from the royal tombs of Vergina thought to depict Philip II of Macedon; Archaeological Museum, Thessaloniki, Greece. Photo by DeAgostini, courtesy of Getty Images.

which the Corinthians accused the Spartans (Thuc. 1.69, 70, 71). Here *hēsychia* means inaction, especially inaction in the face of harm to one's allies. Just as the Athenians were unable to conceive positively of a citizen who removed himself from political affairs, so too the Corinthians were unable to approve of a state that did nothing abroad on either its own behalf or that of its allies. Perhaps this attitude—an expectation of involvement in foreign and domestic affairs, of *action*—lay behind the Greek inability to enter into and maintain a state of peace.

THE ROMANS

What the Romans meant by peace or *pax* was not what we mean by peace today (Woolf 1993; Barton 2007; Goldsworthy 2016; Cornwell 2017). Rather, for them, peace came as the aftermath of military success. It was not a condition that the Romans sought for its own sake; it was a condition they strove for to increase their own military security, might and power (Rosenstein 2007). It was also part of a cycle that guaranteed continued warfare, for the Romans would then have to protect the gains they had made from the peace that had ended the previous war. The Romans did not see an antithetical distinction between states of war and peace the way we do today; the two conditions were inextricably linked and often cycled back to each other (Barton 2007: 246).

Like English "peace," however, Roman *pax* is a word that covers many states, from legal peace to a state of security to tranquility in one's mind or spirit. The meaning of "peace" to the Romans on the international and military level has been well demonstrated already, as noted in the previous paragraph; this chapter will focus on how the Romans themselves viewed *pax*. It was not only a term with many meanings, including meanings that implied the opposite of each other, but it was also far from the only word that Romans used in describing diplomatic agreements and behavior.

Pax as a condition for the Romans usually followed upon *deditio*, a surrender or capitulation. It was a choice the Romans excelled at forcing upon a defeated enemy; for instance, during the Samnite Wars Livy records that, to a besieged city, *levissimum malorum deditio ad Romanos visa*, "it appeared that surrender to the Romans was the least intolerable evil" (8.25.8). Accordingly, the entire city was surrendered to the Romans, the gates thrown open, and no stipulations of mercy were made by their leaders. The result was *deditio*: total submission to the Romans.

The natural result of a *deditio* was *dicio*, power or dominion. Julius Caesar, in the *Gallic War*, indicates the solemnity of such a moment by his phrasing: "At the same season Publius Crassus, whom he had despatched with one legion against the Veneti, Venelli, Osismi, Curiosolitae, Esubii, Aulerci, and Redones, the maritime states which border upon the [Atlantic] Ocean, reported that all those states had been brought into subjection to the power of Rome (*in dicionem potestatemque populi Romani esse redactas*)" (2.34). Caesar makes it clear to whom these states now owe their obligation, and by listing them and identifying their geographical position he delineates more clearly the Roman Empire. His very next sentence begins *his rebus gestis omni Gallia pacata*, "after these things were accomplished and all Gaul had been subjected" (2.35; my translation),[9] and then describes how bringing those final tribes under Roman *dicio* made the tribes across the Rhine more pliable and peaceful. Surrender started a chain of dominoes: it not only brought non-Romans under Roman control, it also set an example for their unconquered neighbors of how best to behave towards the Romans.

The Latin verb *paco*, like *pax*, does not mean to make peace or to pacify, but rather to impose peace terms upon, as Caesar did upon the Gallic tribes here (*pacata*). That this was the path to empire is made clear by Cicero in the Second Catilinarian: "for there is no nation that we should fear, no king who could make war with the Roman people. Everything external [to Rome] has been subjected (*pacata*) both by land and by sea" (*Cat.* 2.11; my translation). *Pacifico*, from which we derive the English verb pacify, is far less commonly used in Latin than *paco*, and does not mainly mean to appease as in English, but rather to negotiate about peace (e.g., Liv. 7.40.14). But to negotiate about peace with the Romans meant to submit to Rome.

The Romans did have treaties that were not peace treaties predicated upon the capitulation of their defeated enemy. The basic Latin word for treaty is *foedus*. These agreements created relationships that were perceived as far more equal than those between the Romans and the surrendered. For instance, the first Roman treaty, the *foedus Cassianum*, was a defensive agreement with the Latin League that recognized both parties as equals after the two had clashed at the Battle of Lake Regillus in 493 BCE (Dion. Hal. *Ant. Rom.* 6.95). Peace in the sense of non-aggression might very well be part of such a treaty, but not peace in the sense of subjugation. There was such a thing as a *foedus iniquum*, a treaty that assumed that one party was superior. The Latin leader Annius complained as early as 341 BCE that often such treaties existed under the guide of a *foedus aequum*, an equal treaty:

DEFINITIONS OF PEACE

For if we are able even now to endure slavery under a shadowy pretence of equal treaty-rights, what is left for us but to give up the Sidicini, and obeying the behest not of the Romans only but also of the Samnites, make answer to the Romans that we are ready to lay down our arms at their beck and call?

—Livy 8.4

Eventually any agreement the Romans made on apparently equal terms might be subverted into a dominant-subordinate relationship.

The Romans' attitude towards war explains at least some of their attitude towards peace. Famously, the Romans only fought defensive wars[10]—yet somehow they ended up in control of the entire Mediterranean basin and parts of Europe. Any number of reasons could provoke a war under such a philosophy: not merely violations of treaty terms on one end of the scale, but pre-emptive self-defense on the other. Cicero articulates the philosophy in his speech *de Provinciis Consularibus*, delivered in 56 BCE, when he states about Gaul: "From the very beginning of our Empire (*imperium*) we have had no wise statesman who did not regard Gaul as the greatest danger to our Empire (*imperium* again)" (33). Fear is cause for war and the abandonment of peace. As Vegetius drily notes in *de Re Militari*, *igitur qui desiderat pacem, praeparet bellum*, "so if one wants peace, one prepares for war" (3 *praef.*). The sentiment is not uniquely Roman,[11] but they lived it.

Pax

Probably the two most famous quotations from Roman authors on "peace" are those of Tacitus and Vergil:

auferre trucidare rapere falsis nominibus imperium, atque ubi solitudinem faciunt, pacem appellant.

To robbery, butchery, and rapine, they give the lying name of "empire" (*imperium*, "rule" or "power over"); they create a desolation and they call it peace.

—Tac. *Agr.* 30; Mattingly translation, slightly adapted

tu regere imperio populos, Romane, memento; hae tibi erunt artes: pacisque imponere morem, parcere subiectis, et debellare superbos.

Do you remember, Roman, to rule imperially over the nations (these shall be your skills), to set the force of habit upon peace, to spare those who submit and crush in war the haughty.

—Verg. *Aen.* 6.851–3; Horsfall translation

Neither quote is unproblematic in terms of revealing Roman attitudes towards peace. Tacitus puts these words into the mouth of the British chieftain Calgacus, who is speaking to his soldiers on the eve of a battle with the Romans. The sentiment is exactly appropriate to a non-Roman rebel, but it is also appropriate to the man who feeds him his lines: Tacitus, Agricola's son-in-law and hagiographer in this work, was part of a disaffected senatorial aristocracy under the Roman Empire, at a time when the honor every noble Roman sought by prowess in war or peace was reserved almost exclusively for the emperor (Woolf 1993: 178–81; De Souza 2008: 95–6). Worse yet, the emperor under whom Agricola served was the hated Domitian, himself quite successful at *auferre trucidare rapere* both at home and abroad. De Souza believes the passage to reflect Tacitus's own ideology of peace: it could only be accomplished by conquest (De Souza 2008: 95). Putting that sentiment in Calgacus' mouth in such bald language only drives the point further home. But Tacitus's insistence on *falsis nominibus* also brings home the point made previously about the shifting and unexpected meanings of *pax*.

The Vergil lines are spoken by the spirit of Aeneas' father Anchises, who, during his son's tour of the underworld, is showing him the great procession of the souls of future notable Romans waiting to be born. There is a similar attitude here to the passage in Tacitus—note that in both authors *imperium* (power or rule) is closely associated with peace—in that both envision the Romans as a conquering people. But what is also telling about the Vergil passage is that the custom or habit of peace is for the Romans to teach or instill in the world (*pacisque imponere morem*).[12] Teaching is very much a superior-subordinate relationship here; the implication is that were it not for Roman conquest, the world would not know what peace even was. Peace, therefore, is ineluctably Roman: only they can create it and instill respect for it in their subjects and enemies. The *pax Romana* is the source of the idea of "hegemonic peace" or the *pax imperia* in modern studies of peace and imperialism.[13] Since men are not angels, peace requires enforcement; it is therefore in the Roman perspective not based upon the goodwill of two opposing parties towards each other, but on the ability of each to enforce the condition of peace either on each other or on dissidents within their ranks. But, as Greg Woolf notes, the Romans were peacemakers, not peacekeepers (Woolf 2016). If peace was ensured by their *imperium*, they needed to nourish and increase that *imperium*—even by breaking peace for the sake of war.

The "History" of Roman Peace

In retrospect, to many moderns it might seem there was no less peaceful society than the Romans; as noted earlier, building an empire means forgoing peace (a lesson the Greeks also learned). Nevertheless, just as their military counterparts created an empire, so too did Roman authors create a "history" of peace in their works, making clear its association with Roman-ness from the very beginning, all the way through the Republic and Empire and even into the late antique period. Vergil, who writes of Rome even before her founding, makes this point repeatedly in the *Aeneid*. As his Roman descendants always claimed to be themselves, Aeneas is a reluctant warrior; his fear in escaping Troy is on display prominently at the end of the second book. Throughout his journey, Aeneas and his men attack only when under threat themselves and the settlements they attempt to found before arriving in Italy are all founded in peace. Even at Carthage, where Aeneas's visit, affair with Dido, and departure presage Roman war with Carthage many generations later, it is Dido's curse that instigates and sets in motion that future conflict.

When Aeneas and his men arrive in Italy and visit Evander's kingdom, they are greeted by the king's son Pallas with the words *pacemne huc fertis an arma*, "do you bring peace or war?" (Verg. *Aen.* 8.114; Fagles translation).

The answer, of course, is complicated; Aeneas is visiting Evander to seek an ally against the Latins, who under Turnus' leadership have attacked the Trojans. But the alliance is predicated upon mutual amity between Aeneas and Evander, and by Aeneas's mentor–protégé relationship with Pallas. War is but a temporary cloud on the horizon. Likewise, once Turnus is defeated, there will be harmony between Trojans and Latins as well. Latinus himself swears this to Aeneas: *nulla dies pacem hanc Italis nec foedera rumpet*, "the day will never dawn when Italian men will break this pact, this peace" (12.202; Fagles translation).

FIGURE 1.3: Aeneas arrives in Latium, offering an olive branch to King Evander and his son Pallas; detail from the *Stories of Aeneas*, by Pietro da Cortona (1596–1669); Palazzo Doria Pamphili, Rome, Italy. Photo by DeAgostini, courtesy of Getty Images.

These two passages do exhibit differences from Anchises' statement about the Romans teaching peace. While Anchises is speaking in the context of giving his son a survey of the future great men of Rome, he is also speaking within the context of a comparison of Greece and Rome; before he instructs the Romans to impose peace, he comments: "Others may beat out breathing bronze more supply, may draw living expressions from marble, may plead cases better, may expound the movements of the heavens with a pointer and tell the risings of the stars" (6.847–50; Horsfall translation). The strength of the Greeks is in learned skill: casting bronze, carving marble, employing rhetoric, and observing the heavens. The Romans' strength, on the other hand, is in imposing peace, sparing the conquered, and defeating the haughty: behavioral skills and the innate tendencies of the Romans themselves. A Greek sculptor or rhetorician instructs his pupils by imparting information and by allowing them a process of trial and error. The Romans' "teaching" method, by contrast, is modeling, and other nations can only imitate it; they might never achieve the full capability of the Romans for any of these activities.

It is also noteworthy that the only sure way to teach any other nation how to make peace or to spare the conquered would be for the Romans to rise to prominence themselves; and conquest of others, of the proud, was the surest way to do that. The gates of Janus at Rome, the gates whose closure indicated that Rome was not at war, could only be closed by a conqueror (DeBrohun 2007: 259). So, if only to fulfill Anchises' prophecy in retrospect, the Romans had to become conquerors. Once they had done so, and promoted the custom of peace in the conquered, it was no longer the Roman responsibility to maintain peace in an active sense; it was that of the conquered not to revolt, not to rock the boat, not to abandon the Roman *mores* that held them firm.

Anchises' use of *imponere* to indicate the Romans' imposition of peace is telling. *Pacisque morem imponere* means not just to impose peace, but rather the custom or habit (*morem*) of peace—and surely it is the Roman idea of what the custom or habit of peace is that prevails. While in Latin *impono* can have a neutral meaning of simply placing something upon something, such as saddlebags on a horse (Cic. *Nat. D.* 2.151) or to load a ship (Cic.*Div.* 2.84), when it is used in a military or legal context, it implies at least a threat of force or constraint if not its actual use. The Romans will educate others in the ways of peace, yes, but it will be an education required for interacting with the Romans.

Seen in that light, Augustus' *pax Augusta* takes on the meaning not of a practical, functional state of relative calm (if not actual peace),[14] but of Rome fulfilling her duty to make the world more Roman.

When Pliny the Elder refers to the *inmensa Romanae pacis maiestate*, "the enormous sovereignty of the Roman peace," he is ostensibly referencing the way in which the Roman conquest of the world has opened up a great deal of new information to scholars.[15] But Pliny's choice of *maiestas* (literally, "greaterness," here referring to Rome's complete domination) is also significant, for by choosing that word he evokes not just the supremacy of Rome but he also gives that supremacy divine overtones, as *maiestas* can refer not only to the state but to the gods.

FIGURE 1.4: The first Roman emperor, Augustus, wearing an oak leaf crown; Glyptothek Museum, Munich, Germany. Photo by PHAS/UIG, courtesy of Getty Images.

And it is the gods who guarantee and grant peace, not only in the sense of guaranteeing an actual peace treaty when the oaths of the treaty are sworn by them or when a text of the treaty is deposited in a certain god's sanctuary as a form of spiritual guarantee, but also in the sense of granting men the boon of a tranquil life without conflict. Under the *pax Augusta*, the Roman emperor took over that divine role well into the second century CE (de Souza 2008: 87). The younger Pliny, for instance, praises Trajan as the one who determines whether there shall be peace or war (*Pan.* 4.4). Naturally, since success in war was also the way in which emperors and the Roman Empire (in both the Republican and Imperial periods) gained authority, there is a strong argument to be made that Roman peace was in fact war; as Greg Woolf puts it, "if war is organized societal violence, then the Roman peace qualifies as war . . . the emperors ruled not by abolishing violence but by channeling it" (Woolf 1993: 191). Peace and war had the same effect on Rome's allies and subjects: it put them under the thrall of the empire.

What the Vergil quotation under discussion makes clear is that *both* war and peace were integral parts of the Romans' nature; a society that claims to value honor, reputation, and duty cannot also be expected to value a concept like peace for its own sake, but only insofar as peace helps its elite to attain and maintain their goals and desires. Augustus' poet Vergil recognizes this, and places this attitude in the mouth of the father of the founder of Rome not to justify or legitimize it, but to enshrine it in the most solemn of contexts: a wise old man prophesying Rome's future from beyond the world of the living.

Ironically, in some ways the Roman self-identification of their national character with peace might arguably be a step in the direction of attaining and maintaining peace in the positive sense. If a nation expects that it will be a peaceful one, it should organize itself administratively to achieve and retain that peace, ensuring that standard tasks go smoothly and that there is as little friction as possible between citizens and between citizens and state. The Romans, of course, also organized themselves to be on a near-constant war footing—and yet that was what assured them that they really had created a *pax Romana*.

Much of the preceding discussion has dealt with peace inside the Roman Empire, indeed peace as a means of empire building. Outside the empire, things were not that much different. As Susan Mattern explains:

> The Romans seem to have perceived foreign relations as a competition for honor and status between Rome and barbarian peoples; by proving its superior force through war and conquest, Rome extracts deference and reverence from other nations, who then remain submissive, refraining from revolt or attack. It is in this way that the empire is supposed to maintain security. Conversely, signs of weakness on Rome's part, such as a show of deference to a foreign people, or failure to avenge a defeat in war or to punish a revolt with sufficient ferocity, are considered invitations to disasters. For these reasons the Romans sometimes seem to react very aggressively to apparently minor breaches of treaty, to exaggerate the threat posed by rivals, and to respond to crises with conquest or even attempted genocide while insisting that their concerns are for their own security.
>
> —2002: 171–172

The same Roman attitudes towards peace that allowed them to acquire and maintain an empire also allowed them to defend it pre-emptively by aggressively pursuing any perceived violations of peace. Above, Cicero noted that any thinking man would realize that Gaul outside the Empire was the greatest threat to the Romans. Inevitably, this threat

FIGURE 1.5a and 1.5b: Aureus of the Emperor Gallienus (r. 253–268 CE); on the obverse, portrait of Gallienus; on the reverse, image of Peace holding branch and sceptre, with legend PAX AVGVSTA. ANS 1944.100.30853. Courtesy of the American Numismatic Society.

led Caesar and others to attempt to conquer and subdue the Gauls. These were defensive wars, not wars of conquest, according to the Romans' idea of security.

States that remained persistently outside the Empire throughout much of its history are hard to find, since most of the Mediterranean ultimately came under her sway. There are, however, two examples of treaties Rome made with powerful Eastern states—the treaty of Apameia with the Seleukid king Antiochos III the Great and the treaty of Rhandeia with the Parthians—that illustrate the point that peace was little different outside the Empire. In the treaty of Apameia (188 BCE), Antiochos did not lose his throne, but was forced to abandon any claim to territory in Europe and also to see Asia Minor west of the Taurus Mountains handed over to his rival Eumenes of Pergamon. He also lost his war elephants, gave hostages, and paid indemnities (Polyb. 21.42). The Romans were

DEFINITIONS OF PEACE 33

able to exact such terms because they had defeated Antiochos, but they did not subdue him. Instead, they left him largely in charge of Asia proper, but too weakened and chastened to pose a threat to Rome, while the pro-Roman Eumenes kept an eye on him.

The treaty of Rhandeia in 63 CE was made on more equal terms between Rome and Parthia. The issue was who would hold the throne of Armenia, a Parthian or a Roman appointee, and with the approval of which state. The treaty stated that a Parthian prince of the royal Arsakid family would hold the throne of Armenia, though the Romans would have to nominate him (Tac. *Ann.* 15.28–30; Cass. Dio 57.21–2). This agreement was reached after the Roman-Parthian War of 58–63 CE, which had ultimately been inconclusive militarily, so the treaty represented a compromise. Although the Roman nomination of the Armenian king theoretically made Armenia a client state of Rome, at Rome the treaty was not viewed favorably, and Nero was accused of losing Armenia (Festus *Breviarium.* 20.1). Telling too is the attitude of Vologeses, the Parthian king, towards Rome when it looked like war would be coming; Tacitus describes him as reflecting on the greatness of Rome (*Ann.* 15.1), and notes that it was his policy to avoid war with Rome (*Ann.* 15.5). Vologeses' attitude shows the fear and respect upon which the Romans relied, both within and without the Empire, on keeping subjects loyal and potential opponents quiescent.

MAKING WAR AND PEACE AFTER THE FALL OF THE WESTERN ROMAN EMPIRE

The traditional date for the fall of the Western Roman Empire is 476 CE. It was ultimately "replaced" by the Holy Roman Empire, while in the East the eastern division of the Roman Empire survived as the Byzantine Empire for almost another thousand years. The division of the empire itself indicated the weakness that the later Roman Empire had faced; its particular diplomatic danger zones were to the east in Asia, where the Sassanian dynasty ruled Persia, and to the north, where the tribes of Germania were beginning to unite and so present an even greater threat to Rome than their ancestors had. In the later Roman Empire and especially in its western division, then, warfare became increasingly necessary for survival, and so correspondingly did diplomacy.

It was noted earlier that the Romans were peacemakers, not peacekeepers. Their attitude may have shifted as their survival became more and more precarious. As one scholar notes, during late antiquity Roman diplomacy came to seek "to substitute itself for war and to treat war not as its precondition but as its outcome" (Blockley 1992: 151). A number of features were introduced into the Roman diplomatic process, or, if previously present, were given greater emphasis in the making of a peace treaty. For instance, diplomacy might be conducted by the emperor and foreign leaders face to face, instead of through the exchange of embassies.[16] This also meant that negotiations were often not conducted in one or the other capital, or even a major city, but on the frontier (an almost-neutral area) where the two leaders were present with their armies. The exchange of hostages was emphasized, but often it was a short-term exchange, not conducted with the earlier intent to "Romanize" hostages.[17] While oaths had always been a standard of ancient treaties, the Romans now begin to quote oath texts in the actual texts of the treaties made, a practice that they had not pursued with regularity before, but which was certainly useful as a guarantee of greater security for a treaty (Heather 1997: 69). All of these elements suggest less of a diplomatic focus on maintaining power and more of a focus on maintaining a lack of hostilities.

In the West, the Romans faced a particular problem: the unreliability of the Germanic tribes on the Danube frontier in keeping to the terms of diplomatic agreements. This was not for the Romans' own earlier reasons for regarding peace terms as flexible, namely imperial ambition, but because the loose social structure and hierarchies of the Germanic tribes prevented the kind of centralized authority that could commit to the maintenance of peace. Moreover, the land hunger the tribes faced constantly had a more serious impact on them than the moral obligations of observing their agreements (Blockley 1992: 45). Emperors could and did pay for peace; for instance, the Byzantine emperor Maurice paid the Avar tribe 100,000 *nomismata* per year for peace, an increase over the 80,000 his predecessor Tiberius II Constantine had paid (Theophanes *Chronographia*, 301–2). The Avars were not the only tribe to enjoy such subsidies, nor were such "tributes" limited to the northern tribes, but were also paid to Persia and the Arabs.

In the East, the Roman and subsequently the Byzantine Empire found itself well balanced with the Sassanian Empire. Diplomacy therefore gave a much more equal appearance than it would have earlier in Roman history; the importance here was to maintain a balance of powers while taking what opportunities came the way of each state (Whitby 2008: 125–40). Possibly for the first time since the Punic Wars, the Romans found themselves facing a state that could well be their match. Under such circumstances, diplomacy became a matter of survival, not a means for expansion.

The comparative weakness of the later Roman Empire and its Byzantine successor dictated changes in the Roman conduct of diplomacy. The Romans no longer used diplomacy as a means to war; sometimes it did still serve that purpose, of course, but if diplomacy and efforts at peace were unsuccessful, it was no longer because they were meant, or hoped to be, such, but because what were essentially temporary defensive measures had failed.[18] The relative weakness of Rome in late antiquity, compared to Rome from the beginning of the third century BCE through the end of the second century CE effected these changes in Roman diplomacy and ideas of peace and war.

CONCLUSION

The difficulty of defining peace and all its implications in any historical era appears particularly acute with the Greeks and the Romans. Like most Western societies, overall, to them peace was a good thing, a positive if it happened to exist. But because both societies were also agonistic and honor-based, peace could never quite find a home: it is hard to have a competition to see who can be the most peaceful city or empire without risking annihilation at the hands of others. And so for both civilizations peace became even more of a dream than it is today, a dream subordinate to each society's need to compete.

The Greeks often made peace treaties that were clearly intended to be temporary, whether they were meant to last for a few hours or for fifty years. These served merely as a respite, and were openly acknowledged to be such by historians like Herodotos. Although accusations of breaking a peace or who was first to do so might fly fast and furious between Greek states—such as Athens and Sparta after the Peace of Nikias—the Greeks do not actually seem to have expected the peace times to last. To be able to blame a state for initiating war was the actual goal in such exchanges. Isokrates' dream of a Panhellenic peace, promoted by him for a good forty years, lacked one component: a strong military leader. Isokrates thought that such a leader would be needed to launch the requisite expedition against Persia, but in fact, such a leader was needed to unite the

Greeks in the first place and force an uneasy peace on them, as Philip of Macedon eventually did. Greek "peace" was very much a tool of war or a by-product of tyranny or imperialism.

For the Romans, peace came after a defeated enemy had subjected themselves to the Romans. It was not an equal state, as peace is conceived of today. It was a top-down, dictated effort, much as the King's Peace was dictated by the Great King of Persia to the Greeks. Furthermore, it had to be enforced, like the King's Peace, by future war or the threat of it. The Romans saw themselves as a warlike people in defense of their homeland, but they also saw themselves as a peaceful people. The two attitudes are not opposite sides of the same coin; they go hand in hand, as a peaceful nation would only fight in defense of itself. Where the Greeks recognized the futility of peace, the Romans integrated it into their national character. Only as the Empire declined in late antiquity do we see Roman attitudes towards peace and diplomacy changing.

CHAPTER TWO

Human Nature, Peace, and War

KURT A. RAAFLAUB

HUMAN NATURE AND THE ORIGINS OF WAR AND PEACE: BIOLOGICAL, PSYCHOLOGICAL, AND ANTHROPOLOGICAL PERSPECTIVES

The concept of human nature defies a clear and simple definition, especially in its connection with war and peace. It alludes to certain character traits or instincts that predispose humans to react to aggression, violence, strife, war, and their opposites in certain ways that are often believed to be so deeply ingrained that they become predictable. I use the concept in this very broad and unspecific understanding that is also closest to ancient discussions of it, omitting debates among philosophers, sociologists, and anthropologists from David Hume (1739–1740) to Jürgen Habermas (2003). The relationship between human nature and war or peace is a large, complex, and rapidly evolving area of research among many disciplines. The sketch offered here necessarily is very rough and selective, and only a fraction of the huge and diverse bibliography on the subject matter can be referenced.[1]

In order to understand why humans incessantly engage in violence and wars, students often ask whether the answers lie in human nature and whether humans are natural predators. For a long time, scholars used to answer this question positively. As Robert Ardrey put it succinctly, "Man is a predator whose natural instinct is to kill with a weapon" (1961: 316). This view is highly controversial, and is challenged by (for example) the essays collected by Douglas Fry in *War, Peace, and Human Nature: The Convergence of Evolutionary and Cultural Views* (2013). A more cautious response might be that humans are part of the natural world and thus part of the struggle of all beings to survive and improve their chances to do so. In the long process of evolution, some animals became predators, topping the food chain but still being part of it. In several species, these struggles at times also aim at more than mere survival: at power through domination of others and at wealth through accumulation of territories and resources that make expanded domination possible.

Due to the unique features and abilities humans developed, they mastered the general struggle for survival, power, and wealth more successfully than all other species. Eventually, they developed tools and methods that enabled them, on an ever-larger scale, to oppress or destroy their enemies and victims, whether human or animal. Still, although they have enormously changed the methods, goals, scale, and intensity of their fights, allowing for ever more detrimental consequences and even raising the potential of complete self-destruction, humans still share behaviors and attitudes that pervade the natural world; they occupy the extreme end of a scale onto which every living being can be placed.

I take war to be the collective, organized, and lethal use of violence by one group against another to attain a group's needs and goals (e.g., Ferguson 2008: 15). Some scholars distinguish between "primitive war" (Turney-High 1971), fought by "crowd armies," and "true/organized war," the latter characterized by strict leadership, the use of formation, and the imposition of discipline (Keegan 1976: 173–74; Ferrill 1997: 11). In the view outlined above, war in its earliest forms was not unique to humans and possibly even predates humans; at least, it was common to humans and some other species like chimpanzees and wolves. War in the form that is recognizable in the archaeological record developed out of earlier forms that we can at least deduce from the modern observation of animal group behavior and surviving instances of tribal group behavior among hunter-gatherers.

This is the view developed, for example, in the influential work of the twentieth-century zoologist and ethologist Konrad Lorenz (1966), who, on a Darwinian basis, emphasized the evolutionary advantages of intra-species fighting among higher animals and the dangers of the "aggression drive" inherited from our "anthropoid ancestors." In contrast to many social animals, in which this aggression drive is controlled by inhibitions, the specific nature of human evolution prevented the development of inhibitory mechanisms (but see below), thus making ever more refined killer capabilities especially lethal.

As David Barash observes (2000: 19), such "instinctivist theories of human aggressiveness have been criticized, especially because [they] seem to promote the notion that warfare is 'in our genes' and, hence, cannot be prevented." In a detailed re-examination, David Livingstone Smith (2012: 339; cf. Fry 2013) concludes that many common assumptions about the origins of warfare are based on minimal and questionable evidence and that a predisposition to war cannot reasonably be regarded as a component of human nature, although it may be an expression of certain features of human nature or of human male nature. Already in the mid-twentieth century, the anthropologist Margaret Mead (1940) argued vigorously against the idea that war is a "biological necessity" or "sociological inevitability," claiming instead that war is a "bad invention," introduced at some point in human evolution and, once introduced, applied ever more frequently and violently. Being a social invention, however, like others (such as the duel or vendetta), it can be recognized as such and replaced by a better invention.

In 1986 the "Seville Statement on Violence," published by eminent social and natural scientists in the context of the United Nations Year of Peace and subsequently adopted by UNESCO, aimed in the same direction:

> It is scientifically incorrect to say that we have inherited a tendency to make war from our animal ancestors. Although fighting occurs widely throughout animal species, only a few cases of destructive intra-species fighting between organized groups have ever been reported among naturally living species, and none of these involve the use of tools designed to be weapons. Normal predatory feeding upon other species cannot be equated with intra-species violence. Warfare is a peculiarly human phenomenon and does not occur in other animals.[2]

This is correct if the definition of war involves the use of tools designed for killing. If we use a more unspecific definition of war, the idea that war developed from modes of intra-species group fighting shared by some species of animals, proto-humans, and early humans still seems feasible.

This all the more if we take into account the insights of evolutionary psychology that emphasize the primary role of men in using violence and being the victims of it "because men have evolved to compete more intensively than women in the race for status, material wealth and sexual partners . . . [Men] are also more likely to do so in groups"; here again humans share with certain animal species (such as chimpanzees) the propensity "to form coalitions that kill members of neighbouring communities . . . By dominating or eliminating neighbouring communities, aggressors can expand their range, which means a better food supply, healthier adults and faster reproduction" (Jones 2008: 513–14, summarizing the results of Williams et al. 2004; see also Lambert 2012; McDonald et al. 2012; Van Vugt 2012). Despite these analogies, however, it is important to take into account the human ability to develop in-group cohesion and a moral sense that reduces in-group violence while allowing lethal conflict with other groups (Jones 2008: 514–15).

Such considerations perhaps make a frequently voiced alternative view less compelling. This view takes the absence of evidence for war to indicate the absence of war and postulates that human warfare emerged from a warless background (e.g., Ferguson 2008: 16). Instead, we might link the gradual emergence of unambiguous evidence for intergroup warfare not to the inception but to the intensification of war. Such intensification is often connected with increased sedentism and population density, social organization (segmentation) in distinct groups (e.g., in clans), hierarchization (such as the formation of chiefdoms) and competition for status and power, control of trade and the sources for precious goods, and ecological change (in particular, reduction of food producing capacity by climatic deterioration; Ferguson 2008: 24–6). In such contexts, the causes of war are generally seen in intensified competition for resources, in attacks on others' resources and their defense by those holding them. What Patricia Lambert (forthcoming) writes about the American Indians might be fairly typical at least for early prehistoric war:

> Striving for enhanced status, raiding for women, slaves, or stored foods, and competition for arable land, fishing grounds, or well-watered spaces—particularly in the context of deteriorating climatic conditions—were important causes of warfare at various times and places. Feuding, the ongoing cycle of blood revenge common in many tribal societies, also played an important role in the chronicity of war.

In fact, war seems to have been a major factor in shaping the development of human societies. As Ferrill writes, prehistoric warfare "was as independently important in early society as the discovery of agriculture, the development of proto-urban settlements and the emergence of organized religious systems" (1997: 13). Since by the end of the prehistoric period war was well established in many parts of the world, the origins of war must date far back in prehistory.

THE PREHISTORIC ORIGINS OF WAR AND PEACE

"Prehistory" is generally understood as the period before the emergence of written records. Its beginning is connected variously with the emergence of life on earth, the appearance of hominids, or the invention of stone tools and weapons, among other proposals. Its end varies enormously among major civilizations that invented writing independently: the end of the fourth millennium BCE in Mesopotamia and Egypt, *c.* 1300–1200 BCE in China, *c.* 300 BCE among the Maya in Central America. Evidence for prehistoric civilizations is primarily physical and material, found and evaluated above all by archaeologists and anthropologists. In script-less societies that were and are still accessible to modern researchers, including some Central and South American civilizations that were both destroyed and recorded by their European conquerors, oral traditions open a sometimes deep window into earlier wars and war making.

War has left traces in the prehistoric archaeological record (Haas 1990; Carman and Harding 1999; Lambert 2002; Otterbein 2004, 2009). Reliance exclusively on archaeological evidence, however, severely limits the amount and types of information we can expect to find. Such evidence fits into four main categories: "bones, settlements, weapons, and art" (Ferguson 2008: 15): it includes settlements established in easily defensible rather than convenient positions, defensive arrangements and fortifications around settlements, the violent destruction of sites, weapons, burials with multiple skeletons showing signs of wounds caused by weapons, and depictions of warriors and fighting. In addition, "longitudinal trends in violence on the order of millennia—including changes in scale, causal relationships between war and economic and political change, impacts of climate change—as well as the demographics of war, changes in technology of war and practices such as the taking of human trophies" (Lambert forthcoming; also, e.g., Geib and Hurst 2013: 2055) offer clues about the development of and changes in warfare (see Ferguson 2008: 16–23 for a brief global survey of such evidence).

Not all this evidence, however, refers specifically to war. Settlements were destroyed for reasons other than war. Weapons for hunting and fighting initially were identical; the appearance of specialized war weapons (such as war clubs, the mace, and refined arrowheads) and the context of the finds offer more certainty. Unless quantity and context reveal clues, it is difficult to determine with certainty whether skeletons with weapons-inflicted wounds reflect the death of individuals in a personal fight, by execution, by a crime, or death in battle or a massacre (e.g., Lambert 2007; Coltrain et al. 2012). In a growing number of cases, though, both the quantitative and the contextual evidence convincingly point to a massacre (e.g., Ferrill 1997: 23–24; Vencl 1999: 57–64; Geib and Hurst 2012).

Defensive arrangements range widely, from modest efforts found in many places all over the world (and often indistinguishable from structures intended to protect animals or property) to highly developed defensive architecture—such as pueblos in the North American south-west or the arrangement of houses to form a contiguous window- and door-less outside wall, for example, at Çatal Hüyük in Anatolia (Ferrill 1997: 31), fortifications, and massive walls of several sites in the ancient Near East (e.g., Jericho). In China, villagers began to protect themselves by deep ditches already around 4000 BCE (Yates 1999: 9). Among depictions of war, several instances of Neolithic cave art stand out, illustrating the use of the newly invented bow and arrow in human intergroup conflicts (summarized by Ferrill 1997: 19–20; a spectacular example in Ferguson 2008: 14). The Moche civilization (on the coastal plains of modern Peru, *c.* 100–800 CE) produced large quantities of painted vessels illustrating multiple scenes of war, from fighting to the treatment of captives and their eventual sacrifice (Donnan and McClelland 1999). Warrior figurines (ceramic or carved in stone) are common among the Moche, Maya, Inca, and Aztecs. Even rock art and painted buffalo hides of native North Americans yield precious information.

All this evidence attests to human actions. The thinking underlying these actions is revealed only indirectly, by evidence that requires active, deliberate intervention, such as the relocation of a settlement from a place along a coast or riverbed to a place with difficult and easily defensible access (like the American cliff dwellings), or the development of defensive architecture. At any rate, the history of war can be traced in human actions for millennia before the origins of writing, beginning perhaps around 10,000 BCE.

Peace, as Sarah Bolmarcich observes, "is a word slippery with meaning" (Chapter 1 of this volume). In a very general and unspecific understanding, peace is the absence of war. As such, it is a passive condition and as old as war. In a more specific understanding, peace is a condition aspired to or achieved by means of avoiding or ending war. This kind of peace is an active condition, resulting from thought, deliberation, and planned intervention, and accomplished through communication and negotiation. Roman coins show, apart from personifications of Peace (*pax*) and Concord (*concordia*), the clasp of hands that symbolizes the unity of previously opposed armies (Kent 1978: figs. 219, 253).

Such images prove that there were nonverbal possibilities to depict peace. Prehistoric humans had apparently not discovered this possibility; this may be one reason why peace is not visible in the physical or archaeological record.

Another explanation is that in some societies, especially in the early Americas (most famously among the Aztecs), fighting was highly valued because, apart from supporting the formation of empires, it provided the captives who were sacrificed to nourish the gods and thus to secure the continued existence of the universe and the prosperity of society. Moreover, such sacrifices, especially in ceremonial contexts, served to demonstrate to lower classes, subjects, and visitors the power of the Aztec gods, kings, and state (Smith 2003: 215–20). Under such conditions, peace among independent polities was not a viable option. At any rate, before the introduction of writing, peace left no recognizable traces and thus cannot be identified. The prehistoric record of peace is not accessible to us.

FIGURE 2.1: A Roman coin of the imperial period, with two clasped hands and the legend CONCORDIA AVGG ("Harmony of the Emperors"). Glevalex © 123RF.com.

ANCIENT THOUGHTS ABOUT HUMAN NATURE, WAR, AND PEACE

The ancient Near Eastern civilizations, as reflected in the medium of cuneiform writing, "never developed any form of meta-discourse, so that there are no essays, no meditations on how things should be done, and no philosophical texts" (Michalowski 2014: 145). Myths, "epics," and other narratives inform us about what was thought about the place of humans in relation to the gods and in the world order. Literary texts and inscriptions tell about wars. In such texts we cannot expect abstract reasoning about human nature. This is true for other highly developed civilizations that developed forms of writing, such as those of the Maya and Aztecs in Central America. In kingdoms and empires from Mesopotamia and Egypt to India, China, and the Americas, wars were initiated by kings and often self-perpetuated by the established social and political system's dynamics. In the Biblical narrative of ancient Israel's history, leaders and kings were selected by God; wars were God-given, God-driven, and God-regulated, whatever man's own propensity to engage in them.

In early China, the issue of human nature began to be discussed seriously only after Confucius (551–479 BCE). Mencius (372–289) argued that it was good, Xunzi (*c.* 310–235) that it was evil and had to be controlled by teachers (Knoblock 1990: 2.211–34). With regard to human nature and war, the *Spring and Autumn Annals of Lü Buwei,* presented to the later First Emperor in *c.* 239 BCE, state that "weapons originated in high antiquity, appearing at the same time as mankind"; hence, presumably, humans and the use of weapons are connected by nature. Another statement is more specific: "As a general rule, weapons inspire fear, and they inspire fear because they are powerful. That the people become fearful when confronted with power is due to their essential nature as humans. Their essential nature is what they receive from Heaven. It is not something a man can contrive, a soldier overturn, or an artisan change."[3]

The issue of human nature as such and of its reciprocal relationship with war—human nature's impact on war and war's impact on human nature—was of great interest to thinkers in fifth-century BCE Greece. This century was framed by two great wars: the Persian in 490 and 480–479, and the Peloponnesian from 431–404. Both wars profoundly affected every aspect of life in Greece and far beyond. The same century witnessed the emergence of democracy that placed decision making in the hands of all male citizens (Hansen 1999), a dramatic cultural upswing in all areas of the arts (Boedeker and Raaflaub 1998), and rapid changes in the frequency, intensity, and brutality of wars.

"Human nature" was understood in various ways. Physicians speculated on the nature or composition (*physis*) of the human body—thus an anonymous treatise in the Hippocratic corpus titled *On the Nature [Physis] of Man* (Lloyd 1978: 260–71). Physicians also discussed how climate, prevailing winds, and the quality of water and soil in a specific area influenced the physical properties and character of the inhabitants. In another treatise in the same corpus we read:

> The constitutions and the habits of a people follow the nature (*physis*) of the land where they live. Where the soil is rich, soft and well-watered and where surface water is drunk, . . . and where the seasons are favourable, you will find the people fleshy, their joints obscured, and they have watery constitutions. Such people are incapable of great effort [and], for the most part, cowards . . . But if the land is bare, waterless and rough, swept by the winter gales and burnt by the summer sun, you will find there a people hard and spare, their joints showing, sinewy and hairy. They are by nature (*physis*) keen and fond of work, they are wakeful, headstrong and self-willed and

inclined to fierceness rather than tame. They are keener at their crafts, more intelligent and better warriors.

—*Airs, Waters, Places* 24; cf. 16 (Lloyd 1978: 160, 167–9)

The theories of physicians and other intellectuals, especially sophists (philosophers and teachers, often focusing on rhetoric and politics), became part of a pool of ideas that influenced the thoughts and works of others, including the historians (Thomas 2000).

In particular, the theory that the nature (*physis*) of a country shapes the physique and character of its inhabitants helped Herodotos explain the unexpected victory of a few tiny Greek poleis (citizen-communities) over the armies of the mighty Persian Empire. He formulates the principle in an anecdote at the very end of his *Histories*: when the Persians had conquered their empire, they proposed to their king, Cyrus, to move from their barren country to a better one among those they now controlled. Cyrus warned them, if they did so, "they must prepare themselves to rule no longer, but to be ruled by others. 'Soft countries,' he said, 'breed soft men. It is not the property of any one soil to produce fine fruits and good soldiers too'." The Persians "chose rather to live in a rugged land and rule than to cultivate rich plains and be slaves to others" (9.122). What Herodotos does not say but implies, is that even so, the Persians could not avoid being spoiled by the riches of their empire and thus, by the time they tried to subject the Greeks, they suffered the fate of a soft country confronting the soldiers of a poor but tough country.

Herodotos has an exiled Spartan king explain to the Persian king Xerxes why the Greeks are going to fight even against a vastly superior army: "Poverty is Greece's inheritance from of old but valour (*aretē*) she won for herself by wisdom and the strength of law (*nomos*). By her valour Greece now keeps both poverty and despotism at bay" (7.102). In other words, the Greeks have enhanced their natural disposition to be brave, a result of their poor environment, by acquired traits such as insight and learning (*sophiē*), and by subjecting themselves to the discipline imposed by law. Such natural disposition is called *physis:* Persians too, fearing their king and the whips of his officers, might excel beyond their *physis* (Hdt. 7.103.4). In late-fifth-century Athens chauvinistic views circulated about the innate superiority of Greeks, born to be free, over the subjects of the Persian king who by nature were destined to be ruled and thus unfree. "It is proper that Greeks rule over barbarians but not barbarians over Greeks. For that kind [of human] is slavish, the others are free" (Euripides, *Iphigenia in Aulis* 1400–1, my translation; cf. Hdt. 7.135). This comes very close to saying: barbarians are by nature slaves!

Such statements reflect an intellectual debate going on at the time between those who attributed certain distinctions among humans (such as aristocratic or slave status) to nature, and others who considered them the result of cultural developments (conventions, *nomoi*). One of Euripides' characters says:

Our speech is a waste of words
if we praise high birth in humans.
For long ago, when we first came to be,
the earth that gave birth to mortals decided
to rear us all to have the same appearance.
We are nothing special:
the well-born and ill-born are one race,
but time and custom (*nomos*) brought about this haughtiness.

—*Alexander TGrF* F61b; trans. GW 70; cf. 275

While some denied any share of reason or the laws to those who were "slaves by nature" (e.g., *TGrF* F304, 326, GW 75), the sophist Alkidamas said: "God set all people free; nature has made no one a slave" (GW 276).

The most famous advocate of "natural slavery" is Aristotle. He knows but rejects the alternative view that slavery is based on convention (*Politics* 1255a3–b4) and claims that, since all basic forms of human association (family, village, and polis) exist by nature (*physis*), the components of the family too exist by nature. Just as there has to be by natural necessity a union between the male and female for the reproduction of the species, so too there must be a "union of natural ruler and natural subject for the sake of security— for one that can foresee with his mind is naturally ruler and naturally master, and one that can do these things with his body is subject and naturally a slave; so that master and slave have the same interest" (*Pol.* 1252a; see Smith 1983; Dobbs 1994). This theory is relevant to our exploration because it was applied to justify Greek subjection of barbarians, "for by nature barbarian and slave are the same" (*Pol.* 1252b7–9; my translation). I single out only one of the contradictions this attempt at justifying slavery raises: many Greek communities used slaves to bolster their armed forces (Welwei 1974–1988), although fighting for the community was generally considered the privilege of the free citizens. This was ideologically embarrassing and prompted historians to fudge it or suppress it entirely (Hunt 1998).

Another debate that is relevant here focused on the role of *nomos* and *physis* (convention and nature) in determining justice. This debate had various facets (Kerferd 1981: 111–30). In its extreme form it stimulated the theory of the natural right of the strong individual to break the shackles imposed on him by conventions and laws, and to assert himself fully, establishing his own standards of justice based on his power ("might is right"). This theory provides the justification of imperialism in Thucydides' "Melian Dialogue" (5.84–113), a set piece inserted into a confrontation between the all-powerful Athenians and the tiny island of Melos. Against the Melians' insistence on justice, the Athenians say: "The standard of justice depends on the equality of power to compel, and in fact the strong do what they have the power to do and the weak accept what they have to accept" (5.89). Countering the Melians' trust in the gods' support, the Athenians insist: "Our opinion of the gods and our knowledge of men lead us to conclude that it is a general and necessary law of nature (*physis*) to rule whatever one can" (5.105).

In Thucydides' historical interpretation, human nature plays a crucial role. He defines his purpose as providing something useful to those who want to clearly understand past events which ("human nature being what it is") will, at some time and in similar ways, be repeated in the future (1.22.4). History is composed of an infinite kaleidoscope of constantly changing events and persons: the one stable element is "the human condition" (*to anthrōpinon*: what is typical of humans or human nature). Humans act in typical ways: confronted with similar challenges, they will react similarly. This makes the future to a certain extent predictable; it enables us to learn from history and makes history useful (De Ste. Croix 1972: 29–33; Raaflaub 2013). In a dense political analysis of what typically happens in civil strife (*stasis*), the historian writes that these fights among citizens "were the cause of many calamities—as happens and always will happen while human nature (*physis anthrōpōn*) is what it is" (3.82.2). The lessons to be learned from Thucydides' view of human nature were relevant to most of his readers for whom war was a constant threat or reality.

Moreover, history is driven by two antithetical motives that are deeply rooted in human nature and incessantly cause war: the desire for power, wealth, and domination,

HUMAN NATURE, PEACE, AND WAR

and the desire for liberty. This conflict is exemplified by the confrontations between Persians and Greeks in Herodotos and between Athens and Melos in Thucydides. Hope and greed, supported by overconfidence and the belief in fortune, tempt individuals to take the greatest risks; it is impossible "for human nature, when once seriously set upon a certain course, to be prevented from following that course by the force of law or by any other means of intimidation" (Thuc. 3.45.6–7). Yet the "human condition" is affected by war in other ways as well. In Thucydides' analysis of *stasis* we read: "War . . . is a violent schoolmaster and tends to assimilate men's character to their conditions" (3.82.2; trans. Hornblower I 1991: 482). War thus prompts an adaptation of character among those frequently fighting it. In a starkly contrasting collective character portrait of Athenians and Spartans, Thucydides has the Corinthians, Athens' archenemies, say:

> [An Athenian] is always an innovator, quick to form a resolution and quick at carrying it out . . . Athenian daring will outrun its own resources; they will take risks against their better judgement, and still, in the midst of danger, remain confident . . . They never hesitate . . .; they are always abroad; for they think that the farther they go the more they will get . . . If they win a victory, they follow it up at once, and if they suffer a defeat they scarcely fall back at all . . . And so they go on working away in hardship and danger all the days of their lives, seldom enjoying their possessions because they are always adding to them . . . They prefer hardship and activity to peace and quiet. In a word, *they have developed a nature* that is incapable of either living a quiet life themselves or of allowing anyone else to do so.
>
> —1.70; my emphasis

Two words sum up the Athenian national character: *pleonexia* (the desire for more) and *polypragmosynē* (hyperactivism, "the tendency to do a lot"). The Thucydidean Perikles emphasizes: "We consider a citizen who does not participate in the city's affairs not passive (*apragmōn*) but useless (*achreios*)" (2.40.2; my translation; cf. 2.63.3). How does this collective character relate to human nature? In the italicized phrase above, Thucydides does not say, "they are by nature (*physis*) incapable"; rather, he uses the perfect tense of a related verb (to grow): "they have grown to be incapable"; perhaps even: "it has become their second nature".[4] At issue here is not the stable human nature discussed above but the result of the Athenians' adaptation to their constant involvement in aggressive interaction with others and, often enough, war.

Once established, this theme too serves as a leitmotif in Thucydides' historical interpretation. In the great debate in 415 BCE about the expedition the Athenians are about to send out to conquer Syracuse and Sicily (6.8–26), both primary speakers take the Athenian character traits as a given. Nikias, experienced and cautious, understands their impact: "I know that no speech of mine could be powerful enough to alter your characters (*tropoi*), and it would be useless to advise you to safeguard what you have and not to risk what is yours already for doubtful prospects in the future." Hence Nikias limits himself to warning his fellow citizens not to undertake this expedition at this precarious stage of the war (6.9.3). His opponent, Alcibiades, young, ambitious, and hotheaded, encourages the Athenians to follow their inclinations: this is the way they have gained the height of power.

> [3] We have reached a stage where we are forced to plan new conquests and forced to hold on to what we have got, because there is a danger that we ourselves may fall under the power of others unless others are in our power. And you cannot look upon

this idea of a quiet life in quite the same way as others do—not, that is, unless you are going to change your whole way of living and make it like theirs is . . . [7] [A] city which is active by nature will soon ruin itself it if changes its nature and becomes idle (*apragmosynē*), and . . . the way that men find their greatest security is in accepting the character (*ēthos*) and the institutions (*nomoi*) which they actually have, even if they are not perfect.

—6.18.3, 7

Alcibiades' insistence that the Athenians would have to change their entire way of life if they wanted to change from "aggressive hyperactivism" (*polypragmosynē*) to peaceful (inactive) policies (*apragmosynē*) is particularly relevant here. It alludes to another prominent debate of the time (Raaflaub 2016d: 130–2): whether and how a power that was "programmed" for war and conquest could be "reprogrammed" for moderation and peace. Herodotos (3.142–3) and Thucydides (2.63.1–2) make clear that such a radical change of policy was both extremely difficult and dangerous for the ruling power.

In one of his model speeches, *On the Peace* (written around 355 BCE, when Athens was involved in a futile war with its allies), Isokrates, rhetorician and Plato's teacher, contrasts the positive reputation Athens had once enjoyed as the savior of Greek freedom in the Persian Wars with the hatred it had later encountered through its oppressive imperial rule. Pursuing a dream it had never been able to realize (predominance in Greece), it had paid an enormous price in lives and resources. The only way out of this cycle of evils was to abandon imperial policies and adopt those of peace, generosity, and collaboration for the common good. But a fundamental change of deeply ingrained attitudes was necessary if the goal was not to end one war through yet another peace treaty but to break once and for all the cycle of self-perpetuating wars and all the misery they caused. "This cannot happen until you are persuaded that tranquility (*hēsychia*) is more advantageous and more profitable than meddlesomeness (*polypragmosynē*), justice than injustice, and attention to one's own affairs than covetousness of the possessions of others" (Isokrates 8.26). This may sound naïve but is profoundly correct. In their inability to realize this prescription for peace, the Athenians ran up against the limitations imposed on them by their customs (*nomoi*) and what had become their national character (their "second nature")—and perhaps also, they might have said, those set by human nature (*physis*).

Considering barbarians slaves by nature, Aristotle also claims that wars against barbarians—human beings who "though designed by nature for subjection refuse to submit to it"—are by nature (*physei*) just (*Politics* 1256b23–26). To the Greeks, wars needed to be just because this determined divine support but, generally, the concept of "just war" itself lacked definition and remained subjective. By contrast, to the Romans the justice of war was determined by the enemy's wrongful actions and refusal to pay restitution, following the age-old rituals that were in place for such cases, executed by the priestly college of the *fetiales* (Harris 1991: 166–75). Here too, just war was pious war, respecting the will of the gods, but it was encapsulated in legal terms as part of the "laws of war" (*iura belli*). By tradition and ideology, Romans fought only just wars. In *On the Republic* (*De re publica*), the Roman orator and statesman Cicero (106–43 BCE) lets one of the interlocutors say: "our people by defending their allies have gained dominion over the whole world" (3.35; cf. Cic. *Off*. 2.27).[5]

Any connection in Roman thinking between war and human nature is, at best, tenuous. In his late work, *On the Laws* (*De legibus*), Cicero emphasizes that nothing is "more valuable than the full realization that we are born for justice, and that right is based, not upon men's opinions, but upon nature." Vices are thus nothing but the result of ignorance and corruption of true human nature (1.28–33). War is not mentioned here. In the treatise *On Duties* (*De officiis*), Cicero discusses in some detail the "laws of war" (mentioned earlier, but rather meaning rules, norms, or duties; 1.11.33–1.13.41), distinguishing between wars for survival and wars for supremacy and glory. It does not occur to him to declare any type of war just by nature. Nor are the duties to be observed in war based on human nature; they correspond to conventional norms sanctioned by religion (in deciding and declaring war) or moral constraints (in treating the submitting or defeated enemy; see Clavadetscher-Thürlemann 1985: 141–52; Bederman 2001: 242–63). In *On the Nature of Things* (*De rerum natura*), the poet Lucretius (*c.* 99–55 BCE), writing from the perspective of Epicurean philosophy, describes human nature as simple, demanding nothing more than the banishment of pain and freedom from anxiety and fear, which suffices to create a sense of happiness. Here too, ambition for power and greed for riches are thus nothing but ignorance and corruption of the elementary needs of human nature (2.1–61).

By extension, this could mean that unjust wars are caused by corrupt human nature. This view seems to be confirmed by the historian Sallust (86–35 BCE) who contends (to a considerable extent wrongly) that the Romans of the early and middle Republic gained their victories and empire by competing in virtue and for honor, avoiding avarice, and maintaining unity among themselves while fighting only with their country's foes. "Right and decency prevailed among them, thanks not so much to laws as to nature (*natura*)." Eventually, though, "a craving first for money, then for power, increased; these were, as it were, the root of all evils," resulting in unfettered ambition, arrogance, cruelty, neglect of religion, and all kinds of depravity, both in dealing with each other and with the outside world (*Cat.* 9–11). Moral decline and, again by extension, unjust wars (not mentioned and contrary to Roman ideology) and the unjust treatment of the defeated (emphasized strongly) must thus have been the consequence of the corruption of human nature.[6]

WAR AND PEACE IN ANCIENT CIVILIZATIONS

This is a huge topic and I have to be selective (for comprehensive surveys of war and peace, and societies not covered here, see Raaflaub and Rosenstein 1999; Raaflaub 2007a). From "the beginning of recorded times, at the earliest appearance of civilization, war was an established pattern of behaviour" (Ferrill 1997: 11). In Egypt, war and securing the borders, and vital natural resources even beyond these, were the pharaoh's domain. A rich textual and pictorial dossier informs us of these wars which, in the "New Kingdom" (*c.* 1550–1070 BCE), established control over large areas along the Levant (Gnirs 1999; Spalinger 2005).

> [In the Egyptians'] ideological construct, supported by economic needs, the peaceful and orderly Egyptian interior was opposed to a wicked and criminal outside world that constantly aimed at attacking the Egyptian order. For the longest time, ideology, not real threats, thus justified wars that kept reaffirming the pharaoh's divinely sanctioned mission. Hence, there was no need to develop a concept of peace in opposition to warfare.

What symbolized peace was the conquered and crushed enemy (Raaflaub 2016b: 5, summarizing Bickel 2016). One famous exception, a negotiated peace following a

FIGURE 2.2: Cuneiform copy of the peace treaty signed between the Egyptians and the Hittites after the Battle of Kadesh; Archaeological Museum, Istanbul, Turkey. Photo by PHAS/UIG, courtesy of Getty Images.

stalemate in war, is the peace treaty between Ramesses II of Egypt and Hattusili III, king of the Hittites, sixteen years after the battle of Kadesh in 1274 BCE (Bell 2007).

Throughout Mesopotamian history, countless monuments, relief panels, and inscriptions as well as texts on clay tablets inform us of the constant need of kings to demonstrate and justify their power through military accomplishments (Stillman and Tallis 1984; Trimm 2017; Radner forthcoming; see also Kuhrt 1995; Van de Mieroop 2007). Especially in the periods of imperial expansion, peace was usually possible only through the submission of the weaker or defeated (Fales 2010). Even so, and although war clearly dominates in the sources, a large number of treaties illustrate various methods used to establish and maintain peace (Foster 2007).

From the late second millennium, between the Levant and the Jordan River, Hebrew tribes, tenuously united by fragile monarchies, fought almost constantly to maintain their independence between the large powers that competed for control of the area. Israel's god was a warrior god who brought victory if king and people followed his precepts, but defeat and punishment if they did not. Little space was left here for peace (Krüger 2007). Israel's wars are amply described, though in late versions marked by much religiously and ideologically motivated revision, in the Hebrew Bible (Niditch 1993, 2007; Eph'al forthcoming).

In early China, before 722 BCE, war mainly served the purpose of capturing enemies, whose sacrifice appeased the ancestors' spirits and guaranteed the continued fertility of the soil, protecting territories, and seizing new ones. Unlike the comparable but much more elaborate practice of sacrificing war captives among early American societies (especially the Aztecs), in China this practice remained relatively low-scale and essentially disappeared when the scope and purpose of wars changed in subsequent centuries. No peace efforts are visible in the record. During the "Spring and Autumn" Period (722–c. 450) that was dominated by wars of city-states or larger coalitions for territory and resources, attempts to impose order were based on a system of covenants (Yates 2007: 34–35). In the "Warring States" Period (450–221) that ended with the foundation of the First Empire under the first emperor, Qin Shihuangdi, "warfare among the regional city-state systems was perpetual and increasingly fierce, and many technological and tactical inventions were adopted on the battlefields. The whole of society, including for the first time peasants, was organized to meet the needs of war and major innovations in social organization resulted. War itself was theorized and integrated into an all-inclusive cosmological system" (Yates 1999: 8–9).

Peace, essentially existing in the intervals between wars, became more permanent only by the capitulation of the defeated and their integration into a shrinking number of growing states. Frequent and devastating warfare provoked leaders and theorists to develop "techniques and rituals to try to maintain peace and harmony between rival political entities, and [to elaborate] theories of how rulers of states should act to ensure the survival of their states and how they should interact with their peers" (Yates 2007: 35). The history, practicalities, and theories of war, and theoretical and practical efforts to find peace are documented by a wealth of extant texts and, at least for war, archaeological evidence (Yates 2007, 2016, forthcoming).

FIGURE 2.3: Terracotta warriors and horses from the army arranged in large pits near the mausoleum of the first Chinese emperor, Qin Shihuangdi; Xi'an, Shaanxi province, China. Photo by Lucas Schifres, courtesy of Getty Images.

The history that is recorded or retrievable about warfare in the pre-Columbian Central and South American civilizations covers only the very last phase before the European conquest. Exceptions include the Moche in lowland Peru (*c.* 100–800 CE), whose prehistoric record of warfare is preserved on painted pottery, and the Maya, whose decline started long before European contact.

Rather than being a peaceful people, as was long believed, the Maya engaged in frequent warfare that was an important factor in the process of social development and state formation (Webster 1999, 2000; Martin 2001). More information on Maya warfare is emerging from increasing numbers of newly readable inscriptions and through an improved understanding of their impressive archaeological remains (Martin and Grube 2000; Carter 2014).

What we know about Inca and Aztec warfare refers to the period of imperial expansion in a relatively short time-span before European contact. For the Inca, archaeological evidence (e.g., warrior figurines and massive fortifications), memories written down by elite Inca survivors, and extensive ethnographic records collected by Spanish missionaries offer insights into a highly developed and effective military system that succeeded in establishing an empire that reached from Chile to Ecuador. To peoples targeted for

FIGURE 2.4: Moche (Mochica) ceramic pot vessel in the form of a warrior clubbing a submissive man over the head; private collection, Lima, Peru. Photo by Nathan Benn/Corbis, courtesy of Getty Images.

attack and annexation the Inca offered the choice between war and peace. "Like other empire builders, the Inca aggressors coerced peaceful submission through threats of extermination—or at least humiliation and dire consequences. Thus the contest for power was rigged in favor of peaceful submission to Inca rule. In effect, both sides wanted and needed peace" (Julien 2007: 345; see generally Jones 2012; D'Altroy 2014).

The Aztec Empire was still expanding when it was destroyed by Cortés in 1519–1521. It suffices here to quote Ross Hassig's summary of war and peace in Aztec society:

[T]he Aztecs lacked a peace god [and any] rites for peace. Conquest was a primary political goal, and war . . . was suitably exalted. Death in war was the most honored status one could attain, and warriors slain in battle went to the heaven of the sun . . . [Virtually everyone benefited from warfare, kings, nobles, commoners, priests, merchants, and artisans. It fueled their economy, permitted their social mobility, and fed their gods.] The question for the Aztecs was not how to coexist peacefully with other polities, but how to bring all other polities into a hierarchical relationship with themselves on top. There could be peace only with the subordinated, the dead, or with those too distant or yet too powerful to be conquered.

—Hassig 2007: 313, 325; see also 1988, 1992

Finally, the Greeks have left a fragmentary but rich and easily accessible dossier about war and peace, the richest from any ancient civilization. The remainder of this chapter will therefore focus on the Greek experience. In their history too, war played a crucially important role (see generally van Wees 2004; Sabin et al. 2007), and the issue of peace rose to exceptional prominence in times of intense warfare (Raaflaub 2016d: 122–57; Moloney and Williams 2017). I leave aside their Bronze Age ("Mycenaean") civilization that is characterized as highly warlike by their mighty fortresses, warrior tombs, weapons, and pictorial representations (Chadwick 1976: 159–79). Despite some vague memories of this period, Homer's epics reflect in their description of the social and political background, in which the heroic actions are embedded, conditions around 700 BCE. The *Iliad*'s story of a great trans-Aegean war is conceptualized according to the contemporary reality of naval raids and wars between neighboring poleis. The soldiers who fight these wars with equipment and in a formation suggesting an early form of the hoplite army also form the assembly (Schwartz 2009; Raaflaub 2008, 2011b; see Figure 7.2). The army is thus communal, and the ideal leader excels in speaking *and* fighting (*Il.* 9.440–3).

The nature of Greek wars changed dramatically in the aftermath of the Persian Wars and in connection with Athenian naval and imperial policies and the increasing competition between Athens and Sparta for primacy in Greece. The employment of large naval forces made it possible to transport troops over long distances.

Wars became long, almost permanent, ubiquitous, and brutal (Raaflaub 2014b, 2016e). Moreover, in the average Greek polis the scope of politics was limited. Outside relations and war demanded almost exclusive attention, most of all in powerful and democratic Athens, where politicians competed for the citizens' approval of their proposals. Here honor, power, and wealth could be gained. In contrast, peace was boring: nothing happened, nothing could be achieved and gained, it was not worth much effort.

Despite the horrific losses the Athenians suffered—by the end of the Peloponnesian War their citizen population had been decimated by half—their imperial ambitions continued unabated and were emulated by Sparta and Thebes in almost uninterrupted wars in the fourth century that ended only with the Greek defeat by Philip II of Macedon

FIGURE 2.5: Greek relief sculpture (fifth century BCE) depicting men rowing a trireme, a Greek warship (the so-called "Lenormant Relief"); National Archaeological Museum, Athens, Greece. Photo by DEA/G. CIGOLINI/DeAgostini, courtesy of Getty Images.

at Chaironeia in 338 BCE. After Alexander the Great's death, wars for primacy among kingdoms largely took the place of wars among poleis and alliances. The Hellenistic world (323–30 BCE) has been characterized as a world of anarchy in which might was right and peace agreements were honored only as long as the advantages they offered were greater than those expected from war (Eckstein 2006a). War was too closely tied into the male and especially elite value system, the sense of honor and spirit of competitiveness were too intensive, the ability to compromise too undeveloped, and confidence in the expected gains too high to allow peace efforts to move to the fore.

Certainly, efforts were undertaken to prevent wars or reduce their impact (Giovannini 2007). Heralds and ambassadors were placed under the protection of the supreme god, Zeus. Diplomacy or arbitration supported attempts to resolve conflicts peacefully. The Delphic oracle of Apollo called for moderation, not least in war. The ideal of a justified war was frequently invoked, especially since divine support depended on it. Many of these tools and ideas are attested already in the *Iliad*. But their effectiveness was limited. A neutral institution supported by all poleis and charged with protecting or restoring peace was unthinkable. The experience of horrendous wars that would in modern times spark the creation of the International Red Cross, the League of Nations, and the United Nations, helped initiate large-scale peace congresses and "common peace" (*koinē eirēnē*) agreements in the fourth century too, but these faltered for multiple reasons. Arbitration was used frequently but failed in conflicts between "super-powers" because there was no superior authority whose verdict would have been acceptable to them. The beginning of the *Iliad* illustrates this on an individual level, the outbreak of the Peloponnesian War on an international level (Raaflaub 2016d: 122–6). And yet, those affected did not simply accept the predominance of wars. War was a necessity, often unavoidable, but certainly not desirable. In the *Iliad*, the poet heroicizes achievements in war but he also brings to life the suffering war causes for the "civilian population." The farewell scene between Hektor and Andromache is among the most moving in world literature (6.390–496; see Figure 3.1).

The extant sources illustrate the continuing importance of the topic of war and peace. Poets motivated the men to fight bravely and die with honor. Early thinkers from Homer and Hesiod to the philosophers used the contrast between war and peace as essential categories around which they organized human life: the Homeric shield of Achilles (*Il.* 18.478–607) and Hesiod's vignettes of the fate of the just and unjust cities (*Works and Days* 225–47) are good examples. In Hesiod's Golden Age there is no place for war, while the Iron Age is dominated by it (ibid. 110–201). Together with her sisters Justice (Dikē) and Good Order (Eunomia), Peace (Eirēnē) represents the central communal values of Zeus' new world order (*Theogony* 901–3). Herakleitos states: "War is both king of all and father of all, and it has revealed some as gods, others as men; some it has made slaves, others free" (DK 22 B53). Fifth-century BCE Athenian tragedies (e.g., Euripides' *Trojan Women*) and comedies (Aristophanes' *Acharnians, Peace, Lysistrata*) highlight war's impact on the population and families. Overall, war was rarely glorified; rejection of war and desire for peace were widespread.

Yet these sentiments seem to have had little influence on decisions that were made in the citizen assembly about war and peace. Peace through negotiation was possible only when both sides were exhausted and convinced that, at least for the moment, more was impossible. Peace imposed by victory was the norm. Still, the new late-fifth-century reality of ceaseless and brutal wars provoked reactions. In *Lysistrata* Aristophanes dramatized the perspective of women: they revolt against the men's "war-mania" and reject their policies that destroy families and communities. The poet thereby contradicts the democratic ideology of war (as formulated in Perikles' Funeral Oration, Thuc. 2.35–46) that demanded of the citizen that he be a lover (*erastēs*) of his polis and subordinate his own interests to those of his beloved (Thuc. 2.43.1–2). Herodotos too condemns war in the strongest possible terms (5.97.3; 6.98.1).

The increasingly fierce competition between the Athenian and Spartan alliance systems was paralleled ideologically by that between democracy and oligarchy and exacerbated civil strife (*stasis*) in many poleis. Sophists developed theories to overcome *stasis* and secure communal peace (*homonoia*). Thrasymachos suggested the reactivation of an "ancestral constitution" that supposedly existed before the emergence of radical democracy and thus should be acceptable to both sides (DK 85 B1). Early constitutional theory proposed a "mixed constitution" combining oligarchic and democratic elements (Thuc. 8.97.2), and early political anthropology identified the middle class of landowning farmers as a crucial force in stabilizing the polis (echoed in Euripides, *Suppliants* 238–45; *Orestes* 917–30). Influenced by such theories, Thucydides added to his detailed description of an extreme case of *stasis* (3.69–81) a penetrating theoretical analysis of the pathology of civil war (3.82–84).

Thus in the late fifth century there emerged an intensive, varied, and largely public discourse on peace that was not purely theoretical but yielded practical proposals especially for ways to overcome *stasis* (Raaflaub 2016d: 136–9). This must be the background for a remarkable solution that was successfully applied in Athens at the end of the fifth century, when, after military defeat and oligarchic tyranny, civil war threatened (ibid. 132–3). A decree of reconciliation, passed in the assembly and secured by oaths, separated the parties and designated a large district as an autonomous oligarchic enclave. The oligarchs moving there maintained their Athenian citizenship and property rights. Both sides swore to forget previous evil deeds through an amnesty. This made it difficult to prosecute political opponents for crimes committed under the previous oligarchy and facilitated lasting internal peace that soon obviated the need for an oligarchic asylum. As a modern parallel, one thinks of the "truth commission" that in South Africa tried to overcome the fallout of apartheid policies.

This solution was possible because the citizens controlled the sphere of domestic politics. This was not the case in inter-polis relations. Although many arguments circulated that praised the advantages of peace, and although the master rhetorician Gorgias proclaimed, "Trophies [victories] against barbarians demand hymns of praise, but those against Greeks lamentations" (DK 82 B5b), concrete proposals were rare. Isokrates (4.3, 115–16, 172–77; 5.7–9, 15–16) and to some extent Plato and Aristotle (Ostwald 1996) condemned the evil of inter-Greek wars but were able to come up only with a desperate solution: to unify the Greeks for a great war against their archenemy, the Persians, and thus to divert their warlike energies towards the outside. This is what Philip II and Alexander the Great achieved after defeating the Greeks and founding the "Corinthian League" in 337, but at the expense of Greek independence.

CONCLUSION

The lack of success the Greeks experienced in finding concrete solutions to the problems of endemic war and stasis should not obscure the significance of the effort and the seriousness of debates about peace and the nature of humankind; as we have seen, together with the Chinese, the Greeks were in fact unusual among ancient civilizations in addressing these questions at all. One of these debates (discussed earlier) focused on the problem of whether and how a power that was "programmed" for war, conquest, and imperial rule, as Athens was, could change to pursue policies of peace and collaboration for the common good. Success in the quest for peace and control of war has eluded humankind to this day, despite much progress in raising awareness and preventing worldwide conflagrations of the type that dominated the first half of the twentieth century, and despite the existence of all-encompassing international organizations that were created with exactly this purpose in mind.

CHAPTER THREE

Peace, War, and Gender

LYNETTE MITCHELL

In book 6 of the *Iliad*, in a tender scene on the walls of Troy, Hektor tells Andromache not to grieve excessively for him at the prospect of his death, since he, like other men, cannot escape his fate:

> Poor Andromache! Why does your heart sorrow so much for me?
> No man is going to hurl me to Hades, unless it is fated,
> but as for fate, I think that no man has yet escaped it
> once it has taken its first form, neither brave man nor coward.
> Go therefore back to our house, and take up your own work,
> the loom and the distaff, and see to it that your handmaidens
> ply their work also; but the men must see to the fighting,
> all men who are the people of Ilion, but I beyond others.

> *—Il.* 486–93

This famous scene, known as a *teichoskopeia* (viewing from the walls), as we shall see, becomes an intertextual reference point for the gender roles of women and men in war. In fact, in Aristophanes' "peace play" *Lysistrata*, produced in 411 BCE, the heroine Lysistrata, whose name means "Dissolver of armies", repeats Hektor's words:

> For a long time previously, thanks to our self-control, we endured <in silence> whatever you men did, because you wouldn't let us utter a sound; but we certainly weren't satisfied with you! . . . Later on we'd come to know of some other even worse decision of yours, and then we'd ask "Husband, why are you carrying through this policy in such a stupid way?" And at once he'd give me an angry look and tell me to spin my thread or else he'd see I had a headache for weeks: "War is for men to take care of."[1]

> *—Lys.* 507–20

Nevertheless, the women, under Lysistrata's leadership, unite to save Greece and bring about a reconciliation between the warring cities by means of a two-part plan: a sex strike and the seizure of the Athenian acropolis.

By taking together these passages from Homer and Aristophanes, it might be easy to assume that war is the concern of men, and peace of women. However, Hektor, before he bids Andromache return to her loom, had prayed to Zeus that his baby son might one day come back from war more pre-eminent than his father, bear the blood-stained spoils of his enemy, and make his mother's heart rejoice (*Il.* 6.476–81). Likewise, although it is the women of *Lysistrata* who achieve peace and reconciliation, they do so by the reminder that the men should not necessarily cease fighting, but should be fighting together against a common enemy (*Lys.* 1108–61), and recalling the memory that they fought together

FIGURE 3.1: *Andromache intercepting Hector at the Scaean Gate*, by Fernando Castelli, 1811; Pinacoteca di Brera, Milan, Italy. Photo by DeAgostini, courtesy of Getty Images.

against the Persians in the past (*Lys.* 1248–65).[2] It is too easy to assume that war was only the preserve of men, just as it is also too easy to say that women were too powerless and politically ineffective to act as peace negotiators, or that women as peace negotiators were necessarily ridiculous and funny—it is sometimes said that this is part of the joke of *Lysistrata*. We will return to this later in the chapter.

In the Greek world, peace (feminine *eirēnē*) and war (masculine *polemos*) may have been fairly simple opposites (e.g. Hom. *Il.* 2.797; Hes. *Works and Days* 228–9; Thuc. 1.40.2), and the characteristics of peace often represent attributes that are positive for the community in opposition to the destructiveness of war.[3] In Hesiod's *Theogony*, the goddess Eirēnē is the daughter of Zeus by Themis (Law), and is sister to Eunomia (Good Order) and Dikē (Justice), and the Fates (901–6), though the *Theogony* itself is not unambiguously positive about the feminine, as the story of Pandora makes clear (570–612; cf. Marquardt 1982: 283–91). In Aristophanes' play *Peace*, produced in 421 BCE, the goddess Peace is a passive figure who is imprisoned by Polemos (War) and needs to be freed by the hero Trygaios and the chorus of the Panhellenes with the help of Hermes (223–6, 292–525). In Athens, originally possibly a fertility goddess and a figure predominantly of interest to farmers, peace was also associated with justice and prosperity (Ar. *Peace* 571–600; cf. Hom. *Od.* 24.486; Hes. *Works and Days*, 225–37; Theognis 1.885).[4] The state cult of Eirēnē in Athens was probably first established in the 370s BCE, and a statue group by Kephisodotos, much copied in the Roman period, was set up in the agora, with the goddess holding the infant Ploutos (Wealth) (Paus. 1.8.2, 9.16.2).[5] On the other hand, in *Lysistrata* the sexualised Diallagē(Reconciliation) is probably a naked young woman that Lysistrata uses to taunt the men of Greece, who are now willing to make peace (1114–21; cf. Ar. *Acharn.* 989-90),[6] a Panhellenic peace among supposed kinsmen (cf. 1128–34).[7]

In Latin, as in Greek, "peace" (*pax*) is a feminine noun. At Rome, *pax* was understood in two different ways: on the one hand, in domestic terms, as the end of civil war, and on the other, in regard to external wars, as a peace enforced by military power on foreign peoples (e.g. Vell. Pat. 2.89.3; *Res. Gest.* 12–13, 25–6). Internal peace was celebrated by temples for *concordia* (concord, harmony), rather than *pax*, perhaps as early as the fourth century BCE (Raaflaub 2011a: 323–38). The continued pressure to achieve military success meant that external peace was not "peace *per se*, an abstract ideal of peace, but peace as the result of military success and victory," so that it was this second kind of peace that the *Ara Pacis Augustae* celebrated, as also Vespasian's *Templum Pacis* (Noreña 2011: 127–8; Raaflaub 2011a: 333). Nevertheless, this military aspect of peace was usually suppressed, and *Pax* on coins was personified as a female figure, often holding an olive branch, although she could also be associated with a sceptre, the cornucopia, and the caduceus as a symbol of commerce.[8]

WOMEN AND THE HEROIC IDEOLOGY OF WAR

The ancient world was intrinsically heroic and competitive, and martial values were important. In Homeric epic, the Lykian Sarpedon says to Glaukos that they above all others receive honors in Lykia because the Lykians say "these are no ignoble men who are lords of Lykia, these kings of ours, who feed upon the fat sheep appointed and drink the exquisite sweet wine, since indeed there is strength of valour in them, since they fight in the forefront of the Lykians" (*Il.* 12.318–21). Nevertheless, the Greeks knew and hated war. Again in the *Iliad*, Hera asks Zeus whether she might drive away her son, "this maniac" Ares, the god of war, who knows no law, but has destroyed the army of the Achaians (5.757–63; cf. 5.829–31, 887–90). Herodotos has the Lydian Kroisos say to Cyrus of Persia that "no one is fool enough to choose war instead of peace—in peace sons bury fathers, but in war fathers bury sons" (1.87.4). Thucydides was clear that war was the result of ambition, greed, and a desire for power (e.g. 3.82.8, 4.61.5, 5.105.2, 6.18), and for that reason there seemed to be an inevitability about war at the end of the fifth century BCE (1.33.3, 144.3, 2.61.1).[9]

While courage (*andreia*) was a "manly" virtue, it was a virtue that the whole community valued, the women as well as the men: through the courage of their men women shared in glory. Lysistrata, in Aristophanes' eponymous play, complains bitterly that women bear sons who in times of war become hoplites (*Lys.* 588–9), but Thucydides' Perikles exhorts the parents of the war dead not to grieve too much: for those who are still of an age to bear children should hold firm to the hope of further sons, and those who are too old should take comfort in the glory (*eukleia*) of the war-dead, since only love of honor (*to philotimon*) is ageless (Thuc. 2.44). Nevertheless, Euripides' Medea, railing against the treachery of Jason, complains to the Chorus that while men say that women face no dangers in living in the home when they have to go out to fight, she would rather "stand beside a shield three times than bear children once" (*Medea* 248–51).

The warrior is embedded ideologically in the *oikos*, in the world of women, as well as the battlefield. The many departure scenes on Greek vases bring women into the center of the ideological field of the warrior-culture as the man receives his armor from a female figure, either his wife or his mother, in order to become a hoplite (Lissarrague 1989: esp. 45–6; Lewis 2002: 39–42).

FIGURE 3.2: Attic white-ground lekythos depicting a departing warrior being handed his armour by his wife or mother, fifth century BCE; National Archaeological Museum, Athens, Greece. Photo by DeAgostini, courtesy of Getty Images.

PEACE, WAR, AND GENDER

It is in this context that we also need to understand the "Sayings of Spartan Women" preserved in Plutarch (and elsewhere), such as the well-known aphorism of the Spartan woman who hands her son his shield and says, "Either this or on this" (Plut. *Mor.* 241.16). Figueira has argued that these "Sayings of Spartan Women" represent the female "monitoring" of men at Sparta, and illustrate "an obliteration of the customary division between *polis* and *oikos* and between *politēs* and *idiotēs* 'private individual'", as well as "a congruence of aspirations of mothers and sons in the achievement of *aretē* in the ultimate test of combat." (2010). In these "Sayings", Sparta might seem to represent an extreme example, but there is evidence from elsewhere (not least Homer, as above) that war was a principal arena for the acquisition of honor, which reflected on the whole community, and the glory of the son could bring glory to his mother and to the rest of the household. The pre-Socratic philosopher Herakleitos says that "*Polemos* is father of all and king of all, and reveals some as gods and others as men, and makes some slaves and others free" (DK 22 B 53; Kirk, Raven, and Schofield 1983: 193–4).

Apparent weakness or treachery could be severely punished by the whole community without compunction. At the beginning of Book 9, Herodotos tells the story of Lykidas, a member of the Athenian *boulē*, who in 479 BCE was stoned to death because he suggested that the council should refer to the assembly the proposal of the Persian Mardonios to accept peace and alliance. "With all the uproar in Salamis over Lykidas," Herodotos says, "the Athenian women soon found out what had happened; whereupon, without a word from the men, they got together, and, each one urging on her neighbour and taking her along with the crowd, flocked to Lykidas' house and stoned his wife and children" (9.5). The community acted together, and the story was remembered into the fourth century as an act of treason on the part of Lykidas and an act of communal honor on the part of his and his family's killers. Demosthenes says that this event was an example of the way that Athens as a city always strove for the first prize, for honor, and for glory (18.204–5), and Lykourgos that it showed the nobility of the ancestors not only in their characters but also in that they obtained vengeance on wrong-doers (1.122).

Even to survive battle could be seen as an act of treachery, particularly by the mothers of the dead. More than one of the "Sayings of Spartan Women" relate how mothers either killed sons or required them to commit suicide because they had survived battle through exposed or implied cowardice (Plut. *Mor.* 241.1, 3, 6, 17, 242.19; cf. 241.13, 14). Herodotos tells a story about a man who was the sole survivor of a battle between the Athenians and Aiginetans: when he returned to Athens and told the story, the wives of the dead were so incensed that they seized him and stabbed him to death with the brooches that held together their clothes, each of them asking where her husband was (5.87.1–2). In this case, the Athenians (as the story goes) decided to punish the women and forced them in future to wear broochless clothes. It is probable that neither the "Sayings" nor the story in Herodotos have any actual historical credibility,[10] but they do provide an indication of what was ideologically acceptable, at least to a point. The Athenians did think that the story of the Athenian women was at some level representative of community feeling. There is some sense that the story itself might represent an over-reaction, at least in so far as it acknowledges that the subsequent deeds of the wives were worse than the original defeat. However, that the prohibition on clothing was the most acceptable punishment which could be found also speaks not only to the fact that the community was prepared to accept that community norms were being acted out, even if in a slightly exaggerated way (Hdt. 5.87.3), but also to the desperation of war (the Athenian women ask: "where is my husband?").

FIGURE 3.3a: Attic white-ground lekythos depicting a woman handing spear and helmet to a dead warrior seated at his tomb, fifth century BCE. Fitzwilliam Museum GR.55.1896, Cambridge, UK; © The Fitzwilliam Museum, Cambridge.

So while peace might have been a desideratum, it was difficult to achieve, not least because there were other communal ideologies which gave value to war. War meant the death of sons for mothers and loss of husbands for wives, but community ideologies, and the practical realities of the limitations of conflict resolution apart from war, meant that this had to be accepted, and to a certain extent embraced. Virtue and glory could be demonstrated in war, even if the need to glorify death in war meant that the grief of mothers and wives and the hardships they suffered as a result of war had to be suppressed. In this sense the image on the mid-fifth-century Athenian lekythos where the woman presents a helmet and a spear to the dead young man who sits at his tomb, dating to the 450s or 440s BCE, is most telling and most poignant.

A step on from the warrior departure scenes, this painting demonstrates on the one hand the importance of the glorious martial death, and on the other the continued importance of that death as an indicator of the role of the dead in continuing to look after the living. It also implies the acceptance by the family, including the women, that death in war brought a reflected glory for the whole household.

WOMEN AT WAR AND WOMEN IN WAR

It is generally taken for granted that, apart from some mythical women like the Amazons, women did not play an active part in war, at least as regular warriors. Nevertheless, it is

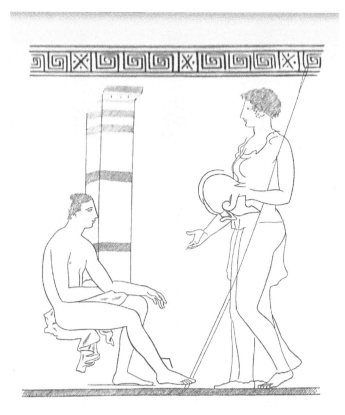

FIGURE 3.3b. Line drawing of Figure 3.3a; from Ernest Arthur Gardner, *A Catalogue of Greek Vases in the Fitzwilliam Museum*, Cambridge University Press, 1897, plate xxxi. Courtesy of Cambridge University Press.

well known that women did take part in defending the city, such as when the women and slaves of Plataia helped during a Theban invasion of the city in 431 BCE by shouting, and throwing rocks and roof tiles (Thuc. 2.4.2). A few years later, the women of Corcyra did likewise, "with a courage beyond their sex" (Thuc. 3.74.1; Schaps 1982: 195–6). When the Carthaginians attacked the city of Selinous in 409 BCE, the women and children helped in the defense of the city by throwing stones and tiles (Diod. 13.56.7), though the city was taken and sacked and all the inhabitants killed, except for those women and children who escaped to the temples for sanctuary (Diod. 13.57.2–6).[11] In 272 BCE Pyrrhos king of Epiros was killed during his attack on Argos, either directly by a roof-tile thrown by an old woman (Paus. 1.13.8; Polyainos *Strat.* 8.68), or by the enemy after he was stunned by the roof-tile and unseated from his horse (Plut. *Pyrrh.*34.2–6).

This willingness of women to take part in war in defense of their cities and their households is not at all surprising, given the consequences if their city was taken. In 422 BCE, when the Athenians took the city of Torone, the men were sent to Athens, and the women and children were enslaved (Thuc. 5.3.4); in 421 BCE, after the Athenians broke the siege of Skione, they killed the adult men and enslaved the women and children (Thuc. 5.32.1). Similarly, when Melos surrendered to the Athenians in 416 BCE,

Thucydides says the Athenians killed the men and enslaved the women and children (5.116.4). Euripides, in a number of his plays in the 420s and 410s BCE, explores the miseries and humiliations of slavery that the Trojan women experienced after the fall of Troy. The *Trojan Women* is the most bleak of all, as Hekuba watches Troy burn with her dead grandson at her feet; the play was produced in 415 BCE after Melos and among the preparations for (what was to become) the disaster of the Sicilian expedition.

Whether the *Trojan Women* is a play about a specific event (the subjugation of Melos) or about the miseries of war in general is a matter of debate (Croally 2007: 231–4). Although the Trojan women may appear noble in the face of their adversities (e.g., Gregory 1997: 155–83), there is no doubt that the actual experience of women after the fall of their city could be brutal: the fate of mass rape and enslavement no doubt inspired the women of Plataia and Corcyra to participate actively in the defense of their cities. While some women could be rescued from slavery by relatives and friends,[12] Demosthenes also recounts a story (that he claimed was told around Greece) of a party at the house of a certain Xenophron, the son of one of the Athenian "Thirty Tyrants", at that time resident in Macedonia. At this party, a young Olynthian slave girl was brought in; she had been born free but was enslaved when her city was taken and destroyed by Philip II of Macedon in 348 BCE. According to Demosthenes, she was whipped within an inch of her life by two Athenians at the party, Aischines and Phrynon, who were with Demosthenes as ambassadors to Philip, because out of modesty and in confusion she refused to sing for them (19.196–8). Demosthenes tells this story because he wants to defame his political enemy, Aischines, but the vulnerability of a Greek captive slave, even in a Greek household—not non-Greek "barbarians" like the Trojan women—is particularly striking, even if the story itself is exaggerated or only partially true.

As well as being prepared to come to the defense of their city, there were women who were prepared to take a leading part in battle if there was need, especially in the absence of, or in defense of, their husbands and sons. In Ktesias' account of the war of Cyrus the Great against the Sakians in the mid-sixth century BCE, once the king Amorges was captured, his wife Sparethe assembled an army of 30,000 men and 200,000 women and defeated the Persians in battle to secure the release of her husband (fr. 9.3). Telesilla of Argos, a poetess, is said by late sources, in the absence of the men (who had just fought the battle of Sepeia against the Spartans), to have led a defense of the city against the Spartan Kleomenes in 494 BCE (Paus. 2.20.8; Plut. *Mor.* 245c–f; Polyainos *Strat.* 8.33).[13]

Another early example is the sixth-century Pheretime of Cyrene, the mother of Arkesilas III, who, when her son went into exile, sought an army from Euelthon of Salamis (cf. Mitchell 2000: 92). Although he gave her many gifts, including a golden spindle and distaff with wool on it (of course a reference back again to the Homeric *teichoskopeia*), Euelthon refused her an army on the grounds that the gifts he gave her were appropriate for women, but an army was not (Hdt. 4.162). However, a few years later, after her son had been assassinated in the city of Barke, she finally did persuade the Persians to take an army against the city, which she accompanied. When the city surrendered she ordered those most responsible for her son's death to be impaled at intervals around the city wall, and the breasts of their wives to be cut off and displayed on the wall also (Hdt.4.165–7, 200–2).

Other royal women were also known for their active involvement in military matters. In addition to building works of great magnificence and splendor, especially at Babylon, Semiramis, queen of the Assyrians, allegedly conducted wars against the Egyptians, Ethiopians and Indians to extend her empire (Diod. 2.4.1–20.5). Tomyris, queen of the Massagetai, was said to have defeated the Persian ruler Cyrus the Great in battle, and in revenge for the death of her son to have cut off Cyrus' head and put it in a wineskin filled with human blood, with the words: "Though I have conquered you and live, yet you have ruined me by treacherously taking my son. See now—I fulfil my threat: you have your fill of blood." (Hdt. 1.214). In the third century CE, after her husband's death, Zenobia, queen of Palmyra, cemented her control of the Roman East, including an advance against Egypt, before she was finally taken captive by the emperor Aurelian (*Historia Augusta*; Zosimos, *Historia Nova* 1).

The fame of Semiramis, Tomyris, and Zenobia was enduring. Justin's epitome of Trogus, composed at some point between the 140s and the 390s CE, includes the innovation that Semiramis achieved her great deeds dressed as her son (1.2.1–10), a story which Orosius, writing in the fifth century CE, also preserves (1.4.4). In Justin, Tamyris (rather than Tomyris, and now queen of the Scythians) tricks Cyrus in battle.[14] Unwomanly

FIGURE 3.4: *Queen Zenobia's Last Look on Palmyra*, by Herbert Schmalz, 1888; Art Gallery of South Australia, Adelaide, Australia. Photo by Fine Art Images/Heritage Images, courtesy of Getty Images.

in her lack of fear at the approaching enemy (1.8.2), and her willingness to use vengeance rather than tears to assuage her grief at the loss of her army and the death of her son (1.8.9), Tamyris completely overcomes Cyrus and his army (1.8.10–12, 37.3.2).[15]

Semiramis, Tomyris, and Zenobia might be highly mythologized characters, but even indubitably historical women of the Macedonian and Hellenistic royal courts were prepared to lead armies, especially in defense of their male relatives (who because of their own position gave the women status; cf. Carney 2000: 36). Thus Olympias, the mother of Alexander III, was prepared to lead armies on behalf of her grandson Alexander IV, and Adea Eurydike was not afraid to take military action on behalf of her husband Philip Arrhidaios. In 317 BCE, Olympias and Eurydike possibly even confronted each other in battle, although the Macedonians in Eurydike's army defected to Olympias, and Olympias subsequently arranged the execution of Eurydike and her husband.[16]

Nevertheless, royal Macedonian women were involved directly in battle only relatively rarely,[17] although Kynnane, the daughter of the Illyrian Audata and Philip II, is reputed to have fought in his battles against the Illyrians and may have trained her daughter Adea Eurydike to fight (Polyainos *Strat*. 8.60; Douris of Samos, *FGrH* 76 F 52 = *BNJ* 76 F 52; Carney 2000: 69). Similarly, Arsinoë (later to become Arsinoë II of Egypt) seems to have had control of armies and territories in the early third century at Kassandreia, before her short and disastrous marriage to her half-brother Ptolemy Keraunos (he killed her children by Lysimachos at the wedding and she was forced to flee to Samothrace: Justin 24.2–3; Carney 2013: 52–3).

However, in order to understand military women, the men who wrote about them had to make them (like the Amazons) into pseudo-men (Sebillotte Cuchet 2015: 228–46). Artemisia I of Karia notoriously fought on the Persian side at the battle of Salamis in 480 BCE (Herodotos says she joined the battle because of her "spirit" [*lēma*] and "manly courage" [*andreia*]: 7.99.1). Xerxes is said to have declared, "My men have turned into women, my women into men" (Hdt. 8.88.3), though this is in fact a Herodotean joke against Xerxes. Artemisia demonstrates her guile, or, as Dewald calls it, intelligent *andreia* (1981: 125), tricking the Athenian commander in pursuit of her ship at the battle of Salamis by ramming a ship of the Kalyndians, Persian allies. The Athenian thought her ship must be either Greek or that of a deserter so he gave up the pursuit, although Xerxes did not understand in the confusion that this was what had occurred (Hdt. 8.87).

Likewise, the formidable Fulvia, wife of Marc Antony (her third husband) and sometimes called the "first empress of Rome" (cf. Münzer 1910: col. 284), was said to have girded herself with a sword and led an army against Praeneste in the Perusine Wars of 40 BCE (Cassius Dio 48.10.3–4; Vell. Pat. 2.74.2–3). Plutarch says she "took no thought for spinning or housekeeping" (*Antony* 10.5), and Velleius Paterculus that she "had nothing of the woman about her except her body" (*nihil muliebre praeter corpus gerens*).[18] It is clear from the tradition of paradoxographical lists of women warriors that date from the Hellenistic period, such as the anonymous *Tractatus De Mulieribus Claris in Bello* (Gera 1997), that female warriors were objects of fascination.[19] Just as Euelthon of Salamis (if the story is reliable) was not prepared to countenance a woman in charge of armies, and essentially told Pheretime that a woman's place was in the home, so male writers writing about women at war needed to understand them in transgendered terms.

Nevertheless, ideas of gender were not necessarily static. If a woman was to be a warrior, then, for our ancient writers, she had to become a man. The alternative, perhaps even more tellingly, as for Vergil's Camilla, who was not accustomed to the distaff or wool-basket (*Aen.* 7.803–7), was to become an Amazon (*Aen.* 11.648–51, 659–63).[20] However, the female Amazonian warriors do not have male counterparts. Instead, in the late Roman Empire eunuchs ('men made soft') were thought not fit for war or high office, as Claudian in his invective against the consul of 399 CE made clear (*In Eutropium*). Even though the eunuch Eutropius had led a successful military campaign against the Huns in 398, he was deposed and his name removed from the consular lists as a result. In fact, a eunuch so outraged ideas of male identity that he was worse than a woman: "for if a woman took the *fasces* illegally, it would be less disgusting" (*In Eutropium* 1.341–2; Long 1996; cf. Nathan 2015).

WOMEN AND PEACE

The ancient world was a world embroiled in war, and, although peace was an object of desire and there were mechanisms for achieving it, lasting peace was difficult to maintain (Raaflaub 2016c). Women suffered as a consequence of war, and, as much as they might participate in the glory of war, they also desired that peace should be achieved. Lysistrata complains of the loneliness of women who are left at home to grow old, or who never marry at all, because the men are at war (*Lys.* 591–7).[21] Xenophon's *Memorabilia* bears testimony to the dire straits to which households of women could be reduced by the consequences of war, especially in early fourth-century Athens, which had been starved into subjection by the Spartans (2.7.2–4). In Euripides' *Suppliants* of 423 BCE, Evadne throws herself onto the funeral pyre of her husband, Kapeneus, one of the seven Argives who died at Thebes.

Women could be the instruments of peace, even if usually passively rather than actively. Certainly, marrying off daughters and sisters (and even wives!) was a way that rulers commonly used to cement peace treaties, or to "buy" peace. For example, in the early 420s BCE, Perdikkas II of Macedon was able to bring a Thracian invasion of Macedon to an abrupt end by giving one of his sisters in marriage to the nephew of the Thracian king (Thuc. 2.101.5–6). Likewise, Philip II of Macedon, the father of Alexander the Great, was notorious in antiquity for "marrying with war in mind" (Satyros, *ap.* Athenaios 13.577b–e). The marriage of women in the Hellenistic world was an important part of the power-games of the period, although it was also the case that some women were able to arrange their own marriages (although not always successfully): against the wishes of her son, Arsinoë arranged the disastrous marriage with her half-brother Ptolemy Keraunos, probably in order to try to secure the position of her sons by her first husband Lysimachos (Carney 2013: 54–64).

Royal women, and especially royal wives in the Hellenistic and Roman imperial periods, at times appear to have had a surprising degree of political independence and agency, and were able to bring to bear influence on their husbands. For example, Apama, the first wife of Seleukos I, was honored by some Milesian mercenaries and ambassadors because she intervened on their behalf with Seleukos in relation to the sanctuary at Didyma (299 BCE; McCabe 1985: no. 8; Harders 2016; Ramsey 2016). In the Chremonides decree of the 260s BCE, Ptolemy II says that he will act in accordance with the policy of his (now dead) sister/wife Arsinoë II (*IG* II[2] 687).

Royal women were often also highly educated, and so were able to negotiate their way in the male-dominated corridors of power. Carney suggests that many Hellenistic royal women were—and needed to be—literate (Carney 2000: 28–9). At these great courts royal women would have been exposed to some of the great intellectuals of their age, such as Kallimachos, who wrote poems for his compatriot and queen, Berenike II, at the court in Alexandria (Clayman 2014: 3–4). For this reason, these royal women were quite capable of and equipped for taking part in high-level court politics and diplomacy, as were other educated women, especially of the elite. The sixth-century CE Gothic queen, Amalasuintha, who was given a Roman education and known for her abilities in multiple languages, was first regent for her young son Athalaric, before on his death becoming queen and raising her cousin, Theodahad, to the position of co-ruler (Vitiello 2017). Inevitably, contemporary sources described her virtues in masculine terms: in her regency Procopius says she displayed "the excessive manliness of her nature" (*de Bellis* 5.2.3). In the *Secret History*, he elaborates that Theodora (wife of Justinian I) was jealous of Amalasuintha's "magnificence and excessive manliness" (16.1). Cassiodorus, likewise, says she "satisfies the excellence of both sexes (*uterque sexus*): for she both gave to us our glorious king [Athalaric] and defends with fortitude of mind your [the Romans'] expansive empire" (*Variae* 11.1.14; La Rocca 2012; Vitiello 2017: 22–8).

Nevertheless, transgressions of the boundaries when intellectually equipped women were elevated from private roles to the position of political counselors (even if informally) could prove dangerous. In the early fifth century CE, the Neo-Platonist philosopher Hypatia, of whom Socrates Scholasticus says, "All men had a great regard for and were in awe of her excessive self-control (*sōphrosynē*)" (*Historia Ecclesiastica* 7.15.3), was an advisor to Orestes, the prefect of Egypt. Nevertheless, she was torn to pieces by the Christian mob because it was said she prevented a reconciliation between Orestes and Cyril, the bishop of Alexandria.[22] As for Amalasuintha, she was deposed, imprisoned, and assassinated by her cousin Theodahad within a year of making him her co-ruler (see Vitiello 2017: 157–62).

Although there are relatively few specific examples, we do have some instances where women actively intervened to prevent war or secure peace. In early fifth-century Sicily, the wife of Gelon, Damarete, was involved in the peace negotiations with the Carthaginians after their defeat at the battle of Himera in 480 BCE, and bargained on their behalf, achieving for them very favorable terms (Diod. 11.26.2–3).[23] Gorgo, the daughter of the Spartan king Kleomenes, was also reputed to have influenced her father not to take part in the Ionian Revolt of the early 490s BCE (Hdt. 5.51; Mitchell 2012: 10). In the Old Testament book of *Esther*, the queen risks her life by going into the presence of the Great King of Persia without his permission in order to save Mordecai and the Jews (*Esther* 4.4–5.8). In the first century CE, another Jewish royal woman, Berenike, the sister of Agrippa I, is said by Josephus to have tried to intervene in the conflict between the Jews in Jerusalem and the Romans (*Jewish Wars* 2.309–14, 333–4, 402–6), although other Roman sources are more hostile (Leiber 2012: 339).

Carolyn Dewald has written about the awareness in antiquity that the world of women was integral and essential to the political world of men, despite the discourse of separation of male and female spheres that tried at the same time to make distance between them (1980). In the Roman foundation myth of the "Rape of the Sabines", as told by Livy, when the Antemnates tried to take revenge for the capture of their women, it was Hersilia, one of the captured Sabine women, who persuaded Romulus as his wife (*coniunx*) to make peace (here *concordia*: Livy 1.11.3). Moreover, it is the Sabine women, rushing into the middle of the battle, who persuade their fathers on the one side and their husbands on the other to turn their anger against them (the women) as the cause of the war (Livy 1.13.3).

FIGURE 3.5: *The Intervention of the Sabine Women*, by Jacques-Louis David, 1799; Louvre Museum, Paris, France. Photo by Leemage/Corbis, courtesy of Getty Images.

At once both sides stop fighting, the leaders come forward to make an alliance, and "not only did they agree on peace (*pax*), but they made one people out of the two (*sed civitatem unam ex duabus faciunt*)" (Livy 1.13.4). Robert Brown argues that the emphasis on the role of the women is probably original to Livy: "it is the women who break the cycle of violence suited to this role by their unwarlike and relational social function as wives and mothers ... the women thus hold for Livy a symbolic significance as embodiments of a *concordia* which complements the Romulean qualities of *virtus* and *pietas*." (1995: 314).

In this story, Livy presents us with his ideal of the relationship between men and women, war and peace: women ought to have a conciliatory role in the public sphere precisely because they are set apart in real life (cf. Finley 2002). Whether or not Livia, the wife of Augustus, modeled herself on Hersilia or Livy's Hersilia was modeled on Livia, a connection was made between them, and it is likely that Livia herself encouraged the link. In this regard, it is significant that Livia was responsible for building the Shrine of *Concordia* in the *Porticus Liviae* (Ovid, *Fasti* 636–7; Angelova 2015: 72–3). Furthermore, Augustus was associated with Romulus as a founder of Rome and a restorer of peace (Scott 1925), and in Ovid's *Metamorphoses*, like Romulus (who is deified as Quirinus: *Met.* 14.805–28), the deification of Augustus as bringer of peace (*pax*) is foretold (*Met.* 807–51). For that reason, it is likely that Hersilia's deification (which seems to be original to Ovid: *Met.* 14.829–50) was intended to suggest that Livia too would be deified.[24] The implication must be that as Augustus brought peace, Livia was his helpmate in achieving this goal, and that this is the way she wanted to represent herself, as the Shrine of *Concordia* seems to demonstrate.

In fact, it is evident that women could use religion and religious activity as routes to political and diplomatic agency. Olympias, the mother of Alexander, for example, made at least one dedication, of a bowl to *Hygeia*, at Athens (Hyperides, *Eux.* 19, cf. 27), which must have been intended as a benefaction but was used to create a political stir during a period in Athens when Alexander and Olympias were out of favor. As Carney notes, that the charge could be made against Euxenippos for allowing her to make the dedication "indicates the political aspect of religious dedication" (Carney 2006: 95–6). Sarah Pomeroy has argued that the royal women of the Hellenistic period enjoyed a reduction in the disparity of standing between themselves and their husbands, had much greater status than the women of Classical Greece, and even surpassed the power in real terms enjoyed by Roman imperial women (Pomeroy 1984: xvii-xix). One of the reasons for this, she argues, was their involvement in their religious roles, especially in ruler cult.

But routes to power, or at least influence, also lay open for non-royal women, even in the Classical period, especially through their religious activities. Herodotos tells the story of the Spartan king, Kleomenes, who, when he tried to enter the temple on the acropolis at Athens in order to take it, was told by the priestess not to enter (5.72.3). Robert Parker is rather sceptical about what this might tell us of the place of women, and remarks: "It is rather startling to find a woman issuing orders to Cleomenes, the most important man in Greece in her day. On the other hand, she is only standing up for principles that her male fellow citizens would have endorsed." (Parker 1997b: 1–4). Nevertheless, she evidently did feel that she had the authority to resist in her own right. Indeed, Connolly argues for the influence and authority of priestesses within civic processes, even in fifth- and fourth-century Athens (Connolly 2007: 213–20). According to Pausanias (5.16.2–5), in Elis there was a college of sixteen women who organized both races for girls at the festival of Hera and the girls' choruses; they also wove the sacred robe for Hera (see Stehle 2012: 202). Although the story is possibly not historical, Pausanias says that the origin of the college lay in the conflict between Pisa and Elis: "they chose a woman from each of the sixteen cities of Elis still inhabited at that time to settle their differences, this woman to be the oldest, the most noble, and the most esteemed of all the women" (Paus. 5.16.5).[25]

Which brings us back, finally, to Aristophanes' *Lysistrata*. In the middle of the last century, David Lewis suggested that the eponymous Lysistrata represented a real-life priestess at the end of the fifth century BCE, Lysimache, the priestess of Athena Polias on the Athenian acropolis (Lewis 1955: 1–12; cf. Connolly 2007: 62–4). Priestesses could be women of authority who operated, at least to some extent, in the civic as well as the religious life of the city (Connolly 2007: 197–221). Whether Lysistrata ("Dissolver of armies") *was* Lysimache ("Dissolver of battle"), or whether she represented a Lysimache-like person and possibly even a priestess,[26] within the play she is a woman of some authority who is in control and directs the action of the play. Part of the point of the play is that Lysistrata's cause is just and right, and that she is able to use her strength and authority to bring about peace, and also her womanly skills and knowledge. Although the *proboulos* mocks Lysistrata, it is significant that she uses the metaphor for wool-carding as the means for achieving peace:

If *you* had any sense, you would handle all your affairs in the way we handle wool. . . . First of all, just like washing out a raw fleece, you should wash the sheep-dung out of the body politic in a bath, then put it on a bed, beat out the villains with a stick and pick off the burrs; and as for those people who combine and mat themselves together to gain office, you should card them out and pluck off the heads. Then card the wool into the work-basket of union and concord (*koinē eunoia*), mixing in everyone; and the immigrants, and any foreigner who's friendly to you, and anyone who's in debt to the treasury, they should be mixed in too. An yes, there are also all the states which are colonies of this land: you should recognize how you now have them lying around like little flocks of wool, each one by itself; so then you should take the human flock from all of them, being them together here and join them into one, and then make a great ball of wool, and from that weave a warm cloak for the people to wear.

—*Lys.* 572–86

In this way, Lysistrata's metaphor takes us back to Hektor and Andromache on the wall above Troy, with which this essay began, but here, rather than being an alternative to war, the distaff and loom become a way of putting an end to war.

Lysistrata is a woman of intelligence, who, like the Homeric Arete, queen of the Phaiakians (Hom. *Od.* 7.72–3), is able through her female wisdom to resolve disputes; she says: "I am a woman, but I have got a mind: I am not badly off for intelligence on my own account" (*Lys.* 1124–5). Lysistrata breaks the bounds of the ideal woman so familiar from other late fifth-century literature: silent, secluded, and for whom the greatest virtue is to "be no weaker than your nature allows, and not to be talked about for good or ill among men".[27] Lysistrata will not succumb to a glass ceiling, and she is as ruthless as Pheretime in pursuing what she wants. Although Lysistrata may have broken the *oikos* apart through her sex strike, at the end of the play she reunites the Greek world, just as she also reunites the *oikos* (*Lys.* 1273–8).

CONCLUSION

The world of antiquity was a world often at war. Because of the terrible consequences of war, peace was desired, but it was rarely achieved except through military force. War devastated families not only by taking away husbands and sons, but also by causing misery and hardship for those defeated in war and for those left behind to suffer the consequences of war. Nevertheless, one of the reasons why war was difficult to avoid was because of the inherently competitive nature of ancient society, for which the pursuit of glory was paramount. This was particularly true for those who died gloriously in war, a glory that reflected back on the city of the glorious dead, and for their households. For that reason, although war was dreaded as a "violent teacher" which takes away the comforts of daily life (Thuc. 3.82.2), war was also a necessary element of social validation. War was ideologically important for the whole community, the women as well as the men.

Yet it was ideologically important, and consistently so, that women belonged to the household and were not warriors. Although there was a grudging admiration in literary sources written by men for women who were prepared to fight in war, it was also seen as transgressive and women who did lead armies were seen as "unwomanly" and even as women who had become men. Although our literary sources (written by men) do not provide many examples of women actively working for peace or involved in peace negotiations, there are some, who are all the more surprising and notable because they do exist. Instead, the role of women is often symbolized by their work with wool, and this is as true for Greece as for Rome. Over and again wool-working is used as a metaphor for the proper world of women, who are (or should be) unaccustomed to war. Even Athena, the warrior goddess and patron of Athens, is associated with spinning and weaving.[28] So although women were not necessarily represented as "peaceful" as such, it was assumed that they should be separated from war.

However, in Aristophanes' *Lysistrata* the metaphor is deliberately inverted, and the productive rather than destructive task of wool-working becomes the means of achieving peace. In fact, it is because the worlds of women and men were ideologically separate that a woman entering the world of men with forcefulness, vigor, and authority is so powerful, even if also so vulnerable. So, while it is true that women were not "peaceful" in the way that men could be "warlike", it was also the case that women and womanly skills could be represented as being peaceful by nature (one thinks of Livia and the comparison she seems to have drawn between herself and Hersilia). On occasion that also meant that women who had positions of *auctoritas* within the community, without necessarily *potestas*, could be the agents of peace, as was the sixth-century Sicilian Damarete, who may have even have received hero-cult at Syracuse for her standing in the community, together with her Syracusan husband Gelon (Mitchell 2012: 14).

CHAPTER FOUR

Peace, Pacifism, and Religion

JULIA WILKER

In Greco-Roman antiquity, the concepts of peace and religion—both defined in the broadest sense possible—were inextricably linked with each other. Whereas peace was generally regarded as a desirable state that was granted and protected (but could also be taken away) by the gods, the relationship between peace and religion was the product of specific political, social, and cultural circumstances. It was thus construed and dealt with very differently among the Greeks and Romans. In both cultures, Peace (*Eirēnē/Pax*) was revered and eventually worshipped as a goddess, albeit in different forms and with different connotations. Yet religion had an impact on ancient views and practices of peace beyond the sphere of cults. In the realm of interstate relations, religious beliefs and rituals provided for a framework that made it possible to conclude and maintain peace between states, end warfare, and protect stability and security at home and abroad. In the ancient world, peace, as a value, a state worth striving for, and as the actual relationship between two or more communities, was unthinkable without religion.

GODS OF WAR AND PEACE IN GREECE

The personification of peace played an important role in Greek culture from very early on. In Hesiod's *Theogony*, Eirēnē appears as firmly established in the mythological genealogy as a daughter of Zeus and Themis alongside her sisters Dikē (Justice) and Eunomia (Good Order), the three Horai (Hes. *Theog.* 901–2; cf. Pindar *Ol.* 13.10–11). Although Hesiod does not give any further details, the association of these three personified virtues demonstrates that peace was conceptualized as more than the absence of war and violence; it was also considered a necessity of good life, security, and order. The same idea is expressed in the *Iliad*'s description of the Shield of Achilles, which juxtaposes the image of a city in war with that of a city in peace. Whereas siege, ambush, and battle symbolize war, peace is expressed through justice, political institutions, and festivals as well as the fruits of a good harvest (*Il.* 18.478–607, city at peace: 490–508; city at war: 509–40).

In these early expressions of peace, external and internal components appear in combination. It was only from the fifth century BCE on that the Greeks began to distinguish between internal harmony (*homonoia*, cf. de Romilly 1972), and *eirēnē*, which was primarily associated with external peace. Despite the distinction, both continued to be considered as prerequisites for the prosperity and well-being of a community. Against this background, it is not surprising that Eirēnē was closely associated with Ploutos, or Wealth, a connection that was evident already in the praises of the fifth-century poet Bacchylides:

Peace gives birth to noble wealth for mortals, to the flowers of honey-tongued songs, to the burning for gods of thighs of oxen and fleecy sheep in yellow flame on elaborate altars, to young men's concern with the gymnasium, with pipes and revelry. On iron-pinned shieldgrips are found the spinnings of red-brown spiders, and sharp-pointed spears and double-edged swords are subdued by rust.[1]

—Bacchylides fr. 4.61–73

Whereas Bacchylides and others present Eirēnē as the mother of Ploutos, Hesiod clearly describes Wealth as being the son of Demeter (Hes. *Theog.* 969–70). Despite such different nuances, the relationship remains close in the mythological imagination, and Peace continued to be conceptualized as nursing and nourishing Wealth.[2]

The personification of peace gained further prominence in the following decades, a process that can be best traced in Athens. This prominence is hardly surprising, considering the long and dreadful experiences of the Peloponnesian War. It was within this historical context of seemingly never-ending warfare, devastation, sorrow, and death that Eirēnē became increasingly envisioned and revered as a goddess. In a surviving fragment of the *Kresphontes*, Euripides lauds her as "Peace, with your depths of wealth, fairest of the blessed gods, I pine for you, so long you are in coming; I fear old age may overwhelm me with hardships before I can look upon your graceful beauty, your songs adorned with dancing, your garland-loving revels." (Eur. fr. 453.15–19).

Eirēnē assumes an even more central role in several of Aristophanes' comedies from the time of the Peloponnesian War. The play bearing her name, performed in 421 BCE, tells the story of how the goddess was abducted by War (*Polemos*) and only freed through the initiative of an individual Athenian citizen, Trygaios. In his longing for peace, Trygaios finds himself at odds with the official politics of the polis and its warmongering politicians in particular; yet he persists and eventually succeeds. Such personal longing for peace also takes center stage in several of Aristophanes' other wartime comedies, such as the *Acharnians* and *Lysistrata*. Yet in the *Peace*, this longing is expressed through reverence of the goddess. Trygaios not only liberates Eirēnē but also establishes a cult in her honor and prepares a sacrifice for her (Ar. *Pax* esp. 923–1026).

Aristophanes' wartime plays demonstrate that by the end of the fifth century BCE, peace had gained a prominent place as a revered personified value, and they are not the only evidence for this process. For instance, an altar from Brauron, tentatively dated around the year 400 BCE, presents Eirēnē and other Horai, identified through inscriptions, in a Dionysiac setting.[3] Despite this growing prominence, it was not until the 370s BCE that a formal cult for Eirēnē became established in Athens.[4] The cult of Peace in the Agora is mentioned in several sources.[5] The famous statue of Kephisodotos, of which several copies from the Roman period have survived, is commonly identified as the respective cult statue, and it highlights further the close association with prosperity and abundance, signified through the little Ploutos being nurtured by Eirēnē.[6] The statue is also depicted on fragments of several Panathenaic amphorae from Eleusis, dating to 360/59 BCE, on which Eirēnē is shown on top of a tall column. That the cult statue was chosen to adorn Panathenaic amphorae proves the popularity and prominence of the festival and the cult of Peace.[7] Unfortunately, next to no details are known about the cultic activities that took place in honor of Eirēnē. Apparently, the main event in this context was a public sacrifice at the Synoikia, celebrated on the 16th of the month Hekatombaion and administered by the *strategoi* (generals).[8] Yet although most of the details of the cult remain elusive, it nonetheless offers important insights into the interplay between religion and peace in late classical Athens.

The worship of personified virtues was a growing phenomenon in the fourth century BCE and not limited to Peace alone (Burkert 1985: 186; Parker 1997a: 228–36), yet the political context in which the cult of Eirēnē was established further illuminates the Athenian understanding of Peace as a goddess. Isokrates ascribes its foundation to Timotheos' victory over Sparta in 375 BCE (*Or.* 15.109–10; cf. Nep. *Timotheus* 2.2). However, the clear intention to praise Timotheos and, more importantly, the short-lived nature of said peace has raised doubts in modern scholarship as to whether this was, in fact, the origin of the cult.[9] In any event, the official reverence of Peace was far from promoting pacifism; instead, it was associated with the positive outcomes of military expeditions for the victor, including wealth and interstate stability. Peace was thus revered as the personification of a desirable status, but this status was established through war and secured through Athenian hegemony. Peace for peace's sake remained a foreign concept to Athenian religion and Athenian politics alike (Parker 1997a: 229–30; Hunt 2010: 241–2). As such, the concept of peace through war remained a staple, despite changing political circumstances. An inscription dating to the second half of the second century BCE mentions sacrifices to Peace by an honored official of the polis, and the famous statue of Kephisodotos was still featured on Athenian coins from the second century CE (*IG* II² 1000.6–8; *BMC Attica* 109, 801 pl. 19.5; Stafford 2001: 177).

The institutionalization of a formal cult for Eirēnē in fourth-century Athens highlights an evolution that, at least in its broader sense, can be applied to other Greek communities as well. Independent cults for Eirēnē are, for instance, attested in Thespiai and Erythrai. A coin from Lokroi Epizephyroi in Southern Italy, presumably from the first half of the fourth century BCE, shows on the reverse the goddess, unmistakably identified in the inscription as ΕΙΡΗΝΑ ΛΟΚΡΩΝ ("Peace of the Lokrians"), sitting on an altar and holding a *kerykeion*, a herald's wand, an attribute commonly carried by ambassadors sent to negotiate peace. The symbol was presumably chosen to commemorate an interstate agreement, though neither the content nor the context of this assumed agreement is known.[10]

Whereas Eirēnē was the main personification of peace, other gods of the Greek pantheon were revered as harbingers and guarantors of peace as well. For instance, the passage from Bacchylides quoted earlier is dedicated to Apollo, who is praised for leaving armor and weapons unused to gather cobwebs (Bacchylides fr. 4.61–2; cf. Simon 1988: 59–60). The notion of peace as being provided by the gods in turn required piety among human beings. For instance, a utopian fragment attributed to Theopompos describes a city of peace, pleasure, and wealth that was named Eusebeia (Reverence) (Theopompos *BNJ* 115 F 75C). The same idea was maintained in the postclassical period and, with a particular Hellenistic twist, even aided the emergence of Hellenistic ruler cults. In the Athenian ithypallic hymn to Demetrios Poliorketes, the king is praised as a bringer of peace:

> The other gods are either far away or they do not have ears or they do not exist or they do not pay any attention to us at all, but we see that you are present, not made of wood or stone, but here in reality. And so we pray to you. First bring about peace, o dearest one, for you have the power.
>
> —Douris of Samos, *BNJ* 76 F 13; translation F. Pownall

The primary objective of this praise was, of course, to ingratiate the *demos* with the ruler. However, it would be oversimplifying to discard the hymn as mere flattery. The chaotic

FIGURE 4.1: Votive relief sculpture of Ares with Aphrodite, fifth century BCE; National Archaeological Museum, Venice, Italy. Photo by DEA/A. DAGLI ORTI/DeAgostini, courtesy of Getty Images.

decades after the death of Alexander and the resulting sense of fear and instability prompted the population to turn to new authorities to provide peace and stability. The honors dedicated to Demetrios Poliorketes were situated on a different religious, social, and political level than the cult of Eirēnē; yet the hymn expresses the hope that he will finally bring peace—a task at which the traditional gods seemed to have failed.

War, in turn, was particularly connected with Ares, who ranks among the Greek gods as the one with the worst reputation. Already in the *Iliad*, Ares is described as a troublemaking, evil deity who disregards justice and most other virtues and is even disliked by his own father, Zeus (*Il.* 5.761, 831, 890–1; Burkert 1985: 169–70). Whereas this negative characterization is based on a negative image of warfare in general, it must be stressed that Ares personifies the worst aspects of war: injustice, pure violence, and fickleness. It is hence not surprising that Ares received his first temple in Athens only in the late first century BCE,[11] although there were older temples devoted to him elsewhere in Greece (Raaflaub 2016c: 24). However, Ares was far from being the only god associated with war or war-like features. Most prominently, Athena also served as a warrior goddess, most evidently in the worship of Athena Promachos on the Athenian Acropolis.[12]

Nikē, the goddess of victory, was equally revered for successes in war, and, like Athena, represented war from the perspective of the victor and its positive outcomes. In essence,

FIGURE 4.2: Bronze sculpture of Athena wearing a crested war helmet, fourth century BCE; National Archaeological Museum, Athens, Greece. Photo by DEA/G. DAGLI ORTI/DeAgostini, courtesy of Getty Images.

all gods were, or potentially could be, associated with peace and war. They were imagined intervening on either side in a military conflict, granting victory, inflicting defeat, and enabling or preventing the reach of agreements and peaceful solutions. Accordingly, the victorious community—as well as individual soldiers, especially the commanding generals—would vow sacrifices and votives, monuments, and even temples to secure the gods' support, and spoils were commonly dedicated to those deities who were thought to have contributed to the recent success (cf. Parker 2016: 125–8).

PEACE IN ROMAN CULT AND RELIGION

Many of the features noted for the Greeks are also evident in Roman religion. However, in other respects the relationships among religion, cult, and peace were conceptualized very differently in ancient Rome. The more prominent and overwhelmingly positive role ascribed to Mars as the principal god of war is only one of the immediately apparent distinctions. In Roman mythology, Mars was perceived as the father of Romulus and Remus and thus formed—together with Venus, the mother of Aeneas—the primary divine couple associated with the origins of the Roman people and its city (Dion. Hal. *Ant. Rom.* 1.76–9, 2.2.3; Livy 1 pr. 8, 4.2, 22.10.9; Ov. *Fast.* 3.11–22). Accordingly, Mars held a central position in the Roman pantheon and was honored and revered from early on. Yet the association with war remained equally dominant. The month of March, named after the god, traditionally designated the beginning of the war season, ritually announced through the famous dance of the priestly college of the Salii. The strict Roman distinction between the demilitarized sphere at home and the, at least potentially, militarized and hostile world beyond the city's perimeter—*domi* and *militiae*—meant that sacred sites dedicated to Mars were commonly located outside of the *pomerium*, the ritual border of the city.[13]

According to Suetonius, Julius Caesar had planned to dedicate a sanctuary to Mars within the city of Rome (Suet. *Iul.* 44.1), but it was only under Augustus that the Temple of Mars Ultor (Mars the Avenger) in the Forum Augustum was built (see below). Yet even before that, Mars was prominently present in the city's temples. One of the rooms in the *regia*, considered one of the oldest sacred buildings in the Forum Romanum, housed spears and shields attributed to Mars.[14] These were used in the rituals before the beginning of a campaign, and the rallying cry "Mars awake!" assured the people and departing troops of the god's support.[15] Accordingly, numerous victorious generals gave dedications to the god upon their glorious return, reinforcing the close connection between Mars and the Roman self-concept.[16]

Although Mars was closely associated with war, he was not limited to this aspect.[17] In turn, he was far from being the only god connected to military enterprises, let alone military success. Bellona, for instance, is attested in Latium from the fifth century BCE onward (*CIL* I² 441). Livy also relates that Appius Claudius Caecus built a temple for the goddess that he had vowed to dedicate in the Second Samnite War (296 BCE) near the later Circus Flaminius outside of the *pomerium*.[18] At least from the second century BCE on, it was in front of this temple that the *fetiales* formally declared war by throwing a lance into a spot of land ritually signifying the enemy's territory (see below; Serv. *Aen.* 9.52). Other gods commonly associated with war included, of course, Jupiter, but also Juno, Salus, Victoria, and occasionally even Venus.[19] Although the strict distinction between *domi* and *militiae* dictated that temples directly associated with warfare were located outside the *pomerium*, glorious generals dedicated the spoils to the gods and vowed sacrifices, monuments, or temples to secure the gods' support on the battlefield. The ever-growing number of Rome's military victories thus had a fundamental impact on Rome's cultic landscape, a process that was further accelerated through the intricate connection of military glory, social status, and competition among the Republican elite in the third and second centuries BCE (Harris 1991; Rüpke 1990, 260–2).

Despite these close connections among war, military glory, and religious rituals, the Romans valued peace and prayed to the gods to grant it to their community. Yet in contrast to its status in Greece, peace was not personified in Rome until the second half of the first century BCE and did not receive a cult before the rule of Augustus. In contrast, Concordia, the personification of internal harmony, was already revered from the Middle Republic on, with the first plans of dedicating a temple to her dating to 367 BCE.[20] However, the apparent contrast between the emphasis on concord within the community and bellicose virtues in foreign relations even in the religious sphere should not be interpreted as a general disregard for peace. Rather, the strict distinction between *domi* and *militiae*, especially during the Republican period, furthered a focus on internal harmony that left hardly any room for Pax, the personification of external peace (cf. Raaflaub 2011a: 326–7).

The experiences of the civil wars in the first century BCE prompted the Romans to reconfigure their system of values and value expression through cults and religious rituals. Against the background of almost constant civil strife, violence, and political instability, it

PEACE, PACIFISM, AND RELIGION

is not surprising that Concordia continued to feature prominently in the representation of almost all leaders who promised to reestablish order and internal unity.[21] Yet the turmoil and horrors of the civil wars also gave rise to the personification of peace and its reverence. The first coin featuring Pax was minted in 44 BCE and depicted a wreathed female head with the inscription PAXS (sic!) (*RRC* 480/24); and in the years following Julius Caesar's assassination, Pax was represented on the coins of the triumvirs alongside deities such as Concordia, Venus, and Victoria.[22] Yet in the religious sphere, this new emphasis on peace only came to full fruition after the end of a decade-long struggle for power as Augustus turned the restoration and protection of peace into one of the main pillars that supported and legitimized his power and the new regime.[23]

The prominence of Pax in Augustan poetry gives vivid testimony to both the profound longing for peace after the civil wars and the importance that the newly defined personification of peace received in this new era of Roman history. One of the first extensive descriptions of the personification of peace comes from Tibullus, written during the first years of Augustus' rule:

> Meanwhile, may Peace be tilling fields! Pure Peace first led the oxen to the plough beneath curved yokes. Peace nourished vines and stored grape juice to ensure the father's jug could pour wine for his son. With Peace the hoe and ploughshare glitter, while in gloom rust fills the hardened soldiers' mournful weapons. (. . .) So come to us while holding cornstalks, fertile Peace, and may fruit spring from your resplendent breast!

—Tibullus 1.10.45–50, 68–71

Here, Pax stands for far more than the absence of war, including the assurance of rich agricultural produce and social harmony. A few years later, in 17 BCE, Horace praised Pax in the *Carmen Saeculare* in a similar way by presenting her alongside other values: "Now Good Faith (*Fides*), Peace (*Pax*), and Honor (*Honos*), along with old-fashioned Modesty (*Pudor*) and Virtue (*Virtus*), who has been so long neglected, venture to return, and blessed Plenty (*Copia*) with her full horn is seen by all" (57–60). The mythological and ideological parallels to the Greek concept of Eirēnē are striking. The copies of Kephisodotos' famous statue that were found in Rome and its vicinity give further proof that the Greek presentation of Peace resonated with a Roman audience (Simon 1988: 66; Simon 1994: 206). However, Pax was far more than a Roman synonym of Eirēnē and differed from the Greek concept and deity in multiple respects.

Most important in this context is the focus on Augustus. From his victory over Marc Antony on, peace as a value and a personification was monopolized by the emperor and was consequently revered as Pax Augusta, allowing the emperor to claim credit for and capitalize on the yearning for peace that had grown consistently the longer the civil war had lasted. Yet as the passage from Tibullus quoted above demonstrates, the Augustan notion of Pax went beyond a mere celebration of perils overcome. Even more important was the prospective aspect that underlined the connection between peace and the emperor even further. The Augustan Peace thus not only prevented the outbreak of a new civil strife,[24] it also led to the notion that the Romans could only live in harmony, political and social stability, and peace under and through the all-encompassing rule of the emperor. Finally, the very concept of the Pax Augusta was quickly expanded to incorporate the empire as a whole and thus *pax* in its original, external sense.[25]

The close connections among Pax, the new regime, and the important role that the religious framing of peace would assume in Augustan representation become immediately apparent in the ritual of closing the doors of the Temple of Janus. In 29 BCE, upon Octavian's return to Italy after his victory in the war against Marc Antony and Cleopatra, the senate decreed that the doors of the Temple of Janus were to be ceremoniously closed.[26] Since this ritual was supposed to signify the end of all external wars, the act underlined the official rendering of the civil war as an external conflict with Egypt. Yet the ritual assumed even greater significance in the following decades of Augustus' rule. In his *Res Gestae*, the *princeps* proudly states:

> Our ancestors wished that (the temple of) Janus Quirinus was to be closed when throughout the whole empire of the Roman People on land and sea peace had been won by victories, and although before my birth it is recorded that from the foundation of the city it had been closed only twice, the senate ordered it closed three times with me as *princeps*.

—*RGDA* 13

Janus, the two-faced god, was revered as one of the oldest deities of Rome and connected to different forms of passages.[27] The location of his temple in the Forum Romanum has not been firmly identified yet, but literary sources situate it near the Argiletum.[28] Furthermore, the sixth-century CE historian Procopius describes a temple with two gates, made entirely out of bronze, perhaps dating to a renovation under Augustus (Procop. *Bell.* 5.25.18–25; see Simon 1990: 619). It housed an old cult statue, presumably identical to the one already mentioned by the annalistic historian L. Calpurnius Piso Frugi in the second century BCE (*FRH* 9 F 11). Piso (preserved by Varro) is also the earliest extant reference to explain that the temple's gate was to be closed only when Rome was at peace (*FRH* 9 F 11, *ap.* Varro *Ling.* 5.165). Like Piso, Livy ascribes the building of the temple to Numa, the legendary second king of Rome, who intended it to function "as an index of peace and war, that when open it might signify that the nation was in arms, when closed that all the peoples round about were pacified."[29]

According to the Roman tradition in the time of Augustus, the gates had only been closed once in the Republican period, in 235 BCE shortly after the First Punic War (Piso *FRH* 9 F 11; Livy 1.19.2). The next time a ceremonial closing is recorded was more than 200 years later, when Octavian (soon to be Augustus) returned after the end of the civil war and the conquest of Egypt. The senate's decree was thus clearly intended to mark a watershed moment; however, it also set a precedent for the following decades of Augustan rule. In fact, references to the ritual multiply in Augustan literature and, as the emperor himself stressed in the passage from the *Res Gestae* quoted above, the temple gates were closed two more times during his reign.[30] This sudden prominence has prompted interpretations that the ritual either only gained importance from 29 BCE on or even that as a major ceremony it was an invention of the Augustan period.[31] In any event, this emphasis demonstrates not only the new, official focus on peace as a value and one of the main achievements of the *princeps* but also its framing in religious rites that were, at least allegedly, anchored in the Roman tradition. Later emperors emulated the use of this symbol of empire-wide peace. Coins under Nero proudly featured the temple front with closed gates and the inscription PACE P(opuli) R(omani) TERRA MARIQ(ue) PARTA IANVM CLVSIT: "After he [Nero] had established the Peace of the Roman People on land and on sea, he closed (the gates) of Janus".[32]

Whereas the ceremonial closing of the gates of the Temple of Janus demonstrates the new value given to peace, this should not be mistaken as disavowing warfare, let alone military prowess. To the contrary: the already close relationship between peace and

FIGURE 4.3a and 4.3b: Gold coin of the emperor Nero, 64/5 CE; portrait of Nero on obverse, depiction of Temple of Janus with doors closed on reverse. BM 1946.1004.43. © The Trustees of the British Museum.

military victory in the Roman conceptual framework of external relations became even more strongly expressed under the empire. Already in the passage from Augustus' *Res Gestae* quoted earlier, the emperor explicitly states that peace had been achieved through victories on land and sea.[33] The celebration of peace as an explicitly imperial enterprise, achieved and secured through military virtue, found its expression in other religious sites and cults as well. The Temple of Mars Ultor, dedicated in 2 BCE as the central building of the new Forum of Augustus, signifies this important component again.[34]

FIGURE 4.4: Remains of the Temple of Mars Ultor (Mars the Avenger) in the Augustan Forum, Rome, Italy. Photo by PHAS/UIG, courtesy of Getty Images.

With this temple, Augustus finally realized a vow he had taken four decades earlier, before the decisive battle against the Republican army at Philippi (Ov. *Fast.* 5.573–7; Suet. *Aug.* 29.2). The temple was thus primarily dedicated to Mars as the avenger of the murder of Julius Caesar. However, this purpose soon slipped into the background because the Temple of Mars Ultor was also designated as the central space dedicated to external military expeditions. The temple housed military standards that had been recovered from the enemy; it was also where other tokens of military victories were dedicated, where the Senate decided on military triumphs, and the site from which generals departed for their campaigns.[35] Internal and external peace were merged, yet this time in a temple devoted to the god of war, the first major sanctuary for Mars within the city of Rome.[36] In the *cella*, Mars was flanked by statues of Venus and the Divus Julius (the deified Julius Caesar), reminders that military successes were now monopolized by the imperial family and that the imperial peace as defined by Augustus was never "peaceful" in the modern sense, neither in reality, nor in the religious sphere (Zanker 1988: 195–7).

Pax was not the only deity associated with imperial peace; in fact, the new personification was often featured in conjunction with other gods and goddesses, including Apollo, Ceres, Felicitas, Minerva, Salus, Securitas, and Venus.[37] The specific historical circumstances of the civil wars and the reorganization of the empire from the time of Augustus on also entailed that Concordia and Pax were now considered complements and became almost interchangeable (cf. Livy 9.19.16; Raaflaub 2015b: 114–15). This fusion of internal and external peace also became evident when the senate decided in 13 BCE to establish the first official cult dedicated to Pax in Roman history.

The famous Ara Pacis Augustae (the Altar of Augustan Peace) was decreed on the occasion of the safe return of Augustus, this time from Spain and Gaul.[38] From the dedication of the altar in 9 BCE on, sacrifices were performed at least twice per year, on the day of its decree (*constitutio*) and the day of its dedication (*dedicatio*).[39] This constituted the first official reverence of Pax in Rome; however, it must be stressed that Peace was not revered in its own right but only in and through its connection with the emperor, as Pax Augusta (cf. Raaflaub 2016c: 23). The close connection between the revered peace and the emperor already becomes evident in the dedication of the altar by the senate, but also in its location and visual program. Situated on the Campus Martius (the Field of Mars), the Ara Pacis Augustae was erected in conjunction with the obelisk commemorating the conquest of Egypt and the Mausoleum of Augustus.[40] The famous frieze on the southern wall of the altar's enclosure depicted not only the emperor himself but also his family.[41] Whereas the altar and the respective rituals praised and revered Pax as external and internal stability, security, and harmony, there was no room left for doubt as to whom the Roman Empire owed this peace.[42] Augustus had thus created a powerful ideological concept of imperial peace that reached its full potential within an official religious framework. This precedent was employed and further developed by almost all subsequent emperors.

Celebrating peace in imperial Rome, however, remained inextricably, albeit usually not explicitly, linked with civil war.[43] When, after Nero's fall and the subsequent civil war, Vespasian in 69 CE eventually prevailed and assumed power in Rome, he not only had to restore order and central control, but even more so the trust and confidence of the Roman citizens and everyone else living under Roman rule. He also had to heal the wounds left by yet another civil war, less than a century after Augustus had begun to build his empire. Again, the bloody competition for the throne had nurtured a longing for peace among the population, and like Augustus, Vespasian gave credit to these feelings, capitalized on them, and connected them inextricably to his reign and the new dynasty he was about to create. Among the numerous large building projects of the Flavian emperors, the Templum Pacis (Temple of Peace) was among the first to be completed and inaugurated in 75 CE (Cass. Dio 65.15.1, cf. Jos. *BJ* 7.158; Suet. *Vesp.* 9.1). The Flavian contribution to the imperial fora consisted of large gardens, a library, halls featuring pieces of art and other remarkable objects, and the central temple dedicated to Pax.[44] Details about the cult and related rituals are not known, but coins seem to depict the cult statue of Pax.[45]

How exactly Peace was defined in this context is debated in modern scholarship. Yet this ambiguity was presumably intentional: the end of the civil war was on the minds of most visitors, particularly the urban population of Rome proper, but, as in most other components of early Flavian representation, the recent submission of the provincial revolt in Judaea also featured prominently in the Templum Pacis. There the most spectacular spoils from Jerusalem, including the golden instruments from the Jewish Temple, were put on public display.[46] In accordance with the ideology established by Augustus, Pax was revered as imperial peace, internally and externally, and remained intimately linked with the emperor and his rule.[47]

Although the cultic reverence of Peace developed in Rome considerably later than in Greece, *pax* had already been a central part of Roman religion through the concept of the *pax deorum*. To maintain peace of and with the gods was at the very center of any religious, cultic action in Roman culture (Simon 1994: 204). However, it took the horrors of the civil war and the deep political and social crisis of the first century BCE for the personification of Pax to receive the status of a deity and, eventually, an official cult. As in Greece, the formal reverence of Peace was thus the outcome of a longing for stability and security that grew out of a military conflict that exceeded previous experiences. Yet the

FIGURE 4.5a and 4.5b: Gold coin of the emperor Vespasian, 75 CE; portrait of Vespasian on obverse, figure of Pax, holding branch in right hand and sceptre in left hand, on reverse. BM R.10329 © The Trustees of the British Museum.

circumstances differed significantly in Rome, as the new yearning for peace was prompted by civil war, not external conflict, and the specific political conditions after the rise of Augustus provided for different cultural and religious dynamics. The emphasis Augustus gave to Pax in his self-presentation demonstrates how deep and strong the yearning for peace was, but it also meant that Pax as a newly invoked deity was immediately monopolized by the *princeps*. In the framework of the principate, Pax was and remained linked with the emperor and became a standard part of the language of power. The same dynamic that was monumentalized in the Templum Pacis persisted over the course of the centuries and Peace continued to be most prominently invoked when the empire was in crisis and a ruler needed to reassure the public of his authority. Consequently, the personification of Pax was featured multiple times on coins in the late second and third century CE, when rival emperors competed for power and Roman armies fought each other again (Raaflaub 2015b: 111).

MAKING AND KEEPING PEACE: RELIGIOUS ASPECTS

In the Greek belief system, peace was granted (or denied) by the gods, who then also acted as guardians over any agreements that were reached to end wars or even establish peace. This anchoring in universally accepted religious beliefs and a shared framework of values, cultural codes, and customs made interstate relations possible in the first place. The notion of divine sanction and protection began with the sacred protection for heralds and ambassadors. When the Spartans reacted to the Persian demand for submission in the early fifth century BCE by throwing the Great King's envoys into a well, this was considered such a profound breach of divine law that two Spartan citizens, Sperthias and Boulis, volunteered to surrender themselves to the Persians to rectify their hometown's wrongdoing (Hdt. 7.133–7).

Religious rituals also played an equally important role for the beginnings and endings of war. Customarily, oracles were consulted and omens were sought to confirm and legitimize a decision. Many of the stories preserved in ancient sources tell of instances in which omens were either misread or deliberately interpreted to argue the intended course of actions; however, the frequency of such events does not undermine the importance of such consultations. Instead, the insistence that warfare should be approved and supported by the gods underlines the important role of religious rituals in this context, even if going to war involved working around divinations that appeared to counter one's cause (see, for instance, Xen. *Hell.* 4.7.2; Parker 2016: 123–5). For states that were about to enter a war, religious rituals also marked the process of transformation from peace to war, just as individuals followed certain rituals to ensure the gods' support for the favorable return of individual soldiers (Cf. *Il.* 2.341, 16.225–49, 24.283–314; Hdt. 7.192.2). In ancient Greece, these processes were less formalized than in Rome (see below), yet they still emerge consistently in the historical record and were considered too important to be foregone, even if respecting them meant delaying a battle to first obtain another, more favorable oracle.[48]

Although the support of the gods and connected religious rituals formed a significant component in the process each community had to undergo before war was launched, oaths by the gods were equally important for agreements to form alliances or terminate violent conflicts. In the absence of any superior agency that could enforce the terms of a treaty the parties involved relied on the gods and their authority to guard and sanction any responsibilities and regulations.[49] In the Greek world, real peace treaties were only an invention of the fourth century BCE; before the late classical period, warfare was only suspended through a limited-term truce. Such agreements were called *spondai*, a term commonly denoting libations of any sort. This transfer of meaning emphasizes how profoundly these interstate treaties were based on shared rituals and depended upon a shared belief in the divine sanction of their stipulations.

Most prominent among the gods invoked in interstate treaties was Zeus in his capacity as Zeus Horkios (Zeus of the Oath). In oaths, he is often accompanied by Helios, Gaia, and Poseidon, thus combining the sky, the sun, the earth, and the sea, as well as Athena and Ares as the gods predominantly associated with war.[50] Whereas these main gods were ubiquitously accepted among the Greeks, an oath taken by each party to the specific gods of their own communities enhanced the sanctification of the formal agreement even further (Baltrusch 1994: 87; Bayliss 2013: 160–7). In cross-cultural agreements, the gods most sacred for both parties were invoked. For instance, the oath for the alliance between Philip V of Macedon and Carthage of 215 BCE read:

> In the presence of Zeus, Hera, and Apollo: in the presence of the Genius of Carthage, of Herakles, and Iolaos: in the presence of Ares, Triton, and Poseidon: in the presence of the gods who battle for us and of the Sun, Moon, and Earth; in the presence of Rivers, Lakes, and Waters: in the presence of all the gods who possess Carthage: in the presence of all the gods who possess Macedonia and the rest of Greece: in the presence of all the gods of the army who preside over this oath.[51]

Any violation of such a formal agreement sworn by the gods constituted a sacrilege. Of course, this did not mean that treaties were never broken. Even more frequently, stipulations were interpreted rather freely—especially by the stronger party—but doing so nevertheless required a pretext or reasoning to legitimize such an action. An outright breach of a treaty was considered a serious violation, harming not only the wronged party but also commonly shared beliefs and customs, and the offender was expected to suffer from the gods' punishment.[52] Already in the *Iliad*, the truce that the Achaians and Trojans agreed upon to have the war decided by a duel of Menelaos and Paris is broken. When the Trojan soldier Pandaros interferes by wounding Menelaos,[53] the Achaians blame all Trojans for the renewal of hostilities, and Agamemnon predicts that the sacrilege will cause Troy's demise:

> Dear brother, it was your death I sealed in the oaths of friendship,
> setting you alone before the Achaians to fight with the Trojans.
> So, the Trojans have struck you down and trampled on the oaths sworn.
> Still the oaths and the blood of the lambs shall not be called vain,
> the unmixed wine poured and the right hands we trusted.
> If the Olympian at once has not finished this matter,
> late will he bring it to pass, and they must pay a great penalty,
> with their own heads, and with their women, and with their children.
> For I know this thing well in my heart, and my mind knows it.
> There will come a day when sacred Ilion shall perish,
> and Priam, and the people of Priam of the strong ash spear,
> and Zeus son of Kronos who sits on high, the sky-dwelling,
> himself shall shake the gloom of his aegis over all of them
> in anger for this deception. All this shall not go unaccomplished.
>
> —*Il.* 4.155–68

From the fifth century BCE on, additional clauses were added to oaths, in which the respective parties not only swore by the gods but also included other commitments. In modern scholarship, these new components have often been taken as a sign of diminished trust in the guardianship of the gods and religious rituals in general. Yet it must be stressed that formal oaths citing the gods as the highest and ubiquitously accepted authorities were never rendered obsolete (cf. Thuc. 4.51.1, 86.2, 5.30.1–4; Baltrusch 1994: 61).

The Romans shared with the Greeks (and most other cultures in the ancient Mediterranean) the custom of having their interstate treaties protected by the gods, and like the Greeks, they expected all parties to swear an oath by their gods to conclude an alliance or any other kind of interstate agreement. Although this did not prevent caution or suspicion, invoking the gods as guardians of any kind of interstate agreement lent legitimacy and served as a token of righteousness.[54] The religious framework of rules was not limited to interstate treaties; it was even more important in the context of a declaration of war. Roman customs included a clear set of rituals to declare war. The most important agent in these was the priestly college of the *fetiales*. Their members would formally present to the enemy Rome's claims of injury and redress (*rerum repetitio*) and, if the demands were not met, would announce the failure in Rome. After the senate and the assembly had voted, the *fetiales* officially declared war by casting a spear into the enemy's territory.[55] This procedure was changed in the third century BCE, apparently in connection with the war against Pyrrhos of Epiros (280–275 BCE), the first Roman military conflict fought against a power outside of Italy. Instead of traveling to the border, the priests now threw the spear at a column in front of the Temple of Bellona that served to represent the enemy's territory (Ov. *Fast.* 6.199–208; Stat. *Theb.* 4.4–8; Serv. *Aen.* 9.52). The ritual did not lose its force through this change. On the contrary: instead of a few witnesses, the entire population of Rome was now able to see the act and thus participate in the ritual that denoted the shift from peace to war. This performative appeal became evident again when Octavian himself in 32 BCE threw the spear to declare war against Cleopatra (Dio Cass. 50.4.5).

Politically and socially, these formalized steps helped to distinguish strictly between war and peace, yet they were far from being the only rituals concerned with these questions. In March, the beginning of the war season was declared by the ritual dance of the Salii, and the season traditionally ended in October with the sacrifice of a war horse and the ritual cleaning of the army's weapons (Scullard 1981: 82–95, 193–5; Rosenstein 2007: 230). However, in the Roman mindset, the invocation of the gods in the context of war and peace and the related rituals were far more than just a reflection of ancient traditions. Instead, they formulated and confirmed the belief that the Roman state—its army, leaders, and citizenry—adhered to rules set by the gods. Performing the rituals correctly, just as living up to one's oath, fell within the realm of the *pax deorum*. Maintaining the peace with the gods was considered a common duty because the divine anger would otherwise fall upon the individuals responsible and the Roman state as a whole.[56] In turn, Rome's military successes were considered as relying on Roman piety (cf. Cic. *Har. resp.* 19).

In this context, the concept of the *bellum iustum* was of utmost importance. The definition of what constituted a just war was complex and combined religious rituals and moral concerns with political interests. Many aspects remain elusive, yet Cicero clearly explains that the distinction between just and unjust wars was based on causes for going to war, proper military conduct (*ius in bello*), and performing certain rituals, such as the correct declaration of war by the *fetiales*.[57] This ideological and religious framework was constantly adapted to new political circumstances and Rome's changing geopolitical status, yet the confidence in divine sanction and the importance of the respective rituals never ceased to be important. In ancient Greece and Rome, belief in the gods, cults, and religious rituals thus helped to maintain and sanction peace.

In contrast to later periods of Mediterranean history, classical antiquity lacked a concept of religious war. Philip II of Macedon and his son and successor, Alexander the Great, justified their attack on the Achaimenid Empire on the grounds of the Persian destruction of Greek temples 150 years earlier, but this hardly figured as the main reason for the campaign. At the same time, neither Greek nor Roman religion categorically demanded peace or condemned war.[58] As outlined earlier, the worship of Eirēnē in Athens and even more so the Roman reverence of Pax explicitly embraced military virtues and an expansionist, even imperialist agenda. Instead, religious aspects, rituals, and cults served to legitimize, communicate, and enhance the official agenda of each community. In contrast, the teachings of early Christianity offered at least the potential for pacifistic ideas.

PEACE IN EARLY CHRISTIANITY

The call for peace and rejection of violence, including military violence, were among the central messages preserved in the New Testament Gospels, most prominently expressed in Jesus' *logion* of turning the other cheek.[59] Despite the prominence of such teachings, anti-violence teachings never became normative in the emerging Christian movement. Nonetheless, military expansion and, in turn, the imperial definition of peace remained a debated topic in the early church. To what degree Christians in the earlier periods of the church identified with the empire is impossible to discern. Yet a prominent line of argument is featured in the *First Letter of Clement*, presumably written in the first half of the second century CE and addressing the Christian community in Corinth. God, so the reasoning goes, has endowed the present authorities with their power. Christians are thus obliged to obey them and required to pray for the sovereigns' "health, peace, concord, firmness" and ask God to help them to "administer with piety in peace and gentleness the power given to them" (*1 Clem* 61.1–2; cf. *Romans* 13.1–7; Swift 2007: 280).

Even more complicated than praying for the empire's welfare was the question of whether belief in Jesus Christ contradicted service in the Roman army. This question did not solely pose a challenge to devout Christians; refusal to serve in the military also ranked among the most common allegations raised against their communities. The first elaborate discussion of these issues comes from Tertullian (ca. 160/170–after 212 CE). According to him, faithful belief in the Christian God prohibits service in the Roman army because of the violent deeds that soldiers had to perform and because of the immanent rivalry between God and the emperor.[60] Tertullian acknowledges that this line of teaching may pose a problem for some of his fellow Christians, yet he remains firm in his belief:

> The situation is different if the faith comes to a man after he is in the army, as with the soldiers whom John admitted to baptism and the converted centurion whom Christ praised and the one whom Peter instructed in the faith. Nonetheless, once a man has accepted the faith and has been marked with its seal, he must immediately leave the service, as many have done, or he has to engage in all kinds of quibbling to avoid offending God in ways that are forbidden to men even outside the service. Or, finally, he will have to endure for God what civilian members of the faith have been no less willing to accept.
>
> —*De Corona* 11.4–6

However, Tertullian's position was not unanimously shared by his fellow Christians. For example, Origen (184/5–253/4 CE), in his work written against the attacks by the

PEACE, PACIFISM, AND RELIGION

philosopher Celsus, also defended his fellow Christians against the allegation that they did not fight for the Roman army and the emperor. Like Tertullian, Origen refers to Christians refusing to fight in the imperial army, but there is a significant shift in the argument. Origen insists that pacifism is not to be understood as opposition, or even indifference, towards the official imperial mission and its success. Instead, Christians would contribute to the military endeavors of the emperor in the most effective way they could, through prayer for God's support.[61] Thus, despite his still strong stance of anti-violence, Origen not only preached obedience to the authorities but also embraced the official concept of imperial peace.

Still, the refusal to fight for the empire was not unanimously shared among Christians. Around 200 CE, Clement of Alexandria preached preference for peace but also argued: "if you were in the army when you were seized by the knowledge of God, obey the commander who gives just commands" (*Exhortation to the Greeks* 10.100.2). These statements reflect what must have been a fierce debate within the Christian communities, yet they also give testimony to another process: the growth of Christianity in many parts of the empire, including its military forces. Whereas pacifistic ideas had never been normative in the early church, they became less and less sustainable as Christian beliefs and members of the community moved further to the center and into the higher strata of society.

The tide shifted with the reign of Constantine, who according to the famous legend won the throne in the civil war against Maxentius because of the Christian God's support (Euseb. *Vita Const.* 1.28–31; Lactant. *De mort. pers.* 44.1–9). With the end of the persecutions and an emperor at least sympathetic to Christianity, identification with the empire, including its military and its wars, became the new norm.[62] The new circumstances prompted further discussion about just war, defined now according to the parameters of contemporary Christianity (cf. Swift 1970). This line of thought is most elaborately explained by St. Augustine (354–430 CE). His major work, *De Civitate Dei*, offers lengthy discussions of peace and war, and it is through his learned deliberations that earlier Roman concepts of just war and proper conduct of warfare are known to us in greater detail. Augustine adopted these traditional concepts and made them compatible with Christian beliefs and the Christianization of the empire. He embraces the idea of an imperial peace that must be created, guarded, and guaranteed through sanctioned violence and war.

> To achieve a minimal kind of benefit, it desires an earthly peace and strives to obtain this through war. . . . When victory goes to those who have fought in the more upright cause, who would doubt that such a victory should be celebrated? Who would doubt that the resulting peace is desirable? These are blessings and are unquestionably gifts from God.
>
> —*De civ. D.* 15.4

The goal of war is thus a praiseworthy peace. War is only to be waged if it is just and gains the support of God (Aug. *Epist.* 138.14, 189.6; Swift 2007: 290–1). Building on the Roman *bellum iustum* tradition, Augustine defines the right to wage war as the last resort of the state to rectify a previous violation or to regain what has been taken illegitimately.[63] The call for mercy once a war has been ended victoriously was also well in accord with Roman customs of the pre-Christian era but now justified from a Christian perspective. Consequently, Augustine strongly disagrees with notions that Christians should object to serving in the army (Aug. *Epist.* 189.4–6). Pacifistic tendencies within Christianity that opposed such teachings dwindled under the new political circumstances but never fully disappeared (Swift 2007: 292–3). However, the adaptation of imperial peace to the intellectual and theological needs of a now Christian empire gave proof, first and foremost, to the lasting power of the image and meaning of *pax* created by Augustus that was now readily adopted into a new religious framework.

CONCLUSION

Among the Greeks and Romans, cultic reverence of Peace grew out of a strong and widely shared longing for peace after years under the devastation and crisis of foreign and civil wars. Yet in both societies, this at least potentially oppositional edge against an official agenda that embraced military success and expansion soon disappeared. The public nature of many religious practices and cults meant that Peace—as a personification, a goddess, or a status granted and protected by the gods—was defined in accordance with the official interests of the political community. Religion thus rarely provided a basis or vehicle for oppositional views and ideas. In contrast, personifications, cults, and rituals played an important role in conceptualizing, communicating, and legitimizing the definition of peace embraced by those in power. The pacifism promoted by some groups in early Christianity diverged strongly from these common trends; yet those tendencies and teachings lost their influence with the growth of the church and became even more obsolete from the time of Constantine on.

CHAPTER FIVE

Representations of Peace

JUDITH FLETCHER

Greco-Roman literature and material culture developed a constellation of images that represented peace as a state of natural abundance accompanied by wine, feasts, festivals, and marriages. Probably because words for peace are grammatically feminine (*eirēnē* in Greek, *pax* in Latin), but also because the female body can be associated with landscape and fertility, Peace was personified as a woman, and more specifically at times, as a mother. This chapter will survey the development of images of peace from the Homeric epics of Archaic Greece to the cultural products of the Roman Empire, a span of roughly a thousand years. It will swiftly become apparent that peace means different things depending on political events and specific ideologies. Ancient notions of peace do not always conform to idyllic visions of concord and harmony as imagined by idealists in our era. Accordingly, celebrations or commemorations of peace through artistic media in the ancient world can often encompass events such as military victory, or convey a message of imperialistic dominance.

REPRESENTING PEACE IN EARLY GREECE

The earliest representation of peace in ancient Greek culture occurs in a poem of war, Homer's *Iliad*. This monumental epic was probably committed to written form sometime around 750 BCE after centuries of oral transmission, but the poem reveals a familiarity with the brutality of war that transcends any specific period. The *Iliad* is a tale of anger, as its first word (*mēnis*) denotes. The Homeric narrator recounts, often in clinical detail, the brutality, carnage, rape, and devastation that have erupted for millennia whenever societies fail to achieve an orderly means of dispute settlement. Correspondingly, the description of a city free from war epitomizes characteristics found in representations of peace throughout antiquity, characteristics that still resonate with modern sensibilities. The image is on the shield of Achilles (18.478–608), manufactured by the god Hephaistos at the behest of Achilles' mother Thetis. The text devoted to the creation of the shield is an *ekphrasis* (an extended description of an imaginary work of art), which describes a miniature cosmos replete with sun, moon and stars, and two cities, one at peace and the other at war.

The siege described in the latter city corresponds in many ways to the conflict in which Achilles participates, while the city at peace, described first, is its antithesis. The peaceful city features a wedding celebration, feast, festival, and procession, a contrast to the Trojan War, the context of the poem, fought after Paris' abduction of Helen violated the civilized institution of marriage. On the shield, Hephaistos inscribes women watching the torch lit festivities, dances and music; the new brides are led to their wedding beds with joyful ceremony, unlike the women who have been and will be assaulted and captured as a consequence of the war. In the agora, or meeting place, a trial is taking place to settle a dispute over compensation for a homicide. This is the first representation of a formal arbitration in ancient Greece, and although scholars argue about the nature of the process, the important point is that the city acknowledges the inevitability of conflict, and has a means of handling it institutionally. Elders, perhaps members of the social elite, sit in a circle holding their scepters as the disputants make their cases. In the center are two ingots of gold, a reward for the best judgment. Heralds maintain order as an eager and engaged throng watches the process.

On another part of the shield, not in the peaceful city but in a serene countryside, Hephaistos renders scenes of farming and animal husbandry: workers plough fields and reap crops, vintners harvest grapes amid singing young people, herdsmen tend cattle and sheep. The theme of agricultural prosperity is associated with peace throughout Greek

FIGURE 5.1: The Shield of Achilles (Scuda di Achille), from Giulio Ferrario, *Il Costume Antico e Moderno di tutti i Popoli* ("The Ancient and Modern Costume of All Nations"), 1831. Photo by Fototeca Gilardi, courtesy of Getty Images.

literature, not surprisingly, since warfare inevitably led to the destruction of crops and livestock. Peace and fertility are thus closely aligned concepts. And all the spheres of activity that Hephaistos includes in the city at peace—marriage, festival, justice, and agriculture—recur to some degree in later representations of peace. Despite the lines spent on the city under siege, more text is devoted to nonviolent themes, so that the overall effect of the *ekphrasis* is one of peace and abundance, a contrast to the frame story (Shannon 1975: 75). But it is also significant that Homer's *Iliad*, like much of Greek literature, exploits the tension between war and peace as an integral part of a narrative dynamic; peace is a static concept, while war makes a story.[1] When Achilles takes his shield, with its life-affirming imagery, onto the battlefield it is "Gorgon-like in its effect upon humankind" (Scully 2003: 45). There is an implicit but ominous contrast between its scenes of fertility and festivity and the tumultuous surroundings as Achilles prepares for his ruthless attack on Hektor (22.313–14).

Even in the peaceful contexts of jurisprudence and shepherding on Achilles' shield, the possibility of violence exists. There is no evidence that the arbitration will be successful, and obviously, a homicide led to it. More explicitly, the country scene contains a brief mention of an ambush, perhaps a raid for livestock. The depiction thus contains a reminder that peace is a fragile state of affairs, and that disputes and violence can always erupt. Only the gods enjoy a life of bliss free from warfare: despite petty squabbles or interference in mortal lives their days end with feasting and pleasure. The possibility of complete respite from conflict for mortals is contemplated in Homer's *Odyssey*, set in the years after the Trojan War, but it is neither a realistic nor a desirable prospect. As he makes his way back home to Ithaka Odysseus is trapped on the island of the nymph Kalypso, a veritable paradise, except that he is the only mortal on Ogygia. He rejects her offer of immortality and eternal quietude, and is eventually set free. Washing up on the island of Scheria, in a polis that apparently knows no wars, the former warrior finds himself in a society where, he is assured, "no man living . . . can come into the land of the Phaiakians bringing warlike attack," since these charmed people live too far away from other mortals (6.201–3). In this utopian landscape, there is limitless abundance: orchards where apples, pears, figs and pomegranates grow continuously, vineyards that teem with grapes pressed into wine, gardens in which lush greenery abounds, and two springs of fresh water that maintain its fecundity. Like the Olympians, the Phaiakians end their days with feasting and song; strife and aggression are channeled through athletic competition; there are no beggars, swineherds or lowly peasants such as inhabit Odysseus' home in Ithaka. Leaving this fairytale kingdom Odysseus returns to a more realistic scenario, where he must do battle with his wife's suitors in order to establish himself as master of his own home, and where his aged father Laertes labors to keep his orchards producing fruit. Conflict and toil are part of life, even after the Trojan War.

The imaginary Phaiakian kingdom corresponds in many ways to the mythical Golden Age, a fantasy developed by ancient Near Eastern societies that influenced early Greek narrative (West 1997: 312–19). Hesiod, a poet roughly contemporary with Homer, recounts a myth of five races of humans, each corresponding to one of four metals of declining value, with the age of heroes (who populate Greek myth) wedged in between the last two (*Works and Days* 106–201). In each successive metallic age, human life becomes shorter and less pleasant, while people behave less righteously. During the Golden Age, concurrent with the reign of the god Kronos, mortals live "like gods" free from care and toil, and exist in harmony with each other; the earth puts forth copious fruit and provender. Mortals begin to behave badly towards one another in the Silver Age.

In the Bronze Age they become bellicose and start to kill each other (145–6). In the Iron Age, during which Hesiod lives, men start to sack each other's towns, and life is hard and miserable. The myth of the metallic ages occurs in some form in ancient societies as far east as India, and serves as an explanation for the pain and misery of current lives. In most such narratives, including Hesiod's, humans had no control over when each age came to an end, and can only yearn for the lost Golden Age which corresponds most closely to the impossible ideal of perfect peace.

Yet even in Hesiod's time, the benefits of peace can be seen, and such peace is a consequence of justice. After telling the myth of the ages, Hesiod describes a righteous city that practices justice (*dikē*) for its citizens and foreigners alike (225–47). In this city (in contrast to the unjust city described later): "Peace (*eirēnē*), the nurse of the young, is over their land, and they are never afflicted with anguishing war by far-seeing Zeus" (228). It is a land of plenty where there is sufficient food for all, sheep provide wool in abundance and women are fertile and faithful. Justice is a prerequisite of peace, as the scene on Achilles' shield suggests. It is difficult to ascertain what form civic justice took for Hesiod and his audience, since we know very little about early law. Archaic Greece began to develop written law and public legal institutions some time after this. Nonetheless, the precept endures: justice ensures that disputes are settled without violence.

PERSONIFYING PEACE IN GREEK CULTURE

The Greeks had a god of war, Ares, a contentious and conflict-causing character who participates in the battles of the *Iliad*, and commits adultery with Aphrodite, wife of Hephaistos, in the *Odyssey*. Ares is one of the twelve Olympian gods, but there is no corresponding anthropomorphic peace deity in either poem. It would not be until the fourth century BCE that the Athenians set up altars to Peace, and acknowledged her as a divinity in her own right. The evolution of her embodiment began nearly three centuries earlier when the concept of peace was given concrete form in Hesiod's *Theogony*, an epic poem that narrates the births of a vast pantheon of gods, many of whom are personifications of various abstract virtues and human attributes. Hesiod makes Eirēnē (Peace) the sister of Dikē (Justice) and Eunomia (Good Laws), also feminine nouns (*Th.* 109). The three civic virtues are daughters of Zeus and Themis (Divine Justice), often referred to as the Horai. Dikē and Eunomia are concepts integral to peace, as we saw in Homer's peaceful city where disputes are resolved by an orderly process, and also in Hesiod's description of the Just City; they are therefore appropriate sisters of Peace. Pindar's *Olympian Ode* 13 (464 BCE) extols the victor's home city Corinth wherein the same triad dwells: "For there dwells Order (*Eunomia*) with her sister Justice (*Dika*), firm foundation for cities, and Peace (*Eirēna*), steward of wealth for men, who was raised with them—the golden daughters of wise-counseling Themis" (6–8). Now we encounter a new idea (peace produces wealth) that becomes increasingly more common over the next century. The combination of the allegories for peace and wealth occurs elsewhere, including a fragment by the lyric poet Bacchylides, Pindar's contemporary, in what is referred to as the *Hymn to Peace*. It begins: "Peace gives birth to noble wealth for mortals, to the flowers of honey-tongued songs" (fr. 4.61–3). Another fragment from an unknown author repeats the sentiment: "O sweet Peace, giver of wealth to mortals" (fr. adesp. 1021 *PMG*).[2]

Bacchylides' invocation may suggest that Eirēnē was the focus of prayer and ritual, although there is little evidence of her status as a cult figure in the fifth century. Yet another fragment of poetry (*PMG* fr. 791.240), this one attributed to the musician/poet Timotheos of Miletos (*c.* 408 BCE), calls on the god Apollo to send Eirēnē and her sister Eunomia to an unnamed city, probably Athens which was heading towards defeat in the long Peloponnesian war against Sparta and her allies at this time. Of course, these poetic invocations do not necessarily mean that Eirēnē had her own cult yet, or that she was represented in the visual arts as a goddess.[3] According to most ancient testimonia, a cult devoted exclusively to the worship of Peace was not established until the 370s in Athens, although depictions of her in the plastic arts start to appear earlier than this, often showing her as part of the retinue of Dionysos. No doubt Peace was understood to be a divine figure well before the existence of her cult can be pinpointed. Amy Smith, who has surveyed the allegorical representations of Peace in material culture, detects a correspondence between the infrequency of her appearance in the visual arts, and the popular political sentiments of the time (2011: 129). Since the Athenian democracy favored war during most of the last third of the fifth century, there would be fewer representations of Peace, suggests Smith. It would not be until the fourth century, when the Athenians were more in favor of peace that visual representations of personified Peace start to appear. As we shall see shortly, however, an embodied Peace does appear in the theater in the last quarter of the fifth century, a phenomenon that adds texture to the concept of peace in relation to the Peloponnesian war.

For now let us consider how Peace is represented in the visual arts, limited as these sources may be. While the poets of the fifth century mention her fairly often, as we saw above, she only appears three times in the surviving visual arts of the period. A krater (Vienna IV 1024), used to mix wine and water, which was probably produced between 420 and 410 BCE, explicitly labels a female figure in the retinue of Dionysos as Eirēnē, and another as Opora, "Harvest."[4] Peace is seated, wears a wreath of ivy, and holds a drinking horn in one hand, while an attentive satyr leans towards her. Dating from the same period is a pelikē (Group of Naples 3235) that represents Peace (labeled Irene) in the company of Pannychis, "All night revel." The third example comes from the cult center of Brauron, about thirty miles beyond Athens: a fragment (Brauron 1170) that may have been part of an altar (*c.* 400 BCE) with a labeled representation of Eirēnē in a procession perhaps led by Dionysos, and accompanied by two other goddesses.[5] Thus at least two, and probably all three, of the fifth century visual representations of Peace show her as an attendant of Dionysos: i.e., she is a maenad. There are good reasons for this: both divinities are associated with fertility, and wine was an essential component in peace treaties. It is also worth remembering that all the extant representations of Peace in the visual arts at this time come from Athens at a point when the city-state was engaged in a long and devastating war.

Evidence for the worship of Eirēnē, and her most significant manifestation in visual art, comes from Athens a few decades later: in 375/4 her cult was established after the general Timotheos (to be distinguished from the musician mentioned earlier) defeated the Spartans in a major battle and negotiated a favorable peace treaty that restored Athens' control of the seas. To commemorate this, according to the orator Isokrates (15.109–11), who was writing twenty years later, yearly sacrifices were instituted. Robert Parker notes that the quality celebrated by these yearly sacrifices was Athenian military strength, not peace per se, and thus the cult of Peace functions more like a "war memorial" (1997a: 143).[6] These sacrifices took place during the Athenian festival of the Synoikeia, a celebration of the early unification of a cluster of villages into the single city-state of Athens. The festival occurred soon after the grain harvest, a crop most at risk if the countryside was ravaged by the Spartans (Stafford 2001: 177); again then Eirēnē is associated with Opora, Harvest, and more generally with prosperity and fertility, but now in a religious context.

According to the records, lavish offerings of oxen were made to Eirēnē, signifying the high prestige of her cult (Stafford 2001: 177). It is tempting to believe that this regularized sacrifice, and Eirēnē's cultic identity, were behind the Athenians' decision to commission the sculptor Kephisodotos to create a monumental freestanding bronze statue depicting Peace holding the infant Wealth (Ploutos) in her arms, arguably the most famous image of Peace from the ancient Mediterranean world.[7] Sadly, no records remain to connect the statue decisively to the cult, but it is safe to assume that by this time Peace was recognized as part of the Athenian pantheon. This monument was in the Agora, at least when the travel writer Pausanias viewed it in the second century CE (1.8.3), and another statue of Peace was erected inside a public building known as the Prytaneion. Both statues are lost, but the former (by Kephisodotos) was apparently much admired and copied by the

FIGURE 5.2: Roman copy of the fourth-century BCE Greek statue of Eirēnē holding the infant Ploutos, by Kephisodotos; Glyptothek Museum, Munich, Germany. Photo by DeAgostini, courtesy of Getty Images.

Romans. Thirteen of these marble copies survive, the best of which is currently housed in Munich. A group of Panathenaic vases (given to victors in athletic competitions honoring Athena) from this period feature images of the statue and help to identify the Roman copies. The monument was also featured on coins, gemstones, and other objects, all of which corroborate the identification of the surviving statue with Pausanias' description.

This iconic representation shows a maternal-looking woman, garbed in heavy, dignified robes, tilting her head down and gazing fondly into the eyes of the infant Wealth who holds a cornucopia filled with fruits in one arm (the cornucopia does not survive in the Munich copy), and reaches upwards with the other towards Eirēnē's face. She probably held a staff, a signifier of authority, in her left arm, as the Panathenaic vessels suggest. The statue group is noteworthy because it is the first example in monumental art of any two allegorical figures together (Stafford 2001: 182). Kephisodotos has captured an intimate moment between a mother (or possibly nurse) and child with charming realism: the obvious message is that peace will nurture wealth. As we have already noted, the connection between the two went back at least as far as the early fifth century.

An important aspect of this statue group, and an issue that we consider again in a Roman context, is how the figure of Peace manifests as a form of syncretism. In other words, she amalgamates elements of Demeter, a mother goddess who is connected with the harvest and who in other contexts is represented as the mother of Wealth (Hes. *Th*. 970–2). Peace, as we have seen, is also associated with harvests (as her attendant Opora indicates). In the earlier representations discussed above she is a youthful maenad in the company of Dionysos; now she is represented as a maternal figure. Presumably a statue base, or some other publicity, would have identified Kephisodotos' sculpture as Peace, but viewers would also be able to project upon her their sentiments about Demeter, whose Eleusinian Mysteries were one of the most significant religious observances of the ancient world. Thus while the statue itself may well have been erected to augment the cult of Peace and notionally commemorated an Athenian military victory—although the celebrated peace treaty achieved by Timotheos did not last very long—the monument also evoked an emotional response that personalized the figure of Eirēnē.

It is in the dramatic arts of fifth century Athens that Peace attains her most fully articulated form. She came to life, as it were, in the comedies of the Athenian playwright Aristophanes during the Peloponnesian War fought by Athens and Sparta and their respective allies (431–404 BCE). The war was the result of the growing imperialism of the Athenian city-state, and the challenges to Athens' bid for supremacy by Sparta. Its consequences included the devastation of the Attic farmland, notably olive trees and vineyards, and the transfer of farmers and their families into Athens—a period of privation and loss for many Athenian citizens.

Eleven complete comedies survive from Aristophanes' oeuvre: three of these are fantasies of peace; the title of a fourth (a second *Peace*) indicates that he treated the topic in other lost plays; and personified peace treaties (*Spondai*) make an appearance in his *Knights*. Giving voice to the concerns of farmers, vintners, tradespeople, women, and all who had been adversely affected by the war, the poet uses many of the tropes associated with peace that developed in material culture and earlier literature. Nonetheless, Aristophanes is still patriotic in his desire for Athenian supremacy and does not advocate peace at all costs. As most scholars would agree (e.g. Henderson 1990: 271–313), his own political views are difficult to determine, and we should be cautious of reading any consistent message regarding the war in his comedies. Certainly he understood how his fellow Athenians longed for the pleasures of peace, while he also recognized that his audience of citizens often voted against the peace treaties offered by the Spartans.

Acharnians was produced in 425 BCE, in the sixth year of the Peloponnesian War, and in the aftermath of a horrendous plague that wiped out a significant portion of the Athenian population. Like all Old Comedies, the play was originally staged during one of two civic festivals of the god Dionysos in the theater dedicated to him before an audience consisting of thousands of citizens, perhaps even their wives, resident aliens, and at times visitors to the city. Since the poet was competing for a prize, he attempted to appeal to his audience's desire for a cessation of conflict, while also acknowledging their grievances against their enemies. The plot is based on the fantasy that a single individual could negotiate his own private peace with the Spartans. The protagonist, a farmer named Dikaiopolis (Just City), after failing to persuade the democratic assembly to vote for peace, sends his own emissary to Sparta. He returns with an offer, which represents three possible peace treaties as different vintages of wine, a five, a ten or a thirty-year treaty; Dikaiopolis chooses the latter.[8] The metaphor is inspired by the ritual of sealing peace treaties, which involved pouring wine onto the ground (*spondai*). Dikaiopolis and his family then celebrate their own private festival of Dionysos, complete with a phallic procession in honor of the god of wine. As noted above, personified Eirēnē was shown as a participant in Dionysian festivities on Athenian vases produced during this time; their relationship is highly symbolic. As the god of wine (the symbol of peace) and fertility, Dionysos is appropriately associated with peace; indeed peace treaties were often ratified in his theater.

Dikaiopolis, like many real farmers in Aristophanes' original audience, had been compelled to live within the city walls while the Spartans laid waste to his crops. When he returns home he must deal with the ire of the neighboring demesmen of Acharnai, who see his treaty as a form of betrayal. The play thus addresses the tension between these opposing concepts: a sense of justified animosity and a desire for peace. Interestingly, while peace is represented as a delectable vintage of fine wine, War is personified by the Chorus of farmers as a drunken party guest who rips apart their vines and dumps their wine on the ground, the very antithesis of a peace treaty (*Ach.* 978–87).[9] Aristophanes never refers to the loss of human life in this play (since this is a comedy), but he situates the tension between peace and war in an agricultural rather than human context. Yet he alludes to the possible casualties of war more subtly. Dikaiopolis is reluctant to give any of his peace wine to other Greeks, whom he summarily dispatches, until a bride and groom approach him. Now he is happy to share his treaty-wine with the bride so that she can keep her husband alive. The nuptial motif takes us back to the scene of peace on Achilles' shield; a productive marriage is the antithesis of war, as Aristophanes demonstrates in a later play. *Acharnians* ends with a symposium, and the tipsy Dikaiopolis is last seen in the company of two naked prostitutes. With this conclusion, fertility and sexuality are celebrated as the consequence of the special vintage of peace wine that Dikaiopolis has selected.

Later that same year, Athens gained the upper hand with the unexpected capture of nearly three hundred Spartiate and Peloponnesian soldiers on the island of Sphakteria. Athens and her allies established a permanent garrison in the strategic stronghold of Pylos, putting the Spartans and their allies at an even greater disadvantage. The annual ravages of the Attic countryside ceased, and Spartan envoys began to offer peace treaties to the Athenian assembly, which repeatedly rejected them, persuaded (Thucydides tells us) by the advice of Kleon. Emboldened by their advantages, the Athenians initiated military action on several fronts. Thus the war continued, and the Spartans, under the leadership of their brilliant general Brasidas, enjoyed a series of important victories, including capturing the Athenian controlled city-state of Amphipolis, where both Kleon, along with six hundred Athenian hoplites, and Brasidas with only seven Spartans were killed (Thuc. 5.11.2). As a consequence, negotiations resumed in 422/1, during which time Aristophanes wrote his *Peace*. Shortly after its production (probably within two weeks), both sides agreed on a fifty-year peace treaty (known as the Peace of Nikias), although it was to be short-lived.

Aristophanes' *Peace* proposes an even more incredible fantasy than that of *Acharnians*. While the earlier play was staged during the on-going war, this comedy is a celebration of the impending treaty, a Panhellenic peace, rather than one negotiated by a single individual farmer. It opens with the comic hero, an Athenian vintner named Trygaios, "a good vine-dresser," as he describes himself (190), ascending to the home of the gods on a giant dung beetle to demand that Zeus cease the war, only to learn that all the gods, save Hermes, have left Olympos, disgusted by the Athenians' refusal to accept a treaty. Trygaios' task is to release the goddess Peace from a deep cave where she has been imprisoned by War, a personified symbol whose intention is to keep war going in Greece. Thus again, as with Homer's shield and Aristophanes' *Acharnians*, peace is represented as the antithesis of war. With the help of Hermes and the chorus of Greek farmers, Trygaios is able to rescue the goddess Peace by subduing Kerberos (the canine guard of Hades, who is by implication symbolic of the warmongering Kleon). This heroic endeavor is a variation of a story pattern in which a fertility goddess is released from the underworld with the aid of Hermes; the most famous version being the release of Persephone from Hades back to her mother, the goddess Demeter (Bowie 1994: 142–3; Olson 1998: xxxiii–xxxviii).

The reference is apt here, since the ascent of Persephone brings the end of the famine imposed by Demeter on earth. Likewise, Peace is associated with fertility; she ascends from the pit with her two attendants, Harvest (Opora) and Festival (Theoria). Trygaios' first words to her bring into play the association of wine and peace (familiar from the *Acharnians*); he addresses her as "Divine Lady, giver of grape-clusters" (520). Her emergence from the ground suggests that Peace is a fertility goddess, and her return to earth ensures that agriculture will resume, a delightful prospect not only for those Athenians whose farms had been ravaged through war, but for all who enjoyed the pleasures of wine and prosperity. Once again peace is associated with marriage: Trygaios the vintner is rewarded by Hermes with a betrothal to Harvest, who substitutes "grow grapes together" (706–8) for "bear children" in a betrothal formula. One might wonder why he does not marry Peace: the usual explanation is that she is a goddess, who would be beyond his reach.[10] Nonetheless, Peace is referred to as "mistress of marriages" (976); the play ends with a wedding procession replete with torches and dancing, and a wish for fertile fields and wives.

The Peace of Nikias did not last long. Greece was plunged into another fifteen years of devastating war, although Athens rejected several peace offers before the city suffered its humiliating capitulation to Sparta in 404 BCE. The beginning of the end, albeit only one in a series of ill-considered plans, was the disastrous Sicilian expedition (415–413 BCE), which resulted in the loss of nearly the entire Athenian navy and ten thousand hoplites. It was in the wake of this catastrophe that Aristophanes produced a third peace play (411 BCE), arguably his most famous comedy, *Lysistrata*. Now the poet goes beyond the agricultural imagery of *Acharnians*, *Peace*, and several lost comedies, and focuses instead on women's sexuality.[11] The shift may be explained by the new situation in Athens. Two years before the play was produced, the Spartans occupied the fort of Dekeleia in Attica, which put an end to all farming in the area, an event which might explain the lack of farming imagery in *Lysistrata*, whose audience would have now consisted entirely of city-dwellers (Dillon 1987: 100–1).

Notably, instead of the farmer heroes of *Acharnians* and *Peace*, the comic hero whose machinations achieve peace is a woman; and the action is entirely set within the walls of Athens, close to or even on the Acropolis. This is the first of two Aristophanic comedies featuring a female in the central role (although all characters were played by male actors). Some scholars believe that the character of Lysistrata (whose name means "dissolver of the troops") was based on a priestess of Athena named Lysimache ("dissolver of the battle").[12] Aristophanes' heroine is revolutionary for several reasons. The figures of Peace and her attendants Harvest and Festival in Aristophanes' earlier comedy of course were non-speaking parts, and female roles in other comedies before this were very rare. The figure of Lysistrata animates the silent allegorical Peace with an assertive personality. Furthermore, the concept of peace is now associated with maternity and child-bearing: the wives resent giving birth to sons whom they lose to the war (588–90), and cite their contribution to the state as their role as mothers (651–2). These are the concerns that motivate the women of Greece, who gather under the leadership of Lysistrata, a new type of comic protagonist possessed of great intelligence and rhetorical ability that allow her to concoct and enact a plan to bring an end of war.

Her great idea is to convince all the married women of the warring Greek states, Sparta, Corinth, and Boiotia, to go on a sex strike in order to coerce their husbands to make peace. The plot is set in motion when the conspirators swear an oath to tantalize their husbands while withholding sex. The oath scene (181–239) is an artful parody of a peace treaty: the women pretend that a jug of wine is an animal sacrifice, comparing the liquid to blood as it spills into a bowl. Numerous inscriptions from ancient Greece confirm that treaty oaths would feature the immolation of animals such as sheep, goats, boars, or cattle. But Aristophanes has collapsed the practice of pouring wine on the ground to secure a peace treaty and the animal sacrifice that secures public oaths. Of course the women's oath is not explicitly a peace treaty (and they happily drink the wine), but rather a conspiratorial pledge that will achieve peace.[13] Yet Aristophanes has evoked the relationship between wine and peace in a nuanced way. By swearing an oath of abstinence over a jug of wine, the Greek wives, in concert with the older women who have taken over the treasury on the Acropolis, bring their husbands to their knees. Desperate for a reunion with their wives the men of Greece concede to Lysistrata's terms and agree to conciliation. Once again a mute female embodies peace. Lysistrata oversees the new treaty by offering a naked woman, the allegorical figure of Reconciliation (the Greek term *diallagē* is grammatically feminine), whose anatomy the Athenian and Spartan representatives divide up between them. Her buttocks, for example, correspond to Pylos (1162), which the Spartans have "been longing for and probing around for a long time." As A.M. Bowie notes (1994: 202), the scene "can be decoded as the re-establishment of male control of sex (Reconciliation's body) and politics (the Greek world)." The play ends with a celebration of peace, a festival, a dance, and feasting. The reunion of husbands and wives is a type of marriage, and a celebration of fertility, although the ritual agency of women has been accentuated throughout the play.

Aristophanes' three comedies are the most detailed treatments of peace in ancient literature, and they deploy most of the characteristics associated with peace since the time of Homer: just as Homer's peaceful city featured joyful wedding processions, so too the peace of Aristophanes' fantasies concludes with a union of men and women. Marriage is an aspect of fertility, likewise the concept of agricultural abundance, which is another feature of the Homeric city, the gardens of the Phaiakians in the *Odyssey*, and the myth of the Golden Age. The maternal figure of Kephisodotos' Peace conflates human and vegetative fecundity, examples of which she holds in her arms; so too Lysistrata's cohort stress their maternal roles. And of course wine, the product of peace and its most enjoyable symbol, flows in abundance through the theater of Dionysos.

REPRESENTING PEACE IN ROMAN CULTURE

There is much less wine in Roman representations of peace; the conservative citizens of Rome held Dionysos' counterpart Bacchus in lower esteem. The goddess Pax, however, inherited many other attributes from her Greek counterpart Eirēnē, although she tends to be much more "masculine" in her appearance and activities; for example, she is shown on coins driving a chariot and in military costume (Spaeth 1994: 67 n. 21). Since the Greeks had created the embodiment of peace in cult, art, poetry, and theater, the Romans had an archive of images to choose from, and were free to select features that suited their own patriotic ideals. The man most responsible for this ideological finesse was Rome's first emperor, Augustus. After the civil wars in the final century of the Roman Republic, the young Octavian defeated Antony and Cleopatra at the Battle of Actium in 31 BCE. It was a decisive victory that established him as *princeps*, first citizen of Rome, and, with the authorization of the senate, he became *imperator*, the first Roman emperor, known to history as Augustus. The peace and stability that he secured are known as the *pax Augusta*, and his legacy became the *pax Romana* (the Roman peace), nearly two centuries of political security and international domination.

Before we examine how the artists and poets of the Augustan age represented peace, the term *pax* requires some clarification. As Stefan Weinstock points out, *pax* "did not originally mean 'peace', but a 'pact' which ended a war and led to submission, friendship, or alliance" (1960: 45). For the Romans, there was great honor to be gained through wars against foreign peoples, although a carefully crafted ideology represented all wars as just and moral responses to hostilities or provocation. The intention was always to secure or restore a form of peace most advantageous to the Romans through a treaty after a battle, although *pax* could also be negotiated without conflict (de Souza 2008: 76–7). During the period of the Republic the Romans had expanded their borders aggressively; Augustus pressed them even further. His military power effectively discouraged or suppressed rebellion or secession, and insured peace for Rome and her citizens. As he put it, in the *Res Gestae Divi Augusti* (26): "The Gallic and Spanish provinces and Germany . . . I pacified (*pacavi*)" and "the Alps . . . I pacified (*pacificavi*)." Philip de Souza sums up his achievements: "Augustus' record of imperialist expansion was second to none in the whole of Roman history" (2008: 81). Yet as de Souza also notes, Augustus was careful to ensure that his *Res Gestae* represented any military action undertaken as a just war, pursued to secure peace in his empire.

With his unprecedented power (*imperium*), Augustus began an ambitious program of cultural, religious and moral renewal. Newly established festivals, sacrifices, buildings and monuments all reflected confidence in Augustus' ability to maintain peace, and deployed the symbols of peace and prosperity established in Greek poetry and iconography. The Augustan era was celebrated as a return to the Golden Age. Vergil's *Aeneid* (6.792–3) contains a prophecy that Augustus will found an *aurea saecula*, a Golden Age. The poet

Horace expressed confidence in the supreme commander's ability to maintain peace, associating it with agricultural fertility, and also suggesting the return of a Golden Age: "Your age (*aetas*), Caesar, has brought back rich harvests to the fields, and restored to our Jove the standards torn down from the proud doorposts of the Parthian; it has closed the temple of Janus Quirinus, now empty of war" (*Carm.* 4.15.4). Ovid suggests that Augustus is god-like in his ability to bestow peace on earth (*Met.* 15.832). The historian Tacitus (*Ann.* 1.2) writing at the beginning of the next century, paints a less flattering portrait, suggesting that Augustus seduced the populace with cheap food and "the confections of peace" (*dulcedine otii*) in order to increase his own power. However one views Augustus' motives, it must be admitted that no political figure had ever manipulated the concept of peace so advantageously before this.

Visual emblems of the *pax Augusta* were disseminated throughout the empire, always with the implication that the subjugation of foreign peoples was a form of peace. Augustus and his artists took full advantage of the iconography of peace inherited from the Greeks, including most importantly her representation as a goddess. Coinage disseminated Augustan propaganda most effectively since currency was a part of everyday life for the emperor's subjects, both in Italy and in the provinces. For example, a coin from Ephesos (28 BCE) features the laureate head of Augustus on the obverse, while on the reverse the goddess identified as Pax is also surrounded by laurel leaves. She holds the caduceus and stands before an altar.

This was not the first occurrence of the goddess of peace on coinage. Eirēnē appears on a silver stater dated around 350 BCE from Lokroi Epizephyrioi, a Greek settlement on the toe of Italy: she is labeled, seated, and holds a caduceus. The caduceus, a staff entwined with two serpents, is the symbol of peace and of heralds: for the Lokrians therefore, the goddess was associated with truces and treaties (Stafford 2001: 190; Weinstock 1960: 44). The caduceus becomes a common, perhaps the most definitive, attribute of Pax on Roman coinage issued, for example, by Sulla and Julius Caesar. The Julio-Claudians continued to use the caduceus as a symbol or attribute of Pax: an arch built to honor Nero

FIGURE 5.3a and 5.3b: Cistophoric coin issued in Ephesos, 28–20 BCE. Obverse: portrait of Augustus with legend IMP CAESAR DIVI F COS VI LIBERTATIS P R VINDEX; reverse: figure of Pax holding caduceus in right hand, within wreath. RIC I (2nd edn) Augustus 476, ANS 1944.100.39180. Courtesy of the American Numismatic Society.

REPRESENTATIONS OF PEACE

(62 BCE) featured a statue of the emperor in a chariot accompanied by Victoria (victory) and Pax, who holds both the cornucopia and the caduceus; the statue group is recorded on a coin dating from the era (Weinstock 1960: 54). In Weinstock's opinion Augustus aspired to create a cult of Pax, a project that he presumably inherited from his adoptive father Julius Caesar, and he used her iconography to further his project.

Whether this is true or not, it cannot be denied that Augustus exploited the image of Pax to her fullest potential. Among the most striking and enduring monuments associated with the *pax Augusta*, and a stunning example of the power of images as a concrete manifestation of ideology, is the *Ara Pacis Augustae*, the great altar of Augustan peace (Cornwell 2017: 155–77). Upon Augustus' return from military campaigns in Spain and Gaul, the Senate commissioned the altar in 13 BCE, and formally dedicated it in 9 BCE. In design and decoration it is strongly influenced by Classical and Hellenistic public art, although the many artists who created the masterful relief sculptures remain anonymous. Nearly fully restored under Benito Mussolini in 1938, it has been situated in its own museum designed by Richard Meier since 2006. The monument was originally close to what would have been the Campus Martius, where Roman legions practiced their drills, its location serving as an implicit reminder that the *pax Romana* depended on the state's military power. The altar itself is enclosed within an ornately decorated white marble chamber. Running around its four exterior sides on the lower register, is a frieze of stylized plants, fruit and flowers, over fifty species, decorated with motifs and images that signify abundance, fertility and peace, yet arranged in an orderly manner as if to suggest the organizing power of the *pax Augusta*. Pilasters marking the edges of each corner repeat the vegetal motifs. Nestled within the various leaves are small wildlife, frogs, lizards and birds contributing to the sense of tranquil abundance. The outer wall also has four scenes that treat episodes presumably from Rome's mythological origins, beginning with Aeneas, notional ancestor of the Julian dynasty, although there is still controversy about what the historical episodes represent.

On two lateral sides (north and south) are processional friezes representing what art historians have speculated are Augustus, his extended family, various senators, their families, and religious functionaries. Marilyn Skinner points out that this is the first time the interaction between adults and children is depicted on a state monument: "the connection between the overall iconographic program of fertility and the concrete representation of actual Roman families, however idealized, is readily understood" (2005: 257). The implied fecundity of the imperial family is a natural extension of the generative capacity of peace, as seen in Greek culture, but the image has been skillfully incorporated to abet the political ambitions of Augustus. The cumulative effect of all the decorative elements on the monument seems to be that Augustus, putative descendant of Aeneas, was fated to lead Rome into a golden age of prosperity, and that only a member of the Julian gens could maintain this era.

The most visible images on the chamber would have been two panels, one on either side of the entrance on the south side in the upper register, which the ancient viewer would see from the Via Flaminia. The panel on the right hand side of the entrance was probably a female figure seated on a pile of weapons. Although the panel is so badly damaged that reconstruction can only be speculative, art historians believe that she is the allegorical figure of Rome. In much better condition is the beautiful panel on the viewers' left hand side as they enter the chamber. The focal point is a voluptuous seated female with her head covered: she holds on her lap a pile of fruit and two cherubic infants, one of whom offers her some of the fruit. Stalks of grain and poppies, which appear on coins

FIGURE 5.4: The "Tellus Panel" from the Ara Pacis Augustae, first century BCE; Rome, Italy. Photo by DeAgostini, courtesy of Getty Images.

representing Pax, seem to be growing behind her (de Grummond 1990: 666). On either side are two female figures, perhaps representing ocean winds, and at her feet are various forms of livestock.

There has been much controversy about the identity of this figure. She is often referred to as Tellus, or Mother Earth; various scholars suggest that she is Ceres (goddess of the harvest), Rhea Silvia (the mother of Romulus and Remus) or even Venus Genetrix. Paul Zanker justifiably sees her as an amalgam of several deities, and accepts the persuasive suggestion that she is the embodiment of the *pax Augusta* (1988: 172–9; see also de Grummond 1990: 663–77). Although the missing caduceus has troubled some scholars (e.g. Spaeth 1994: 67), it is obvious that this figure represents fertility and abundance, and as we have seen throughout this historical survey, these attributes are associated with peace. Just as the Athenian statue of Peace and Wealth, which also conceived Eirēnē as a maternal figure, evoked the revered goddess Demeter, so too this image of Pax Augusta incorporates Demeter's Roman counterpart Ceres, and other goddesses of fertility. Zanker suggests that: "the whole composition is like a kind of icon, or devotional image, in which each element would evoke manifold associations in the viewer" (1988: 175). Turning back to classical Greek renditions of Eirēnē, the artists employed to celebrate the achievements of Augustus brilliantly exploited the long artistic heritage of peace as a nurturing figure. The lush landscape in which she sits on her rocky throne, the ornamental frieze that suggests images of fertility, and even the family procession all work together in the culmination of a long heritage of representations of peace.

PEACE AND *CONCORDIA*

While all the representations discussed thus far employ the female as an allegory for the benefits of peace, our survey ends with a statue group that emphasizes harmonious relationships between men in a concrete representation of the Roman ideal of *Concordia*. This concept, often closely associated with *Pax*, had been personified as a goddess with her own designated temple since the early days of the Republic. Concordia encompasses the notions of social harmony, cooperation and unity of purpose, all of which complement the notion of peace. Indeed, the goddess is often depicted with the same attributes as Pax including the cornucopia; like Pax, Concordia ensures that a society free from the threats of aggression, both civil and external, can enjoy a life of prosperity and fertility. These ideals are encoded in the distinctive porphyry statue group of the Tetrarchs, the four co-rulers of the late Roman Empire, a sterling example of the use of iconography to express the concepts of peace and harmony, *pax* and *concordia*, while harnessing those desirable attributes to the service of ideology.

By the middle of the third century CE (235–84) the Roman Empire was in crisis with a succession of emperors selected and assassinated by armies, a series of devastating plagues, economic turmoil, foreign invasion and civil wars—the very antithesis of the harmony and affluence that marked the beginning of the Imperial period. The empire was now fragmenting into separate warring units, but Diocletian, after a decisive battle at the Margus River in 285 CE, gained complete domination of the Roman world and restored stability and unity. Diocletian understood that an empire as immense as Rome could not be governed by a single leader, and he also wanted to avoid the succession problems that had plagued his predecessors. Accordingly, he divided the vast conquests of Rome into two and then four administrative units. Appointing his son-in-law Maximian as co-emperor of the West, he made himself emperor ("Augustus") of the East. By 293 CE the Tetrarchy, two Augusti, each with a designated successor or "Caesar", ruled the empire. In the East, the pair was Diocletian and Galerius, matched by Maximian and Constantius Chlorus in the West, a solution designed to prevent the overthrow of the government by a single assassination.

This peaceful resolution was secured, albeit for only two decades (until the rise of Constantine), by Diocletian's well-ordered administrative reforms, including a unified system of coinage with standardized portraits of the tetrarchs. To reinforce the message of unity and stability, Latin panegyric, a genre of prose devoted to political praise, celebrated the *concordia* of the four leaders as evidence of their divinity. This *concordia imperatorum* is given concrete expression in the porphyry group of the tetrarchs originally displayed in Constantinople, and then transferred to St. Mark's Basilica in Venice, where it still stands.

In terms of style, the sculpture represents a significant shift in conventions of portraiture; classical realism gives way to a distillation of the human form now rendered as four nearly identical, stylized male figures. Each Augustus and Caesar have their arms around each other suggesting a sense of brotherhood and harmony, even though in reality the four rulers seldom met, let alone embraced. Only the sparse beards of the Augusti distinguish them from the Caesares; in all other respects, they are indistinguishable, thus announcing to all in very simple terms that the four rulers are a harmonious unanimous entity (Walden 1993: 222). As Roger Rees puts it: "In the group Concordia is established by homogeneity . . . The overriding message of the group is that your strength lies in their unity and solidarity" (Rees 1993: 182–3). Although the tetrarchy was short-lived (284–

FIGURE 5.5: Sculptural group depicting the members of the tetrarchy, the four emperors, early fourth century CE; now in St. Mark's Basilica, Venice, Italy. Photo by Leemage/UIG, courtesy of Getty Images.

311 CE), the effective use of imagery to convey a sense of efficiency and common purpose provides a cogent example of the association of peace with civic order, a concept dating back to the association between Eirēnē and her sister Eunomia in Archaic Greek poetry.

CONCLUSION

Our knowledge of the thousand years covered by this chapter has been for the most part organized in terms of military events. Ancient historians such as Thucydides, Xenophon, Livy and Tacitus invite us to define and frame historical periods according to invasions, conquests, battles, and civil wars. Great literary works including Homer's *Iliad*, Greek tragedy, and Vergil's *Aeneid* articulate the brutal disruption and tragic carnage of war often by describing its effect on family life, yet peace becomes not only a cessation of, or freedom from, these horrors, but also a reward for prevailing, surviving, and winning. Its representations are often within the context of war, be it the Homeric city inscribed on the shield of Achilles or the voluptuous maternal figures that celebrated the imperial agenda of Rome and the *pax* obtained through conquest. In contrast to the confusion and disorder of war, the blessings of peace in the ancient cultural imagination encompass fruitful marriages, maternal plentitude, and a well-ordered family exemplified by the fraternal or paternal *concordia* of the tetrarchs. Peace is a state of abundance and justice, but as the politically inflected art and literature of the Greeks and Romans suggest, it is also a condition that must be maintained by human endeavors that keep its borders secure.

CHAPTER SIX

Peace Movements

CRAIGE B. CHAMPION

Throughout Greek and Roman antiquity, interstate warfare was constant, and "peace movements" usually concerned temporary cessation of hostilities, addressed particular two-party conflicts (often by means of third-party arbitration), and imposed peace terms of limited duration.[1] Aside from lofty and illusory utopian visions found in literature, strains of which we may detect in Aristophanic comedy, peace initiatives were never peace movements in the sense of serious attempts to bring about a permanent universal peace as the inviolable order of things. Jaundiced (Neo)-Realists could argue that classical Greek and Roman antiquity offers nothing new in this regard, but simply gives us prototypes for human history as it has played itself out in subsequent centuries. Human societies have been free from war only in the constructions of fanciful dreamers or in theories driven by tendentious politico-cultural agendas, such as the "New Age" archaeologist Marija Gimbutas' fantasy of a peaceful, ecologically-attuned, communally-agricultural Old Europe centered on the worship of a pre-Indo-European Mother Goddess (see, for example, Gimbutas 1991). Sober scholars are less optimistic. As Michaela Kostial has reminded us, there were 159 wars worldwide in the roughly forty-year period between the end of the Second World War and 1984, for an average of some four new wars each year (1995: 25 and note 70). Yet some present-day social scientists and public intellectuals continue to ignore brutal facts such as these and generally consider war to be a gruesome abnormality, an international disease, and a perversion of the natural order of things.

In early Greece, "Peace," or Eirēnē, was personified as a goddess. She was said to be one of the Horai, or daughters of Zeus and Themis. Her sisters were "Justice," or Dikē, and "Good Governance," or Eunomia (Hesiod *Theogony* 901–2, Pindar *Olympian* 13.6–8). As early as Homer, Eirēnē was paired with "Wealth," or Ploutos.[2] In Athens, Kimon, hero of the Persian Wars, celebrated his resounding naval victory over the Persians at the Eurymedon River with a statue and altar of Eirēnē, an early example of the goddess' public cult (Plut. *Cim.* 13.6). In early Greek cultural representations, then, "Peace" was a desideratum and a state of affairs worthy of receiving personified deification. In terms of peace movements broadly conceived, we can pause to consider invocations of Eirēnē in the civic education of public dramatic performances at Athens. Euripides' *Trojan Women*, for example, first performed in 415 BCE, is a savage indictment of the Athenian atrocity committed on the tiny island of Melos in the preceding year, but we are justified in also seeing it more generally as a repudiation and condemnation of the Athenian war then raging against Sparta and its allies. Aristophanes' *Eirēnē*, produced in 421 BCE, had earlier urged an end to the war, and it both reflected and generated public sentiment that led to the formal but short-lived truce in that year, brokered by the Athenian general Nikias.

While it is wise to mention literary objections to war such as these in our consideration of peace movements (more on this later), their actual influence was minimal. The examples we have considered from Euripides and Aristophanes conform to the general pronouncement made at the outset: they primarily advocated the end of hostilities in a particular conflict, not any sort of plan for an everlasting, universally peaceful humanity. On this last point the plot of Aristophanes' *Birds*, performed in 414 BCE at the City Dionysia and staged shortly after the launching of the disastrous Sicilian Expedition, is instructive. Two middle-aged Athenian men, tired of the bustle of the city, decide to retire to the countryside in search of a more tranquil, peaceful mode of life. But they soon find themselves scheming to create an airy embargo by the birds, which could block interchanges between mortals and gods. What started off as a quest for tranquility and peace ends up as a grandiose plan for an empire of the sky. There is no help for it— Athenians will be Athenians, and Greeks will be Greeks. Unfortunately, as we shall see, peace movements in Greek and Roman antiquity, if we can even think of such a thing, were about as effective as the search for a peaceful and contemplative solitude by Peisthetairos and Euelpides, the protagonists of Aristophanes' *Birds*.

CONSTRUCTIVISM, (NEO-)REALISM, AND THE ANCIENT PARADIGM

Albert Einstein once made a suggestion for understanding his own colleagues: "If you want to find out anything from the theoretical physicists about the methods they use, I advise you to stick closely to one principle: Don't listen to their words, fix your attention on their deeds" (Einstein 1949: 30). Following Einstein's cue, we can posit that pride of place in thinking about peace movements in antiquity must go to the actual behavior of Greeks and Romans in interstate relations. But there is good reason for beginning our consideration of peace movements in ancient Greece and Rome with the idealizations and fantasies of ancient literary texts, if we frame our study within present-day scholarly debates on the nature of interstate relations. This is because a trend in recent scholarship on the questions of peace, war, and international diplomacy, which we could label as the Constructivist School of Interstate Relations, emphasizes ideological constructions (such as the ancient literary texts with which we began) as engines for actual political, diplomatic, and military behavior on the part of sovereign states. This approach is in sharp contrast and opposition to the older Realist/ Neo-Realist School, whose modern founder is Kenneth Waltz and honorary ancient exemplar is Thucydides (and, to a lesser extent, Polybios), which attempts to undertake a no-nonsense, empirical analysis of interstate dynamics and the underlying structures of interstate systems (Waltz 1979). To simplify, Constructivists see ideological productions as shaping and directing international realities; (Neo)-Realists see a brutal, zero-sum game, whose default condition is systemic international anarchy, in which ideology merely follows and reflects the dictates of raw international power relations and hierarchies. The Constructivist School is characterized by greater optimism. If we can use more pacific and conciliatory discourses in our international political rhetoric, the theory goes, we can hope that the very terms in which our discourses are couched will have salutary and peaceable outcomes in the actual unfolding of world political events and the global issues we all are facing. The (Neo)-Realist School is more deterministic and pessimistic, not allowing scope for the ameliorative powers of words and ideas over behaviors.

PEACE MOVEMENTS

Let us consider some recent work in ancient Greek and Roman history within this framework. In a brief article on "Peace" in the award-winning Wiley-Blackwell's *Encyclopedia of Ancient History*, Martin Dreher writes,

> It is now generally accepted that, for an ancient state, peace was the desired normal relation to all other states, which could be interrupted by a declaration of war or by the beginning of war. The limitation in time of many peace treaties to five, ten, thirty, or fifty years, which used to be regarded as proof of the precarious and exceptional character of these treaties, presupposes a developed juridical concept.[3]

This statement suggests that Dreher may fall into the Constructivist camp. For an in-depth study of ancient Greece utilizing this approach, we can turn to Polly Low's 2007 monograph, *Interstate Relations in Classical Greece: Morality and Power*. In that work, Low suggests that in classical Greece there existed "a developed normative framework, visible in a range of ancient sources, which shapes both the conduct and the representation of interstate relations" (2007: 3). Both international law—to the extent that it existed—and conventional diplomatic expectations, undergirded by traditional moral precepts, encompassed multiple normative systems: Panhellenism, ethnicity, ideological commonalities, kinship politics, reciprocity, and *philia* (friendship), all of which statesmen employed in accordance with the rhetorical and diplomatic demands of the moment.

For Roman history, Paul Burton has taken a similar line of approach in his 2011 book, *Friendship and Empire: Roman Diplomacy and Imperialism in the Middle Republic (353–146 BC)*. Burton takes the power of diplomatic language seriously as being capable of directing and shaping outcomes in interstate relations. "Perhaps the most important normative expectation of personal friendship across cultures and across time is that friends must trust each other, as comparative scholarly research and popular surveys alike reveal. In the absence of any formal constraints (such as juridical law), friendship relies on a culturally shared notion of a compact of trust for its practice and efficacy" (Burton 2011: 39). As this passage suggests should be the case, the Roman diplomatic term that demands most of Burton's attention is *amicitia*, or "friendship." In seeing Roman diplomatic conceptions and practices as echoes of Roman social relations, Burton's study has affinities with Ernst Badian's 1958 classic, *Foreign Clientelae*. But while Badian believed that Romans used the language of friendship (*amicitia*), alliance (*foedus aequum, socii*), and trust (*fides*) as a Machiavellian cloak for sharp practice, Burton believes that this sort of discourse actually enabled diplomatic rather than military solutions to interstate tensions, fostering reconciliation, compromise, and cooperation.

All of this stands in the sharpest of contrasts to the (Neo)-Realist interpretation of ancient Greek and Roman history. The idea that we should not wear rose-colored glasses when we view how Greek states interacted with one another or how the Roman Republic rose to hegemony over peninsular Italy is nothing new (indeed, a bleak perspective on human society as merciless competition in which power is always the final arbiter goes back to Thucydides), and Badian's *Foreign Clientelae* is itself an epitome of ancient history as *Realpolitik*. Arthur M. Eckstein is nonetheless the first ancient historian to employ the conceptual apparatus and analytical terminology of (Neo)-Realist international relations (IR) theory explicitly and in a sustained fashion to the ancient Mediterranean world (2006a, 2008). For Eckstein, the stage for ancient Greek and Roman history was a multipolar international anarchy, in which all states were highly militarized, bellicose, and in a ceaseless struggle for power and security. The stakes were high: survival or annihilation. On this view, the efficacy of diplomatic overtures was negligible. As Eckstein and I wrote in the Introduction to *Roman Imperialism: Readings and Sources*,

> Institutions of diplomacy were primitive. Ancient states did not send out permanent ambassadors to other states to keep them abreast of their actions and perhaps give early warning to both sides of problems that might arise, heading them off while they could still perhaps be resolved—the type of activity moderns consider to be an essential process of conflict reduction. On the contrary, ancient ambassadors were sent out to other states only when relations had already reached crisis point, and most often what then occurred were harsh mutual demands made in public fora. Such "compellence diplomacy" often actually had a negative impact on the chances for peace. No one was willing to back down in public; and no one was bluffing. This came from a widespread belief that a fierce reputation for upholding one's rights and one's "honor" helped ensure real security, for then others would fear to interfere with your interests.
>
> —Champion and Eckstein 2004: 6–7

Constructivism or (Neo)-Realism: these are diametrically opposed views on how the ancient world worked, and they lead to wildly divergent assessments of the possibilities for peace and the prospects of peace movements in that world.

These terms beg a question: are they applicable to ancient Greece and Rome, and how helpful is the very concept of 'peace movement' in attempting to understand Greek and Roman antiquity? David Weigall provides a brief and basic description of the term "peace movement":

> This term has been used to describe numerous movements committed generally to the preservation of peace, to the ending of war and to disarmament, or specifically in relation to particular conflicts such as the Vietnam War (1960–75). With the mechanization and increasing destructiveness of war, such movements developed notably in the nineteenth century and as a consequence of the impact on public opinion of the carnage of the First World War. The inter-war years saw a significant increase and mass mobilization of opinion for movements embracing pacifism, disarmament, and campaigns for avoidance of military entanglement. In the period since 1945 the growth (or revival) of peace movements has coincided with periods of major international tension and acceleration of the arms race, notably at the height of the Cold War.
>
> —Weigall 2003: 176

Weigall's summary emphasizes the view that peace movements are essentially a modern phenomenon, and it is certainly true that there was no such thing as a "peace movement" in the modern sense of the word—particularly one embedded in a sophisticated philosophical or theoretical framework—in antiquity. Nevertheless, we can detect moments in Greek and Roman history when there were groundswells of anti-war emotion, usually in the context of a particularly bitter or long-standing conflict (cf. Raaflaub 2016b: 4). In this respect, ancient "peace movements" do resonate with Weigall's classification of movements in response to a specific conflict such as the Vietnam War. These feelings found expression, as we have seen, in the peace plays of Aristophanes, which are full of the yearning for the fundamental blessings of peace. It is in this sense—an upsurge of popular feeling, at times conjoined with a rational recognition by politicians that the financial and human resources for war have been exhausted—that this chapter will explore peace movements in the ancient world. Several case studies will be examined in order to test the two propositions of Constructivism and (Neo-)Realism described above.

PEACE MO(VE)MENTS IN GREEK AND ROMAN HISTORY

The Peloponnesian War (431–404 BCE) is one of the most famous, and most studied, of the wars of classical antiquity, and we are fortunate to have the exacting account of Thucydides as our main source for it. The historian underscores the monumentality of his subject matter in his preface:

> This was the greatest disturbance in the history of the Greeks, affecting also a large part of the non-Greek world, and indeed, I might almost say, the whole of mankind. For though I have found it impossible, because of its remoteness in time, to acquire a really precise knowledge of the distant past or even of the history preceding our own period, yet, after looking back into it as far as I can, all the evidence leads me to conclude that these periods were not great periods either in warfare or in anything else.

> —Thuc. 1.1.2–3

In the lead-up to the outbreak of hostilities, a Corcyraean embassy arrived at Athens in 433 BCE with the offer of a naval alliance. The Corcyraeans stressed that the combined naval powers of Corcyra and Athens would be nearly invincible, and that this force would serve the Athenians well in the immediate future, since the Spartans would soon be declaring war against Athens. They went on to point out that the proffered alliance would not be a breach of the existing treaty between Athens and Sparta, since one of its express provisions was that any neutral Greek state was free to join whichever side it should choose (Thuc. 1.35.1–2).

The latter treaty was struck in the year 446 BCE. By its terms, the Athenians were to relinquish their strongholds on the Isthmus of Corinth and in the Peloponnesos. The peace between Athens and Sparta was to last for thirty years, but Athenian meddlesomeness and aggression continued under the leadership of Perikles, until crises at Corcyra and Potidaia precipitated the formal beginning of the Great War in 431 (with Corinthian lobbyists pushing a hesitant and reluctant Sparta hard for a war declaration). The Thirty Years' Peace was troubled almost from the start, and it ended after fifteen years. This was the first of several failed peace movements in the war.

During the first ten years of the war, the Spartans annually invaded the region of Attica, destroying crops and damaging propertied estates. This was the policy of the Spartan king Archidamos, and in response Perikles called all Athenians within the city's protective walls. This first decade of the war (431–421 BCE) is referred to as the "Archidamian War," after the Spartan king who conducted these yearly invasions of Attica. By the latter stages of this phase of the war, two "hawks" had appeared, wielding considerable influence on their respective war councils, Kleon at Athens and Brasidas at Sparta. But when both of these men perished at the battle of Amphipolis in 422 BCE, the way was opened for negotiated conflict resolution. The Athenian general and statesman Nikias and the Spartan king Pleistoanax emerged as proponents of peace (Thuc. 5.16.3–17.1), and historians have named this peace initiative of 421 BCE the "Peace of Nikias," after the Athenian who brokered it.

In light of the facts that the war had raged for a decade by the time of the treaty and that Athenian war strategy forced Athenian landowners to allow their estates to be devastated in the annual Spartan invasion, we are justified in seeing the treaty as a reflection of widespread desire for peace at Athens. Furthermore, and as a nod to the Constructivists, we can read Aristophanes' anti-war play *Lysistrata*, produced later in the war (411)—along with his *Eirēnē* and Euripides' *Trojan Women* (discussed earlier)—in the same vein. Perhaps at this juncture it will be useful to remind the reader that the approach adopted here is to assess peace movements in Greek and Roman antiquity in concrete terms by concentrating on actual behaviors in the sphere of international relations, subordinating intellectual and philosophical aspects to this overriding criterion.

Thucydides provides an editorial comment on the Peace of Nikias (421–413 BCE): it was not a genuine peace between wars but rather an interval of limited aggressions during a single, protracted war (5.26). Machinations and intrigue at Corinth and at Argos followed hard upon the heels of the peace. By the summer of 421, Athens grew suspicious of Sparta for not observing all of its treaty obligations, while Athens itself retained Pylos and other places the Athenians had promised to give up (Thuc. 5.35). In the summer of the following year, the charismatic, ambitious, glory-seeking Alcibiades was working in Athens to have the treaty overturned (Thuc. 5.43). By the time Alcibiades led a small expedition in the summer of 419 through the territories of all Peloponnesian allies (Thuc. 5.52), it was clear that the peace had broken down. Intended to last for fifty years, it was breached within two years of its inception. A second major peace movement, then, came to no avail.

We can rush along to the war's bitter conclusion and its aftermath. The Spartan admiral Lysander dictated harsh terms to the Athenians after disabling the Athenian fleet at Aigospotamoi in 404 BCE, including a drastic reduction in the number of ships Athens was allowed to possess (twelve) and the destruction of the "Long Walls" connecting the city to its harbor at Piraeus. By 395 BCE —largely because of Spartan aggression—the Greek states were again at war, led by Athens, Thebes, Corinth, and Argos against Sparta in the "Corinthian War" (395–387 BCE). In 387 BCE, enervated by constant military challenges and the shifting and short-lived alliances of the period, Sparta agreed to the "King's Peace," associated with the Persian king at the time, Artaxerxes II. The peace was considered to be a disgrace by many Greeks because one of its main provisions returned the Greeks of Asia Minor to Persian subjection (Xenophon *Hellenika* 5.1.31), in a sense undoing the gains of the stunning Greek victories in the Persian Wars of the early fifth century BCE. But Sparta continued to abuse its position as Greek hegemon, with the Spartan commander Phoibidas seizing the Theban acropolis in 382 BCE, in time of peace, and another Spartan named Sphodrias invading the Athenian Piraeus in 378 BCE, also in time of peace.

In response to Spartan enormities, the Athenians formed the "Second Athenian Empire," or "Second Athenian Sea League," in 377 BCE. Athenian foreign policy in the troubled fourth century BCE was more tempered and far less ambitious than it had been in the fifth century. Its main policies were to try to stay out of financially crippling wars and to secure access to the grain supplies and natural resources of the Black Sea region. After 355 BCE, an individual named Euboulos became increasingly influential at Athens and continued its relatively pacific orientation. A master of finances, he ushered in a time of peace and prosperity at Athens, introducing a law to thwart the use of public funds for minor military operations, ensuring that surpluses were available for public works. In these years, Euboulos was considered to be a leader of the peace party at Athens, opposed after 346 BCE by the hawkish and fiery oratory of Demosthenes' rising star. In the 350s, Euboulos and his associates Meidias, Aischines, and Phokion tried to block the advances of the Macedonian king Philip II by means of a "common peace" (*koinē eirēnē*). When this peace overture foundered, Euboulos consented to the so-called Peace of Philokrates, concluded in 346 and named after one of the Athenian statesmen who negotiated it, which named Athens as Philip's ally and renounced Athenian claims to Amphipolis.

Ultimately, these attempts at peaceful conflict resolution failed, Demosthenes became the most powerful politician in Athens, and under his direction Athens worked with Thebes to build a coalition of Greek states to stand against Philip II. The military confrontation came on the battlefield of Chaironeia in 338 BCE, and the Greek coalition was crushed. Historians have traditionally viewed this battle as marking the end of Greek autonomy and freedom and the beginning of Macedonian subjugation of the Greek poleis. Philip became hegemon of the Greeks and began planning a massive military expedition against Achaimenid Persia. But his common peace and the alliance based on it, known as the League of Corinth, were only secured by Macedonian military garrisons in Greek cities and the threat of force in the case of Greek resistance and independence in external affairs.

The common peace was a typical diplomatic tool of the fourth century BCE (Ryder 1965; Jehne 1994). We first encounter the idea in Andokides' speech *On the Peace* (3.17; 392/1 BCE), in the peace negotiations during the early phase of the Corinthian War. As we have seen, this war ended in 387 with the "King's Peace", which was "sent down" to the Greek poleis by the Persian king Artaxerxes II. This peace is the first actual *koinē eirēnē* in the historical record. In its formal terms, it guaranteed the autonomy of all Greek poleis, except those claimed by the king and three islands ceded to Athens. The Great King even threatened military action against anyone who refused to observe the peace (Xenophon *Hellenika* 5.1.31). Common peaces—also supported by the Persian king— were concluded by Greek city-states in 375 BCE (*SVA* II 265), 371 BCE (*SVA* II 269 and 270), possibly 365 BCE (*SVA* II 285), 362 BCE (*SVA* II 292), and 346 BCE (*SVA* II 331). They honored the terms of the King's Peace, were multilateral or open to all Greek city-states, prohibited assaults against their signatories (but also against third parties), and were not assigned term limits (in stark contrast to "classical" peace treaties).

The common peaces were intended to curb internecine, persistent warring among Greek cities, but in practice, powerful poleis used them to expand their own supremacy. In this period, common peace initiatives provided some equilibrium as the polis-interstate system crumbled, eventually to be replaced by the great Hellenistic monarchies. But on the whole they failed: as we have seen, within a few years of what we can regard as the first common peace, the King's Peace of 387 BCE, Sparta, the very guardian of the peace, violated other states' autonomy. Furthermore, common peaces of the 370s quickly broke down into renewed fighting.

Nevertheless, we should consider common peace agreements more seriously as "peace movements" because, at least rhetorically, they were attempts at lasting peace involving more than two states. The Athenian intellectual Isokrates repeatedly urged the Greek states to recognize their common kinship and cease warring on each other, but ultimately Isokrates' dream was a failure. The last common peace was the treaty of 338/7 BCE, after the defeat of many Greek poleis by Philip II of Macedon. As the Greeks who promised to adhere to the peace became members of the League of Corinth (337 BCE), the common peace was transformed into a hegemonial alliance. Moreover, the point of Greek unity under the Macedonian leadership of Philip II and his son Alexander was to undertake a great war, a massive military campaign against Persia, an idea already bandied about among Greek statesmen early in the century, including Isokrates (*Panegyrikos*, 380 BCE).

After Alexander's death (323 BCE), the geopolitical configuration evolved into an uneasy balance of power among the Hellenistic monarchies and smaller cities and leagues.

Warfare was a constant, as it was in the classical period, with the never-ending struggles for control of Koile Syria between Ptolemies and Seleukids providing a striking illustration, but the size of the armies and the scale of the fighting were unprecedented.[4] A significant feature of the age was the large, professional, mercenary army. Hellenistic kings called their realms "spear-won territory" (*doriktētos chōra*), and some of their royal epithets—such as "Victor," "Bringer of Victory," "Lightning Bolt," and "the Besieger"—made their martial pretensions and ambitions plain to see.[5]

During the fourth century BCE, the Roman Republic was consolidating its supremacy among central Italian states and expanding its hegemony to include all of peninsular Italy by the century's end. In the period of the early Republic, the Romans had struggled to gain control of their immediate environs in battles against the neighboring Latin peoples. This was achieved in the battle at Lake Regillus and by the terms of the bilateral peace agreement between Rome and the Latins struck in 493 BCE, known as the *foedus Cassianum*. But the Latins continued to look for opportunities to reassert their freedom and autonomy and, exasperated by this defiance, the Romans crushed a Latin military coalition and abolished the "Latin League" in 338 BCE. Thereafter individual Latin communities could have formal understandings with Rome, but not with each other. By about 300 BCE, the Romans had subdued the Samnites in protracted warfare and had established Roman hegemony over the Italian peninsula.

In trying to understand this historical process—the Roman conquest of Italy—two crucially important factors must be stressed: Rome's gradated incorporation of the defeated into the Roman political commonwealth, a process I have called the "politics of inclusion" or the "politics of incorporation"; and the requirement of all Italian states with whom the Republic had formal relations that they provide annual quotas of recruits for the Roman military forces. Having created an Italian Confederacy on these terms, and more importantly a military machine that could draw on a seemingly inexhaustible supply of Italian manpower (enabling the Roman Republic to lose many battles but win every war through attrition), the Romans were poised in the early third century BCE to establish Mediterranean-wide hegemony.[6]

This process lasted at least three centuries and precluded anything like a "peace movement" of any durable nature. Arthur Eckstein's monographs (2006a, 2008) have had the salutary effect of making us question ancient Roman exceptionalism and the Romans as a pathologically or exceptionally militaristic and bellicose people. Given the brutal international environment in which the Roman Republic existed, it is easy to see why Rome—like every other state—had to focus on warfare as a means not only to power, but also for survival and security; Eckstein's interpretation thus aligns itself with (Neo-)Realist IR theory. And so the key to Roman imperial success does not lie in the military sphere per se (indeed, the Romans suffered some ninety serious defeats on the battlefield in the Republican period), but rather in what we might call the Roman political genius, and in particular the "politics of inclusion" (hence Polybios devoted his book 6 to the Roman Republican political and military organization). Having acknowledged this much, we should be wary of going too far. After all, the very foundation myths of Rome are permeated with violence and warlike motifs: Romulus gained control of the Roman political community as its first king only after a fratricidal resolution to a power struggle with his brother Remus; the brothers themselves had Mars, the Roman god of war, as their father; in myth the early Roman community was augmented by the abduction and rape of the Sabine women; and various aetiological stories marked out Rome as the conqueror and ruler of the world.[7]

PEACE MOVEMENTS

115

The Roman aristocratic male lived for renown and glory, and this was measured in terms of military achievement and culminated in the public celebration of a triumphal spectacle through the streets of Rome (Beard 2009). The Roman Republican aristocracy's emphasis on military achievement is underscored in the famous epitaph of Lucius Cornelius Scipio Barbatus, Roman consul in 298 BCE: "Cornelius Lucius Scipio Barbatus, sprung from Gnaeus his father, a man strong and wise, whose appearance was most in keeping with his virtue, who was consul, censor, and aedile among you—he captured Taurasia, Cisauna, Samnium—he subdued all Lucania and led off hostages" (*CIL* 6, no. 1287). The doors of the Temple of Janus in the Roman Forum were closed only in a time of complete peace. They were closed twice in the history of the Republic: in 235 BCE after the First Punic War, and in 29 BCE after the naval battle at Actium.

In the year 264 BCE the Romans launched an overseas military campaign to the island of Sicily. This was the first step on the road to Mediterranean-wide Roman hegemony and the first encounter with the Republic's arch nemesis, Carthage. The decision for this military action underscores the anxieties and security concerns of any state inhabiting this hostile interstate system. The immediate issue concerned the strategically important Sicilian town of Messana, on the shore of the narrow strait separating Sicily from Italy. Campanian mercenaries had seized the town from its rightful inhabitants, and both Hiero II, king of Syracuse, and the Carthaginians had become involved in the conflict there. This was to be expected, as these two powers, Syracuse and Carthage, had vied for control of the island for many years, with Greeks controlling the eastern side of Sicily, and Carthage dominant in the western half of the island. The Roman Republic on the long view was the interloper.

Hiero besieged the mercenaries in Messana, who called themselves Mamertines ("sons of Mars"), after their marauding activities had made them a menace throughout a large part of northeastern Sicily (Polyb. 1.8.1–2; cf. Diod. 22.13.1; 23.1.4; Plut. *Pyrr.* 23.1, 5). Although details of the events are far from certain, the Mamertines, hard-pressed by Hiero, appealed to both Carthage and Rome for assistance. Debates on this Mamertine appeal were protracted and agonizing in the Roman Senate. To assist treacherous mercenaries who had unlawfully seized control of a city would be an undertaking of dubious morality, to say the least. But in the end, fear won out over the justice of the situation. The senators felt that if the Carthaginians went unchecked in their operations at Messana, they would soon possess a bridgehead for an invasion of Italy. And so they moved to send a force across the straits, precipitating a war against Carthage lasting about twenty-four years. If we are to believe the account of Polybios, this was a preemptive Roman expedition motivated by security concerns. It demonstrates that warfare, paradoxically, was often thought of as the only avenue to safety; and how little trust could be placed in diplomatic solutions and peace overtures in this world.[8]

Let us pass quickly to the geopolitical scene in the aftermath of the Hannibalic War (the Second Punic War, 218–201 BCE). In addition to Hannibal's terrifying invasion of Italy (217–203 BCE), the war was also fought by proxy in its Greek theater, with King Philip V of Macedonia fighting as an ally of Carthage, and the Aitolian *koinon* in league with the Romans (the First Macedonian War, 215–205 BCE). The Macedonian monarchy and the Aitolian League were inveterate enemies, who had recently fought a bitter conflict, known as the Social War (220–217 BCE), which was temporarily halted by a peace initiative at Naupaktos, just as the war between Hannibal and the Roman Republic was getting underway. In a sense, the military conflict in Greece of Macedonians and Aitolians as allies of the principals of the Hannibalic War was a continuation of seemingly perennial

Macedonian–Aitolian hostilities. In this theater of the war, the enervated Aitolians struck a peace with Philip V (206 BCE) before the Roman war against Hannibal had ended. This unilateral action, without consultation of the Senate or Roman permission, was later to create grave problems for the Aitolians. But for our purposes we must for now focus on Philip V in the years immediately following the successful Roman conclusion of the Hannibalic War.

After the devastating Roman defeat in the early phases of that war at Cannae (216 BCE), in which there may have been as many as 70,000 Roman casualties, Philip had come to an agreement with Carthage. The treaty had been struck when Hannibal appeared to have the upper hand, and its oaths and stipulations are preserved by Polybios (7.9). By the terms of this treaty of 215 BCE, each party pledged to come to the assistance of the other in time of need, and in particular, they promised to work jointly in the present war against Rome. It was in response to this agreement that the Romans had forged an alliance with Philip's old enemy, the Aitolian League, thus setting the stage for what I have called the proxy war in Greece. But once Hannibal had finally been vanquished on the battlefield at Zama in 202 BCE, there was to be a Roman reckoning with Philip, who had, so to speak, backed the wrong horse.

In 200 BCE the Roman consul Publius Sulpicius Galba worked hard and (ultimately) successfully to push a war-weary populace to declare war against Philip V (the Second Macedonian War, 200–197 BCE). After several Roman commanders faltered in the campaign in Greece and Macedonia, Titus Quinctius Flamininus defeated Philip decisively in 197 BCE at the Battle of Kynoskephalai in central Greece. What happened in the following year at the Isthmian Games at Corinth is of signal importance for our theme of peace movements. This was the famous "Isthmian Proclamation," in which Flamininus declared that Roman forces would evacuate Greece and that the Greek states were to be left free and independent, and live in peace at the behest of the Romans.

This was, at face value, a most impressive peace movement, but although Roman military forces did indeed withdraw from Greece, the prospects for a lasting peace in Greece under the Roman dispensation soon proved to be illusory.

By the terms of the alliance between Aitolia and Rome during the First Macedonian War, the Aitolians were to be allowed to incorporate any poleis they captured into their *koinon*; however, the Aitolians, by swearing a separate peace with Philip in 206 BCE, had vitiated their agreement with Rome, at least in Roman eyes. The Aitolians had failed to realize that in treaty relations with the Republic, Rome took the role of imperious patron, and the other party was to assume the position of submissive and dutiful client (Badian 1958). Flamininus was thus enabled to declare that the Greek cities were to be free and independent (and not part of the Aitolian League as per the earlier agreement). The disgruntled Aitolians began to court the Seleukid monarch Antiochos III to come west with a military force as the "liberator of Greece" (their real motivation, of course, was to incorporate subdued Greek cities into the Aitolian *koinon*), setting off a chain of events that would ultimately lead to a showdown between the Roman Republic and another of the great Hellenistic monarchies. And so the "Isthmian Declaration" came to naught as a peace movement. Flamininus' proclamation, we must note, was neither singular nor unprecedented: such international sloganeering, guaranteeing autonomy and freedom, was a commonplace among the successors of Alexander, known as the Diadochoi.[9]

The Roman trial of strength against Antiochos III was preceded by an uneasy cold war and strained diplomatic interchanges, a period during which international "peace" was of a nature akin to the tense decades of the 1950s and 1960s (Badian 1959). The decisive

FIGURE 6.1: Engraving showing T. Quinctius Flamininus granting the Greeks their freedom (the "Isthmian Proclamation"). Photo by Kean Collection, courtesy of Getty Images.

battle between Rome and Antiochos at Magnesia took place in late autumn 190 BCE, and although the battle was protracted and bitterly contested, it ended in Roman victory and the vanquishing of the king. But for our purposes in considering the prospects for peace and peace movements in this world, we need to back-track somewhat. In the tradition of his ancestors and of the other Hellenistic royal courts, Antiochos boasted of his "spear-won" territorial empire, and in his so-called Anabasis he had campaigned to the frontiers of northern India. He returned to Greek Asia Minor in the guise of a great conqueror, taking the sobriquet "Megas," or "The Great."[10]

The images of vast military conquests and invincible military powers were of crucial importance and centrality for the public persona of a Hellenistic king. This ideology, it goes without saying, was hardly conducive to non-violent, diplomatic solutions to interstate tensions, and what happened near the end of the third century BCE between the Antigonid, Seleukid, and Ptolemaic monarchies underscores the aggressive and bellicose nature of Hellenistic kingship, even absent Roman intervention.

FIGURE 6.2: Portrait of a Hellenistic king, often identified as Antiochos III (r. 223–187 BCE); Louvre Museum, Paris, France. Photo by Leemage/UIG, courtesy of Getty Images.

In the winter of 203/2 BCE, King Philip V of Macedonia and King Antiochos III of Syria had made a pact that Polybios considered to be of monumental historical significance (15.20; Eckstein 2005). Polybios roundly condemned both kings for having made a despicable agreement: the kings' plan was to descend jointly upon Ptolemaic Egypt at a moment of weakness, as the boy-king Ptolemy V had assumed the throne, and to parcel out the Ptolemaic realm between themselves. But Polybios assures the reader of the justice of Fortune, or *Tyche*, as she visited a condign punishment upon both kings for their rapaciousness and lawlessness. By this, he probably means the fact that both monarchs were in the end militarily defeated by and subjected to the power of the Roman Republic, and more precisely that Fortune alerted the Romans to the diabolical schemes of Philip and Antiochos.

For the concrete manifestation of this, we must look to the international diplomatic activity of these years. At least four Greek states sent embassies to Rome in the winter of 201/0 BCE in order to complain of the behaviors of Philip and/or Antiochos. These embassies will have attracted the Romans' attention to the unstable geopolitical situation in the Greek east, and probably specifically to the "Pact between the Kings." It is likely that this alarming development, and the prospect of having to fight the combined forces of the Antigonid Macedonian and Seleukid Syrian armies in the near future, pushed the senators to the war declaration against Philip alone in 200 BCE. Their intention would have been to dispatch Philip V in the Second Macedonian War, with only Antiochos III left as a threat for the future (with Hannibal still at large and soon to become an advisor to Antiochos), rather than having to cope with their combined strength later. Although the motivation(s) leading Rome—not just the senate, but also the people—to fight the Second Macedonian War have been much debated, it seems undeniable that the perception of both Philip and Antiochos as very real and present dangers (no doubt heightened by the recent experience with Hannibal) loomed very large in the Roman mind. And so the picture that emerges is again one of aggression, fear, greed, and security concerns for all players inhabiting this interstate system: a cocktail of collective behavioral characteristics inimical to any real prospects for lasting peace.

In the preceding paragraphs, we have assembled selected episodes—that I believe are representative of the historical arc of ancient Greece and Rome—in order to give a concrete dimension to the position taken in this chapter about the potential for peace and the efficacy of peace movements in the ancient world. While we have seen moments of yearning for peace that were strong enough to bring about at least temporary peace treaties in the Greek world, we have seen little in the Roman Republic to support the idea of popular groundswells in favor of peace, though admittedly this has not been a comprehensive account. Moreover, we should acknowledge the distinct differences in our literary records for Greek and Roman antiquity. We have little from Roman literature that might be seen as analogous to the popular works of Aristophanes, who (at least in part) seems to have expressed the views of the "common man", while the historical record of Rome tends to focus primarily on the ambitions and actions of the elite, the very class that benefited most from military success and glory. As far as the small farmer in ancient Italy goes, it would probably not be inaccurate to assume that his concerns were much the same as those of his counterpart in ancient Greece.

We may now proceed with our meditation on peace movements in classical antiquity by returning to the conceptual universe of political scientists and international relations theorists. The interstate system we have tried to describe so far—from the classical Greek poleis on through the period known as the Middle Roman Republican and Hellenistic periods—is what these social scientists would call an anarchic, multipolar interstate system. This type of international scene is a kaleidoscopic, rapidly changing series of alliances and estrangements precariously preserving an unstable equilibrium of power dynamics. As we have seen, warfare is its hallmark.

IMPERIAL ROME

Multipolar, anarchic interstate systems can evolve into hegemonic empires in a new situation of unipolarity whenever one state's superordinate power enables it to subjugate the others, with no single state or coalition of states left to challenge its primacy. Traditionally and more prosaically, we would call this an empire; other chapters in this volume have examined the Roman Empire and the ironic truth that the military dominance of Rome gave the ancient world its lengthiest and most widespread era of peace. In particular, the first two centuries CE, between the reign of Augustus (27 BCE–14 CE) and that of Marcus Aurelius (161–180 CE), were a time of peace among the many polities that made up the Roman Empire, interrupted only occasionally by episodes such as the Jewish War (66–73 CE) and later the revolt led by Simon bar Kokhba (132–136 CE).[11]

We often refer to this period simply as the *pax Romana*, or "Roman peace." Edward Gibbon asserted that in the history of humankind, in terms of peace, prosperity, and felicity, this was the happiest time and place in which to have lived. While we can attribute the flowery hyperbole of such sentiments to the ornamental adornments of the prose style of Gibbon's day, we must take seriously the underlying historical significance of the Roman achievement during this period, known as the High Roman Empire. Whereas we can think of the Roman Republic as an aggressive, expansionist, territorial, hegemonic empire, we should think of Rome in this later time as an "empire of maintenance" or an "empire of consolidation." We can turn to an anecdote as an index of the transformation. On his deathbed, Augustus supposedly told his successor Tiberius that there should be no more major conquests; this was the time, as it were, to take care of domestic affairs.

This new orientation was reflected in concrete terms in the drastic reduction in the number of the Roman legions from around seventy in the civil war period to twenty-eight during the reign of Augustus. The Roman army increasingly became an agent for building infrastructure (roads, bridges, and aqueducts); professional career paths developed in the civil and military service; the Roman citizenship franchise was steadily extended until it included virtually all free inhabitants of the empire (by the *constitutio Antoniniana* of 212 CE); the Roman Empire was a network of cities interconnected by relatively secure roads and trading lanes; and citizens were, formally at least, entitled to the protections of Roman law (one thinks of the trials and tribulations of St. Paul). Conditions of life were, to be sure, harsh by the standards of today's western democratic nation-state: the legal system was frequently compromised by bribery and corruption; the poor in fact had few chances of legal remedy; the Roman world generally was a self-help society; there were no standing police forces as we know them; and the frontiers and borderlands were hardly impenetrable defenses against incursions, raids, and invasions. Nonetheless, for the conditions of the ancient world, the *pax Romana* provided a degree of stability, security, and peace that is remarkable.

Interestingly, the emphasis on military renown and battlefield victory became more pronounced in Roman self-representations in art, literature, and other forms of propaganda, even as Roman wars of imperial expansion subsided. During the period of the *pax Romana*, and far from carrying out anything like a "grand strategy" of empire, Roman emperors sporadically and haphazardly lashed out on campaigns against real or trumped-up enemies in ephemeral and often aimless military operations in order to promote the correct image of indomitable fighting spirit and heroic courage in successful war-making. For example, both in his autobiographical account of his career, known as the *Res Gestae Divi Augusti* ("Deeds Accomplished of [by] the Divine Augustus") and in the works of the literary writers working under his regime, Augustus emerges as an unvanquished world conqueror. His actual record in the military sphere, however, especially in places like Spain and the Rhineland, was checkered. Recognizing the futility and potential disaster of yet another war against the Parthians, in 20 CE Augustus employed the arts of diplomacy to repatriate the lost legionary standards captured by the Parthians at Carrhae in 53 BCE; nevertheless, in his *Res Gestae*, Augustus insists that he "compelled" the Parthians to return the standards and to supplicate Rome for the favor of its friendship (*RGDA* 29).

Of course, Roman propaganda and ideology projected Rome as the defender of the oppressed and the bringer of peace (as in the famous lines Vergil gives to Anchises in Book

FIGURE 6.3: Detail of the breastplate of the Prima Porta statue of Augustus, depicting the return of the legionary standards lost to the Parthians; Vatican Museum, Vatican City, Italy. Photo by DEA PICTURE LIBRARY/DeAgostini, courtesy of Getty Images.

Six of the *Aeneid*), but countervailing representations of Rome as military dominatrix show how deeply entrenched warlike motifs and martial values were in the Roman collective identity (Isaac 1993; Mattern 2002). And as an index of the atrocities the Roman army was capable of as an agent of Romanization, we have the famous critique of the tribal leader Calgacus as rendered by Tacitus, "they create a desolation, and they call it peace" (*Agr.* 30).

With the end of the Antonine dynasty—Commodus, the last Antonine emperor, was strangled in his bath in 192 CE—imperial power in Rome entered a period of dynastic, military, social, and economic crisis that was to last for a century. The Severan dynasty that succeeded the Antonines held things together for a time, but the rivalry between Caracalla and Geta, the sons of Septimius Severus, set the pattern for events in the third century CE: a more highly militarized society, political and military instability, frequent "barbarian" incursions into Roman territory, and a series of soldier-emperors, all circumstances that would only bolster the grim nature of prospects for peace offered here. *Pax Romana*, of the type associated with Augustus, was long gone, and in the fifty years between 235 and 285 CE, there were over twenty emperors, with an average reign of a little over two years for each. The majority of them were killed in battle or succumbed to assassination.

FIGURE 6.4: Engraving from *The Pictorial History of Scotland* (1859) depicting Calgacus delivering his speech to the Caledonians before the Battle of Mons Graupius. Courtesy of Wikimedia Commons.

The tetrarchic system of government devised by Diocletian—the empire was divided into two administrative zones, west and east, and each zone was governed by a senior and a junior emperor (an "Augustus" and a "Caesar")—put an end to the havoc and chaos of the third century (see Figure 5.5). Nevertheless, the deeply ingrained cultural values that identified the emperor as a warrior, not to mention the personal ambitions that swayed these men, meant that the tetrarchy too was short-lived. With the abdication of Diocletian in 305 CE, the empire once again became a battleground of opposing forces, a struggle that ended only with the defeat and subsequent execution of Licinius (325 CE), Constantine's last remaining rival. Constantine reunited the empire under his own control, and took two steps that were to have a profound impact on the Roman Empire and on subsequent western history: the transfer of the imperial capital from Rome to Byzantion (now Constantinople) and the adoption of Christianity.

With the imperial focus now in the east, the western portion of the empire gradually crumbled in the face of increasing pressures from peoples such as the Goths, the Vandals, and the Huns; traditionally, the end of the western empire is dated to 476 CE, the year when the Germanic soldier Odoacer deposed the last Roman emperor, Romulus Augustulus. In the east, on the other hand, the Christian Byzantine empire lasted for close to a thousand years after the fall of the west. But peace was not the hallmark of the

Byzantine empire either, and Christianity did nothing to promote a popular peace movement. Constantine's brand of militant Christianity—the emperor as a soldier of God—was the dominant religious framework. While the Byzantine emperors did at times conduct peaceful international relations of diplomacy and cooperation with their neighbors (Lee 2008; Whitby 2008), theirs was still the age-old dilemma of security concerns and mistrust of other nations (a dilemma shared by their neighbors likewise). To the north, the Huns, the Slavs, and the Avars were all "barbarian" tribes not to be trusted, while in the east, the Sassanid Persians, and subsequently the Arab Islamic caliphate, presented grave dangers to the territorial integrity and resources of the Byzantine empire.[12]

CONCLUSION

The Greek city-states, the Hellenistic Greek federal states and monarchies, and the Roman Republic existed in a brutal international anarchy, in which everyone was preoccupied with being prepared for war in order to maximize power and security. That is a statement that conforms to the bleakest of visions of (Neo)-Realist international relations theorists, but it is in line with the historical evidence from classical antiquity for the frequency and ubiquity of warfare. It is telling in this regard that in the post-classical Greek world there could very well be clauses of inviolability; in other words, a signatory had to promise not to attack an ally in a random fashion (Rigsby 1996). In conclusion, we can concede that any discussion of peace movements in this world must give due attention to the common peace (*koinē eirēnē*) treaties in Greek diplomatic attempts at conflict resolution, the achievements of the *pax Romana* in the Imperial period, and even the shaping, ameliorative powers of diplomatic discourse, as Constructivists would stress. But on the whole, comprehensive and lasting peace and peace movements that could effect this kind of peace were not features of the world of ancient Greeks and Romans.

CHAPTER SEVEN

Peace, Security, and Deterrence

JASON CROWLEY AND CECILIA RICCI

As most of the chapters in this volume have demonstrated, both peace and war were concepts of the utmost importance to the Greeks and the Romans: war because it was a common experience and peace because it was a fondly held desideratum. Peace, as we have seen, meant many different things in antiquity, but rarely did it carry the full spectrum of meaning that it carries in the modern world. In its most basic sense, as "not war", the Greeks and Romans often did seek to maintain it, where they could, through military means. While this may seem paradoxical, it remains true that in any anarchic international system, it only takes one to make a fight, and a belligerent party may only be constrained through the application of force. This chapter examines the use of deterrence and security mechanisms for preservation of peace and limitation of war.

GREECE
Jason Crowley

A modern reader might be forgiven for thinking that the Greeks and their neighbors were addicted to war. Their historical writings, and indeed much of their other literature, revolve around conflict, and yet, the impression is misleading: they greatly appreciated peace, and the distressing ubiquity of war is less the result of human choice, and more a reflection of harsh geo-political necessity. However, if the Greeks valued peace and feared war, why did they so readily engage in armed conflict?

The ubiquity of war is explained by three mutually reinforcing factors. The first is a geo-political environment characterized by cultural unity and political fragmentation. According to Herodotos (8.144.2), the Greeks felt a common kinship, yet their Panhellenic sentiment was undercut by a more immediate attachment to their individual city-states (poleis), a feeling forcefully expressed in Perikles' funeral oration, delivered during the first year of the Peloponnesian War. This speech, reported, or perhaps recreated, by Thucydides (2.35–46), celebrates the patriotic zeal of the Athenians, especially its highest manifestation: the willingness to fight to the death for Athens (Crowley 2012; Loraux 2006).

The Greeks, then, were subject to the competing demands of Panhellenism and polis particularism, but the strength of these forces was by no means equal, as their response to Xerxes' invasion reveals (Lazenby 1993; Mitchell 2007). This is often imagined as the Greeks' finest hour, during which they collectively defeated an overwhelming Persian force, but the truth is that the Greeks did not unite: they looked instead to their own

FIGURE 7.1: Relief sculpture of the goddess Athena contemplating a gravestone (?), known as the "Mourning Athena", fifth century BCE; National Archaeological Museum, Athens, Greece. Photo by DEA/G. NIMATALLAH/DeAgostini, courtesy of Getty Images.

interests. Some, like Argos, stayed neutral, others, such as Thebes, sided with the Persians, and a very small minority, only thirty-one, formed the Hellenic League and resisted. Worse still, the Hellenic League was so infected by polis particularism that its collective aims were continually undermined by its leading states. The Spartans, for instance, were willing to sacrifice all the northern and central Greek poleis, including Athens, as long as they themselves were safe in the Peloponnese, while the Athenians threatened repeatedly to leave the League unless coalition forces were committed north of the Isthmus of Corinth (Hdt. 8.60–2; Lazenby 1993). The Greeks might have shared a common identity, but this identity was much weaker than the attachment they felt for their individual poleis.

The second factor was their inability to regulate interstate relations in any lasting way. In theory, regulation was provided by a widely accepted set of norms and values underpinned by a sophisticated legal framework and advanced mechanisms for conflict resolution (such as interstate arbitration: Thuc. 5.18, 5.79; Sheets 1994: 51–73). Such measures reveal a desire to control inter-communal competition, but they failed largely because they could not be enforced (Low 2007: 77–128; cf. Thuc. 5.89.1). Greek poleis, consequently, formed a horizontal community of states in which the only vertical authority was provided by the gods (Low 2007: 118–26; Hunt 2010: 215–36). Diplomacy, as a result, was conducted under the purview of the divine (heralds, for instance, were protected by Hermes), and interstate treaties were guaranteed by oaths sworn to the gods. These oaths exerted considerable force, since breaking one incurred not just divine wrath, it also risked the gods joining with the wronged party to punish the oath-breaker (Xen. *Hell.* 3.4.11, 5.4.1; Hall 2007: 85–107; Low 2007: 118–26; Raaflaub 2016d). Avoiding this through interstate arbitration, an obligation enshrined in many Greek treaties, was, therefore, compelling (see esp. Thuc. 1.78, 1.85, 1.140, 2.2–7, 7.18). Nevertheless, even if an acceptable arbitrator could be found in the polarized geo-political context of Classical Greece, there was little possibility of forcing any major Greek power to accept an offer of arbitration or of enforcing a subsequent judgment (Ager 1993).

These two factors, furthermore, resulted in a third, namely the way the Greeks felt about war and the warrior. Understandably, given their unstable environment, the Greeks came to accept war as a natural way for a state to resolve disputes and advance or defend its interests (Thuc. 1.76, 2.64; Xen. *Eq. mag.* 8.7, *Mem.* 2.1.28). Moreover, since it was men who fought these wars, the Greeks' concept of masculinity became as militarized as the geo-political environment in which they lived (Crowley 2012: 80–104). Of course, with the exception of the Spartans and serving mercenaries, the Greeks were amateur warriors, and so their concept of masculinity was not entirely martial (Trundle 2004; Roisman 2005: 26–63). Nevertheless, the Greeks felt that the greatest quality a man could demonstrate, and the one thing that undoubtedly defined him as a man, was his ability to overcome his fear and fight in interpersonal combat (Soph. *Ant.* 640–81; Thuc. 2.42; Crowley 2012: 92–6). Consequently, when interstate disputes escalated, it was easier for men to vote for war, since this confirmed their courage, and harder to vote for peace, because that called their courage into question and exposed them to accusations of cowardice (Roisman 2005: 113–17; also Hunt 2010: 108–33).

Security and Deterrence in Classical Greece

The Greeks then, were politically fragmented, they lacked an enforceable system of international law, and, faced by endless conflict, they normalized war and privileged the role of the warrior. Nevertheless, they were not helpless, and while they could not avoid the danger of war, they developed a range of sophisticated strategies designed to minimize the risks they faced.

Some poleis pursued a policy of neutrality, hoping to avoid the wars of others, but, as Bauslaugh (1990) demonstrates, this strategy entailed significant risks. The concept of neutrality was, for the Greeks, not just indistinct, but also contentious and contested. Poleis wishing to remain neutral had to perform a precarious balancing act, seeking *philia* (friendship, see Mitchell 1997; Hall 2007) with potential belligerents while at the same time avoiding entangling obligations. Furthermore, non-alignment could easily become isolation, as Corcyra discovered immediately prior to the Peloponnesian War, when, threatened by Corinth, it found itself with no allies to come to its aid (Thuc. 1.31–2). This risk was exacerbated by the suspicion neutrality attracted: the action-oriented Greeks tended to associate neutrality with selfishness and cowardice, and since belligerents often considered conflict to be a zero sum game, neutrality could easily be construed as aiding the enemy (Bauslaugh 1990: 70–83; Hall 2007). As Thucydides describes (5.84–116), the Athenians demanded that Melos side with them against the Spartans, and when it refused, they violated Melos' neutrality, crushed it militarily, executed its men, and andrapodized the surviving populace.[1]

Neutrality, then, was fragile, and evidence of success is scant. This may, as Bauslaugh observes (1990: 21–35), simply reflect the nature of the extant evidence, which makes neutrality most visible only at the point of failure. Argos, admittedly a relatively powerful polis, was able to remain neutral during some conflicts that marred the fifth and fourth centuries BCE. Nevertheless, it seems clear that neutrality, for the powerful, was a position they violated or upheld as it suited, whereas, for the weak, it was a risky strategy that entailed isolation and the placement of trust in those who often sought to prey upon them.

The alternative, for weaker states, especially those in close proximity to more powerful neighbors, was to bandwagon (Walt 1987). This involved trading some or all external freedom (*eleutheria*) for guarantees of external security and internal sovereignty (*autonomia*), an exchange that allowed powerful poleis to establish themselves as hegemons (Thuc. 1.8.3, 15.2; Karavites 1982: 145–62; Hall 2010: 72–107; Hunt 2010: 154–84). After the Persian Wars, for instance, many Greek states collectivized their security under the leadership of Athens in order to protect themselves from Persia (Thuc. 1.89–118; cf. chapter 8). Hegemonies, however, exist for the benefit of hegemons, and while subject states might sometimes manipulate them for their own interests (see esp. Thuc. 1.67–88), their initial sacrifice of *eleutheria* might lead to further loss of *autonomia*. Democratic Athens, for example, seems to have encouraged and sometimes imposed democracies on allies, and oligarchic Sparta acted similarly among those poleis she enrolled in the Peloponnesian League, which she controlled, in part, by supporting their own oligarchic regimes.

Neutrality and subordination, then, guaranteed neither peace nor security, and it is unsurprising that Greek states sought to maintain their own capacity for defense. As Grundy and Gomme recognized (1911: 240–52; 1945: 10–24), a glance at a map suggests that, for some states, the terrain itself, augmented with judicious use of fortifications, could have been used to deny hostile forces access to friendly territory. This potential, of course, had been actualized by the Greeks during the Persian Wars, when they used the pass at Thermopylai and its rudimentary fortifications to good effect against the invading Persians in 480 BCE. The failure to hold the pass, however, highlights one of the three obvious problems with preclusive defense.

First, no matter how strong a strongpoint is, or how challenging the terrain in which it is located, a determined invader can usually find a way around it (Hdt. 7.213–18). The second problem is even worse: manmade or natural obstacles are only obstacles as long as they are defended. An effective system of preclusive defense, therefore, requires a standing military force as well as the logistical systems required to support it, and both were generally beyond the modest resources of the Greeks (Gomme 1945: 10–24; Krentz 2007). Finally, even if a system of preclusive defense could be manned and supported, there was no way of avoiding the third problem inherent thereto, namely, any state that adopted it placed all or most of its strength at its extremities. This entails such a dangerous degree of dispersal that a numerically inferior enemy can attain relative superiority by concentrating its forces at given location, and, by breaching the defenses at that point, render the entire system useless (Luttwak 1976; McRaven 1995).

These problems could be avoided by allowing a hostile force to violate the integrity of one's territory, a temporary concession that allowed a state to concentrate all available forces against an invading army in the hope of defeating it in one decisive engagement (Hanson 2000). The most famous example from Greek antiquity is probably the Athenian decision in 480 BCE to abandon the territory of Attika and move the entire Athenian population across the straits to the island of Salamis, thereby allowing the invading Persians to take and sack the city of Athens, while making preparations to meet the Persian naval forces in the ensuing Battle of Salamis. In less extreme circumstances, such a strategy avoided the costs of building, supplying and garrisoning static defenses, while at the same time allowing the men of the polis to remain economically productive and politically engaged; and it was still an effective security solution, because the Greeks were able to mobilize and deploy impressive field armies.

Typically, such armies formed around a core of heavy infantrymen the Greeks called hoplites. These warriors took their name from the Greek word for kit (*hopla*; Lazenby and Whitehead 1996: 27–33), and a full set of kit (a panoply) included a large round shield with a double grip, body armor, helmet and greaves for protection, a large thrusting spear as a primary weapon, and a short sword for backup (Hanson 1991: 63–84). Naturally, the weight of this entailed a substantial loss of tactical mobility offset by the adoption of a close-order formation called a phalanx (Schwartz: 2009).

Often eight deep, this formation presented the enemy with a shield wall and an intimidating line of spear points, and although it was strong when engaged head-on, it

FIGURE 7.2: Vase painting depicting hoplite warriors in phalanx formation, seventh century BCE (the "Chigi Vase"); National Etruscan Museum, Villa Giulia, Rome, Italy. Photo by DEA/G. NIMATALLAH/DeAgostini, courtesy of Getty Images.

was vulnerable to attack from flank or rear (Crowley 2012: 49–66). Such a force, in the event of a serious threat, could deploy *pandēmei* (with all available men: Hdt. 1.62.3; Lys. 3.45; Thuc. 2.31.1, 4.42.3; Xen. *Hell.* 2.2.7) or, to meet more limited threats it could be mobilized by age groups (as at Sparta: Xen. *Hell.* 5.4.13, 6.4.17, *Lac.* 11.2) or *katalogos* (Ar. *Peace* 1172–85; Thuc. 6.26.2). The latter method involved the handpicking of men by their commanders, and while it was slow and cumbersome, it enabled a state with an amateur army to mobilize a high quality force containing a high proportion of experienced veterans (Crowley 2012: 22–39).

The hoplite phalanx did not fight alone, but was generally supported by light infantry and cavalry. In an emergency, those too poor to afford the two indispensable items of the panoply, namely the shield and spear, could serve as light infantry, but because that role required proficiency in weapons and tactics, *ad hoc* bodies of light infantry were of questionable worth (Pritchett 1991: 65–7; van Wees 2004: 61–71). Consequently, poleis often hired small contingents of professionals: *peltasts* (javelin-throwing skirmishers), slingers, and archers (Best 1969). Cavalry service was even more demanding: cavalrymen not only required proficiency with weapons (especially the javelin), they also had to deploy those weapons from a horse, as well as operate at speed and in formation (Hyland 2013: 512–26).

FIGURE 7.3: Athenian grave stele with relief sculpture of a cavalryman, known as the Dexileos Stele, fourth century BCE; Kerameikos Museum, Athens, Greece. Photo by DEA/G. NIMATALLAH/DeAgostini, courtesy of Getty Images.

Consequently, effective cavalry forces required a degree of competency that the Athenians, for instance, attained through state oversight of and financial support for a small cadre of semi-professionals recruited from the horse-owning elite (Bugh 1988; Worley 1994: 70–80).

Despite this focus on field armies, however, there was still a role for fortifications. Poleis were usually protected by walls, behind which non-combatants could shelter in the event of an invasion (Laurence 1979; Winter 1971). Some poleis, such as Athens and Megara, augmented these defenses with *makra teichē*, "long walls" that protected a corridor connecting the fortified urban center with the sea. These walls offered significant advantages, especially in Greece, where siege warfare remained under-developed until the Hellenistic age. Accordingly, while attempts to defeat fortifications were not unknown (for example during the siege of Plataia, 429–427 BCE: Thuc. 2.71–8, 3.20–4, 3.52–68), the Greeks tended to rely on circumvallation, that is, encircling their target with a siege wall and letting time and starvation do their grisly work. Long walls, however, were an effective counter-measure, because they allowed a state that was cut off from its own agricultural land to obtain supplies by sea, and this could be prevented only if the attacker went to the additional expense of imposing a naval blockade.

The ability to control home waters was therefore highly desirable, but also extremely expensive. The standard Greek warship, the trireme, was designed for maneuver and ramming, and while it was relatively inexpensive to construct, the cost of crewing such a vessel was exorbitant. Each ship was powered in combat by one hundred and seventy rowers arranged in three vertical tiers who had to work together if their ship was to maneuver effectively in combat (see esp. Thuc. 2.83–92, with Morrison and Williams 1968). Such skills did not come cheap, nor did those of the additional crew each trireme required, namely the naval professionals responsible for actually sailing the ship and the small contingent of marines and archers each vessel carried for protection. Big fleets, then, were a luxury only wealthy states such as Corinth, Corcyra, and Athens could afford, but, despite the cost, most coastal poleis and those located on islands maintained naval forces commensurate with their more modest economic resources, quite simply because their security depended on it (Kallet-Marx 1993).

Credible armed forces and strong fortifications (Arist. *Pol.* 7.1330b–31a; Dem. 14.11), however, only partly satisfied a state's security needs, and most sought additional protection through alliances with others. At the most basic level, poleis formalized reciprocal friendship with other states through open-ended *philia* agreements (Bauslaugh 1990: 36–69; Mitchel 1997: 28–44), but since this provided little positive benefit in the event of conflict, they also sought alliances that included more concrete obligations. According to Thucydides (1.44.1, 5.48.2), there were two distinct types of alliance: an *epimachia* was a defensive alliance which only required contracting parties to come to one another's defense if either was attacked by a third, whereas a *symmachia* was a full defensive and offensive alliance which required the contracting parties to "have the same friends and enemies". Actual practice, however, blurred the distinction between the two types of alliances. Leaving aside aggressive operations, both types of treaty provided participants with a means of increasing their aggregate power, since, once activated, all parties were obligated to provide military assistance to any ally under threat.[2]

Such obligations, naturally, were not always faithfully discharged. When faced with the prospect of war, some states offered excuses and avoided their obligations (for examples, see Bauslaugh 1990: 166–96), but such transgressions came with penalties. It was difficult, admittedly, for the Greeks to compel a state to honor its obligations, but, because interstate relations were governed by reciprocity, any state that failed to aid its allies might well find itself left in the lurch when those same allies reciprocated in kind (van Wees 1998: 13–49, 2004: 3–18; Hunt 2010: 72–107, 185–214). Alliances, then, were taken seriously by the Greeks, and they formed an effective way for a state to enhance its own security.[3]

The Greeks, then, had various means to enhance their security. Some states remained neutral, but the suspicion and isolation this entailed left them vulnerable. Others surrendered a degree of freedom in order to avoid the aggression of more powerful neighbors and obtain their protection. Those, however, with a realistic chance of maintaining their independence, placed their faith in credible armed forces, fortifications, strong allies, and a good reputation, and the way a state used these resources to respond to the aggression of another could also deter future aggression.

As Hunt observes (2010: 108–33, 185–214), a weak response to aggression encourages further aggression, whereas a forceful response reduces the likelihood of further attacks. This situation encouraged small states to fight back against larger opponents (Thuc. 2.71–8, 3.20–4, 3.52–68), but a polis could also deter aggression by exploiting its military victories to the fullest extent possible. Accordingly, the Greeks pursued beaten enemies mercilessly and those unable to evade risked massacre (Hdt. 6.78–81; Thuc. 3.94–8, 4.96, 7.73–85; van Wees 2006: 69–110), not simply because this served to deter future aggression from others, but also because a severely damaged rival lost not just the will but also the capacity for further aggression.

Of course, the poleis of Greece did not simply adopt a strategic posture and then passively await the evolution of events, they also tried to pre-empt aggression by engaging in a constant process of positioning to ensure that they were best placed to meet existing or emerging threats. Some states bandwagoned with emerging threats, but those who could tended to balance (Walt 1987), that is, ally themselves with other states to counter-balance the threat. For example, the rise of Athens after the Persian Wars was opposed by Sparta and Thebes, the rise of Sparta after the Peloponnesian War was opposed by Athens and Thebes, and the rise of Thebes after the Corinthian War was opposed by Athens and Sparta (Hunt 2010: 154–84; Strauss 1991: 189–210). Greece, then, was in many respects a self-balancing system, in which no one state could become predominant, and while this did not reduce the prevalence of conflict, it did allow the Greek poleis of the Classical age to maintain their independence.

The Hellenistic World

This independence, however, came at a price. An acephalous collection of micro-states was, by its very nature, vulnerable to more unified external threats. The Greeks' resistance to Persia was so undermined by particularism that they avoided subordination in the early fifth century BCE by the narrowest of margins (Hdt. 8.60–2; Lazenby 1993). Famously, their response to the rise of Macedon was even worse. Philip II isolated his opponents with a mixture of threats and promises, and although a coalition was eventually formed against him, it was too little, too late. As a result, the Greeks' endless internecine struggles ended in crushing military defeat at Chaironeia in 338 BCE, after which matters of peace, security, and deterrence were determined by the overarching authority of Philip of Macedon, and those who came after.

Alexander's conquest of the Persian empire and premature death created a geopolitical environment radically different from that which came before. This vast expanse was partitioned between Alexander's senior commanders (the *Diadochoi*, the "Successors"), and the super-states that emerged from their competition operated on a distinct dynamic determined by their political evolution. This produced kings whose legitimacy rested primarily upon military success, and while a common Macedonian identity, dynastic intermarriage, and incessant diplomacy went some way towards ameliorating conflict, the Hellenistic kings had to fight in order to survive.[4]

To do this, the Hellenistic super-states were able to draw on economic resources far beyond those of the traditional Greek powers. Macedonia, of course, was by no means poor, and the conquest of the East provided access to the wealth of Asia as well as agricultural land that could be tithed or settled in exchange for military service (Serrati 2007). As a result, the military forces deployed by the Hellenistic monarchs were simply unparalleled (Sekunda and de Souza 2007). On land, they were able to rely on huge armies whose ability to project power was derived not just from their size but also their enhanced professionalism (Roth 2007). Hellenistic navies were similarly impressive. As the fleet deployed by Demetrios I Poliorketes at Salamis (Cyprus) in 306 BCE reveals (Diod. Sic. 20.49–50), ships were bigger, carried more fighting men and in many cases deployed artillery for use against other ships and coastal defenses (Sekunda and de Souza 2007: 357–67). The advances in artillery that made this possible, particularly the widespread adoption of the torsion spring, also provided the Hellenistic monarchs with an unprecedented ability to attack and take fortified positions (Polyb. 5.99.7, with Roth 2007; Sabin and de Souza 2007: 399, 448–60).

Against such power, the poleis of Greece could do little. Some, like the twelve states of Achaia in the Peloponnese, were able to pool their sovereignty, and through the revival of the Achaian League, seek a degree of regional security and independence (Roy 2003). Most, however, accepted their irreversibly changed circumstances and sought security through subordination. Naturally, for the Greeks, given both their history and their culture, this was particularly unpalatable, and they sought to mask their subordination by recasting their successive Macedonian overlords as benefactors whose generosity they celebrated and honored (Billows 2007). This, of course, did nothing to change the reality of the relationship: the Macedonians eclipsed the power of the Greeks and their old enemies, the Persians, but despite their predatory predominance, even they were unable to check the rise of Rome.

ROME
Cecilia Ricci

Rome and Italy: Security, Deterrence, and Integration

Between the seventh and second centuries BCE the city-state of Rome enforced a process of unifying the Italian peninsula. In 493 BCE, the *foedus Cassianum*, signed by Rome and the Latin peoples in the aftermath of the Battle of Lake Regillus, represented a pact of non-aggression and mutual military assistance between the contracting parties.

The importance of the agreement is reflected in the longevity of its application (it shaped Roman-Latin relations of the fifth and a large part of the fourth century), as well as its role as a model for the treaties that individual populations would eventually sign with Rome. Each of these treaties was of a bilateral nature, between Rome and the allied signatory; thus, they were not based on a federation, and the allies involved did not share a common bond with each other. Indeed, the "unequal agreements" with Rome shattered

FIGURE 7.4: *The Battle of Lake Regillus*, by Tommaso Laureti, 1587–1594; Capitoline Museums, Rome, Italy. Google Art Project. Courtesy of Wikimedia Commons.

previous ethnic and federal units: the term *Italicus* was a Roman fiction, designating a multiform reality that may have been considered potentially hazardous (see Harris 1984b).[5] Nevertheless, despite their differences, the treaties did have some common characteristics: although autonomous, the allies undertook not to have their own foreign policy; they did not pay taxes, though they did provide military contingents to Rome's wars; and the ruling classes of their cities were guaranteed political dominance.

To Greek observers, as for instance Polybios in the Republican era or Appian in Imperial times, the capacity to assimilate a defeated enemy was a new and distinctive character of the Roman practice of government (see Eckstein 2006a and 2008). The bilateral agreement and the granting of citizenship were fundamental tools used by Rome to regulate relations with the cities and communities of ancient Italy, particularly between the fourth and third centuries. Initially, the citizenship granted was predominantly that of *sine suffragio*—limited citizenship, without the right to participate in political decision-making—understood by the Romans as granted to non-Latin-speaking neighboring cities and then eventually used as a first step towards obtaining full citizenship. For Rome, it was an instrument used to bind a subordinate community to itself (Gabba 1990).

Another key concept in the era of Rome's expansion in Italy was that of colonization. Rome had already begun to found *coloniae* during the royal period, though the "big Latin colonization" took place during the fourth and third centuries. While its primary purpose was security (a colony could be established to the side of or behind an enemy territory to ensure strategic connections), the sheer number of people involved was remarkable: in founding colonies, Rome may have lost citizens but she acquired allies, who were bound to provide troops when called upon.

By the end of the second century BCE, the full extent of the imbalance between the Mediterranean power of Rome and its Italian allies became clear; it was a consequence of continuous wars, the confiscation of lands, and a reformulation of the alliances that increasingly tipped in favor of Rome. In the Hannibalic War (the Second Punic War,

218–201 BCE)—as in the war against Pyrrhos (280–275 BCE)—the foreign invaders had miscalculated the degree to which the Italian populations shared a sense of common identity or common aspirations that might lead them to rise against Rome. However, the inferior position of the Italic peoples became clear as they were forced—with increasing difficulty—to provide men for the Roman army. They suffered from increasingly severe agricultural crises as small estate holders were overtaken by the establishment of larger estates (*latifundia*) incorporating entire portions of the *ager publicus* (public land).

The tipping point was a proposal by the tribune Tiberius Sempronius Gracchus in 133 BCE to enforce the existing law that prohibited large estate holders from occupying large tracts of the *ager publicus*, and gradually to grant *civitas* (citizenship) to the Italian allies.

The reactionary response against the proposal of Gracchus and the much broader reforms proposed by his brother Gaius a decade later unleashed a political conflict that was only (militarily) resolved a few decades later with the *bellum sociale*. During the Social War (90–88 BCE), a majority of the population of south-central Italy, along with some of the Gallic peoples, turned against the Romans. The outcome was Rome's progressive grant of citizenship to all communities, with the exception of Transpadane Gaul (Galsterer 2006).

By the Roman failure to adopt a more progressive attitude towards its Italian allies over the centuries, a network of alliances—or rather a series of unidirectional connections to the metropole—that was originally intended to promote Roman security and to deter uprisings in the Italian peninsula resulted in a conflict that for the first time in over a century threatened the Romans on their home soil. The most striking effect of the Italic rebellion was that, on this occasion, the insurgents were able to attain connections with each other

FIGURE 7.5: Portrait of Tiberius and Gaius Gracchus, by Jean-Baptiste Guillaume, 1848–1853; Musée D'Orsay, Paris, France. Courtesy of Wikimedia Commons.

that the Roman system of alliances and bilateral agreements had failed to (and were not intended to) produce. The Roman government was fully aware of this, and reacted extremely harshly: first, by destroying or closing the federal Italic sanctuaries, lively centers of economic social and political life, and then by initiating a complex process of administrative decentralization, imposing the municipal model upon various local situations.

The most impressive phenomenon of the municipalization process, alongside the provision of *civitas*, was the Social War's role as a powerful integration tool and disruptor of the status quo. It was a slow and complex process, linked with a need to demarcate the territories, to implant an urban center for administrative and judicial work, and to centralize where once there was scattered settlement. The expression "municipal empire" was coined to define this complex system: at this point in time, during the first century BCE, the geographical and political concepts of Italy were now wedded to the political and the legal-administrative (Gabba 1990).

Security Abroad: the War for Supremacy in the Mediterranean

The opening of hostilities with the western Mediterranean power of Carthage was preceded by the diplomacy of treaties, spanning from 509 to 241 BCE. According to Polybios (3.22), the first treaty was concluded in the first year of the Republic, and contained both military and commercial terms. It was an unequal treaty between Carthage and a Rome that had just experienced an institutional revolution, a transition from monarchy to newborn Republic, and one whose features were not yet fully defined. This inequality was evident: while the Carthaginians could still freely travel in the Tyrrhenian Sea, the limitations imposed on sea traffic for the Romans were remarkable.

The second treaty was in 348 BCE (Polyb. 3.24). The situation had changed after a century and a half, with the imbalance between the two parties narrowing. Carthage kept the freedom to trade and defend itself against anyone who threatened it (at this time, the Carthaginians faced the aggressive policies of Dionysios II of Syracuse in southern Italy and in the Tyrrhenian Sea); Rome kept its commercial prerogatives in the Tyrrhenian Sea and the ability to quell resistance from the Celts in central Italy (Palmer 1997). Both parties employed the peaceful means of diplomacy as a way of enhancing their own security, but as we have seen throughout this volume, the sacralized nature of treaties did not prevent one or both parties from breaking them.

From this point on, two distinct spheres of influence emerged within the western Mediterranean: North Africa/Sicily and Italy, respectively dominated by Carthage and by Rome. Within the Roman ruling class, a growing awareness of being encircled by Carthage emerged; in parallel, Carthage began to fear the danger of a Greek–Roman alliance for anti-Carthaginian purposes (Brizzi 2005). In the *symmachia* (alliance) between Rome and Carthage against Pyrrhos, which the two powers agreed to between 280 and 278 BCE (Polyb. 3.25), the political-military character prevails: we perceive the signals of a more elaborate stage of Roman diplomacy, as they assessed the usefulness of resorting to a new form of agreement to deter a common enemy. The alliance against Pyrrhos was the last diplomatic effort before the outbreak of conflict between Rome and Carthage: in Rome, according to Polybios, *hoi polloi* ("the people"), and not the Senate, decided on the opening of hostilities in 264 BCE. At the end of this First Punic War (264–241 BCE), Rome imposed on Carthage humiliating—in economic and political terms—conditions of peace: this as a strong reaction to the fear of being encircled by Carthage, and as an answer to the economic influence that Carthage had enjoyed in the Mediterranean until that time.

PEACE, SECURITY, AND DETERRENCE 137

For the first time, the Romans tied the idea of war as a profitable activity and the idea of security to that of subjugation of The Enemy.

In the approximately twenty years (241–218 BCE) between the First and Second Punic Wars, the process of change in mentality begun during the late part of the fourth century and the beginning of the third accelerated to the point of causing a crisis in traditional values and Roman attitudes towards wealth (Cassola 1983; see also Richardson 2008). From this time on the change became clear: the hard phase of Roman imperialism has begun. The propaganda message, more or less, was this: Roman rule guaranteed freedom from "foreign" rule (e.g., Carthaginian) and ensured control and security (in navigation, supplies, transport, etc.). Of course, these are slogans underlying a logic of domination: "freedom" was the freedom of Romans to continue the expansionist objectives in Italy, and security was the Roman guarantee of counting on the material support of the allies to pursue those goals.

Security and freedom became a distant memory during the disruptive years of the "kingdom of Hannibal" (217–203 BCE), when the Carthaginian general invaded Italy. In fact, he behaved much as Rome had, signing treaties with cities and peoples (Capua, Lokroi, a part of Tarentum, the Lucani, and some Etruscan cities), and tightening alliances with foreign states (Syracuse and the kingdom of Macedonia) (Toynbee 1965). Yet he failed to build an effective coalition around him with the Gauls, the Etruscans, and the Greek and Italic peoples of the peninsula. He also failed to create the conditions among the Italians for an alliance of their own against Rome.

In the eastern Mediterranean, from 200 BCE on, Rome found itself increasingly drawn into conflict among the Hellenistic kingdoms, the Greek federal states, and the few remaining single polities—such as Rhodes—of any significance. Many of the Hellenistic states turned to Rome in search of their own security; Rome, in turn, initially sought alliances in the east in order to offset threats to its own dominance in the west, such as Illyrian piracy in the Adriatic or a meeting of minds between Hannibal of Carthage and Philip V of Macedon. Opinions in Rome were divided: was it best to encourage a perimeter of free and grateful Greek states who would act in the interests of Rome, or would it serve Rome better to exercise direct military authority in the Greek world? The tension between these viewpoints dominated foreign policy debate in Rome in the first half of the second century, but ultimately the direct approach—and the enrichment opportunities it offered to military commanders—won out (Harris 1991).

In the second century, the character and intensity of Roman warmaking changed, as did the nature of the armies and their leaders and, in a momentous and irreversible change, the very concept and rules of conflict. The *bellum iustum* ("just war") of the first centuries of the Republic, as well as the "chivalrous conception" of international relations that it presupposed (Brizzi 2005), now gave way, in the eyes of many, to unscrupulousness, to stratagem and deceit. The words of Livy (42.47.8) are à propos:

Occasionally a greater advantage is gained for the time being by trickery than by courage, but final and lasting conquest of the spirit overtakes one from whom the admission has been extorted that he has been conquered, not by craft or accident, but by the hand-to-hand clash of force in a proper and righteous war (*iustum ac pium bellum*). Thus the older men, who were less well pleased by the new and over-sly wisdom (*nova sapientia*); however, that part of the senate to whom the pursuit of advantage was more important than that of honour, prevailed . . .

—42.47.8–9

138   A CULTURAL HISTORY OF PEACE

As we saw earlier, the changes in Roman foreign policy in the second century BCE—and the increasing importation of wealth and the resultant inequities—eventually sparked the reform movement of the Gracchi, the uprising of the Italic peoples against Rome, and ultimately the Roman civil wars of the first century BCE. Rome's strategies of security and deterrence failed badly when it came to maintaining peace among the ranks of its own elite.

Security and Deterrence in Augustan Rome

When the Roman civil wars ended with the Battle of Actium in 31 BCE, Octavian (soon to be Augustus) was honored as a bringer of peace. The closure of Janus' temple; the establishment of peace "on land and sea" (a formula already employed by the Hellenistic rulers); the altars of Peace Augusta (*Ara Pacis Augustae*) in Rome and in the provinces: these were all intended as symbols of a definitive end to the permanent conflict of the previous century.

During the Republican era, the subjugation of the Italic peoples had been marked by the *foedera* and the progressive and differentiated granting of the *civitas*; at the end of the conflicts with the great Mediterranean powers (Carthage, Macedonia, Syria), the borders of Roman domination were integrated into a pan-Mediterranean system of security by diplomatic relations and peace treaties. The restoration of order to Italy and the provinces after the civil wars did not change the essential foreign policy of Rome. During the first two centuries of the empire, wars were not lacking, and were characterized by an intolerance and ferocity not dissimilar to that seen in the past. Peace within the borders of the empire was not matched by peace with the empire's neighbors. With Augustus, the *pax Romana* was thus both a slogan of imperial propaganda and an ideological construct (Rich 2003).

Within literary and philosophical circles during the late Republic and early Principate,[6] terms such as *tranquillitas* (quiet, but also peace) or *concordia* (accord, harmony), along with the imperial *virtus* par excellence—*pax*—became key items of vocabulary within cultural debate. These concepts were fed by Hellenistic philosophies, with reference to the state of mind produced by a state of uncertainty—such as that created by the civil wars of the first century BCE—and a subsequent need to gain new balance, in private as well as public life. *Securitas* also gradually gathered pace and gained full value in communicative language. In terms of artistic, monetary, and epigraphic representation, it also signified (along with *pax*) a restoration of normal life after long decades of conflict. The close connection between the two concepts of *pax* and *securitas* during the Augustan age appears in the iconographic and epigraphic program achieved in the ancient city of Praeneste (now Palestrina): the decurions and the people of the City dedicated a richly decorated altar to the *pax Augusta* and/or *Augusti* (*CIL* XIV 2898 = *ILS* 3787), and another one to the *securitas Augusta* and/or *Augusti* (*CIL* XIV 2899 = *ILS* 3788). *Securitas*, usually a mere ancillary motif, in comparison with the great theme that includes all of the *pax Augusta*,[7] here is given equal dignity.

The existence of an Augustan plan for the security of Rome and the imperial family can be reconstructed from (seemingly isolated) episodes and interventions. It matured gradually, predominantly responding to the daily needs of the city's inhabitants and its *princeps*, and was destined to undergo adjustments after the death of the founder of the Principate. The first tool employed was law. Augustus proceeded to define one of the oldest notions of political and Roman legal culture, *maiestas* (treason) and the *crimen*

FIGURE 7.6a and 7.6b: Coin of Nero (64–68 CE); obverse: head of Nero and legend NERO CLAVD CAESAR AVG GER P M TR P IMP P P; reverse: figure of Securitas, seated right, on throne, resting head against right hand and holding short sceptre in left; in front, lighted and garlanded altar, legend SECVRITAS AVGVSTI S C II. *RIC* 1 (2nd edn) Nero 406, ANS 1957.172.1548. Courtesy of the American Numismatic Society.

connected to it (crime of treason) (Levi 1969).[8] *Maiestas* was placed in a political and religious context, and included not just the Roman state in the persons of its magistrates (*maiestas populi Romani*), but also the *princeps* and his family (*principis et domus Augustae*). Augustus' legislative action appears to have coincided with institutional actions, in particular with a security plan based on prevention and deterrence that was put into effect on two separate but converging levels: the organization of military forces to ensure his own safety; and an intervention in the urban fabric to ensure the security of individuals in public places.

With the unscrupulousness that characterized much of his work, though with formal respect for ancient traditions, Augustus created the basis for infringing the principle that forbade soldiers to be stationed in Rome, inside the *pomerium*, the sacred boundary of the city. Acting in substantial continuity with the commanders of the late Republic, Augustus recruited private bodyguards, the *corporis custodes*. He wanted to link a new Praetorian Guard with a representation of imperial power, wherever it was manifested, in the imperial residence as in public spaces, in Rome and outside of it, during his travels within Italy and abroad (Sablayrolles 2001). Several factors allowed the people of Rome and the Senate to accept the profound shifts envisaged in this plan: the gradual nature of the process, along with what can be called (the definition is mine) "an integrated system", where military and paramilitary forces, officials and their subordinates were also called on to participate and contribute, according to their skills and abilities. The Augustan plan would be accomplished within a few decades and, with no significant changes, maintain the original *ratio* (principle) for at least two centuries.

As for the Roman provinces, peace was secured through watchful governance and the strategic posting of military forces. The extension of Roman citizenship to non-Romans throughout the empire was a significant integrative tool that operated to discourage local loyalties from becoming resistance struggles, but the overwhelming military might of Rome was also a substantial deterrent. Occasionally dissatisfaction with

Roman rule spilled over into action, most notably in the case of the Jewish resistance of the later first century CE, but in general, the first two centuries of empire were marked by peace within and a successful combination of diplomatic and military action without.

Diplomacy and War, Security and Deterrence at the Limits of the Empire

The northern and eastern frontiers of the Roman Empire presented quite different sets of challenges: beyond the provincial territories to the north, there was simply the *barbaricum*, with its only partial equilibrium. Pressures from the Germanic tribes began to be felt by the end of the second century CE, and for a long time imperial policies followed a traditional line of maintaining the security of the frontiers by military means. In the east, however, the Romans faced a powerful and structured empire—first the Parthians, then the Sassanid Persians—that was not dissimilar to their own and that demanded quite a different set of international behaviors (Millar 1982; Gabba 1989).

Under Trajan (r. 98–117 CE), the empire reached its maximum expansion, surrounded by natural boundaries and protected by the presence of client kingdoms that were tasked to deal with any low-intensity threats beyond the borders. The legions, distributed in the provinces considered to be at risk, acted as a deterrent against possible attacks. The function of the border armies, and more generally the very concept of a "frontier" (*limes*), have in the last forty years been the subject of intense debate among historians of the Roman world, fueling what is commonly known as the "Strategy Debate" (for an in-depth analysis, see Wheeler 2007). This debate originated in a book written in the mid-1970s by Edward N. Luttwak, a political analyst and US government advisor (Luttwak 1976).

Chiefly interested in the military situation of the Roman Empire during the third and fourth centuries CE, Luttwak ascribed extreme rationality to the defensive policy of Rome. He also used concepts and expressions in his analysis—such as "in-depth-defense" or "systemic threat"—that until then had never been used in studies of Roman imperial policy. Luttwak argued that over the course of four centuries, the Roman Empire went through three phases in its defensive program. The first, which coincided with the Julio-Claudian era (30 BCE–68 CE), was characterized by the presence along the borders of temporary camps and client states that were entrusted with the policy of border security ("shifting zones of expansion"). The second, which coincided with the second and third centuries CE, saw the replacement of temporary camps with permanent ones ("static defensive frontiers" for forward defense) and the gradual disappearance of client kingdoms. The last phase, during the Late Roman Empire (from the fourth century on) was one of in-depth defense, with the development of a military area dotted with fortified points and military forces; enemy incursions were now met and defeated within the militarized zones.

Since the 1990s, for various reasons and with differing methods of analysis, Luttwak's theories have been hotly disputed. The most systematic and coherent contrast with Luttwak's rationalist vision is that of Charles Whittaker, who believes the Roman frontier was largely a zone of interaction between Romans and "barbarians" (Whittaker 1983). Whittaker argues that the use of the term "strategy" in relation to the actions of Rome in the border areas undermines the character of the *limes* as a place of exchange between different worlds, which "represented a compromise between the range of conquest and the economy of rule" (Whittaker 1994: 85). It also belittles the fundamental economic,

PEACE, SECURITY, AND DETERRENCE 141

social, and cultural function of the *limes*, even aside from politics (for a general perspective see Forni 1987).

The character and security functions of the border area vary depending on whether we consider the western or eastern portions of the empire. The scenario that Whittaker describes is substantially that of the frontier between the western empire and its northern boundaries, particularly those along the Rhine and the Danube. The eastern *limes* maintained its own specificity, primarily through geography. Its extent and structure—a long broken line, adapted to the natural boundaries—was influenced by the presence of large desert areas, while military camps were located in urban centers, where possible, and/or along the main roads. Significant also was the existence of a strong and unified imperial power on the other side of the eastern frontier.

The changes to the eastern borders during the Flavian period (69–96 CE, a time of transition, according to Luttwak's theory, between the first and second phases of the defensive strategy of Rome) were not so much the sign of a different military-strategic orientation as an adaptation to shifting political conditions. When the network of semi-independent client kingdoms on which Rome had relied for centuries was absorbed into the imperial system, the emperor's response was based on a redistribution of military forces and improvements to infrastructure: the construction of new ports in the East, along with the reorganization of existing ones; the establishment of a naval base for the new *classis Syriaca* (Syrian fleet) at the site of Seleukeia Pieria, the port of Syrian Antioch; and the strengthening of roads and waterways (Dart 2016).

The other factor affecting the character of the eastern *limes* was the presence of the kingdom of the Parthians, and subsequently the Persian Sassanid dynasty (ruled 224–651 CE). Their empire was the only one to remain for a long time independent of the Roman Empire, apart from short periods of formal submission of part of its territory at the time of the Antonine emperors. Its capital Ktesiphon had been repeatedly destroyed and rebuilt, but its power over many allied and auxiliary desert populations remained undisputed even in times of internal civil war between the lords of Persia. Moreover, the Parthian Empire retained part of the heritage of the ancient empires of the Achaimenids, Alexander, and his Successors. The great imperial dynasties, especially the Sassanids, gave the empire a "mission" to retrieve and reunite the Persian Empire.

In 53 BCE, the defeat of the Roman general Crassus by the Parthians at Carrhae had cost the lives of 20,000 men, in addition to their general, and the loss of the legionary standards. The consequences of the conflict went far beyond the military defeat, and produced a reconceptualization of the empire and its limits. The Romans had long pondered a response to the affront they received, as well as the appropriate attitude towards an empire of equivalent strength and power. The *imperatores* often opted for military campaigns (first Julius Caesar, then Marc Antony, and centuries later Lucius Verus, Severus, and Caracalla), though never with entirely satisfactory results.

More often, the diplomatic solution proved to be the most effective one. Thus Augustus, in 20 BCE, proceeded to rearrange the kingdom of Armenia (a dispute that occupied both the Roman and the Parthian empires from the time of Marc Antony up to Trajan, and took considerable investment in terms of political commitment and infrastructure). He reached an agreement with the Parthian king Phraates IV, and one of his greatest diplomatic victories was to negotiate the return of the eagles lost at Carrhae. Several decades later, in 66 CE, the emperor Nero gave evidence of the high profile the east had in Roman perceptions of their empire and its frontiers by inviting the Armenian ruler Tiridates to Rome to receive the diadem from the emperor's own hand. The ceremony also underscored the importance of Roman *maiestas*, in its literal sense of "greaterness": the semiotics of Nero's actions successfully communicated the superior power and authority of Rome (Tac. *Ann.* 15.25–30, 16.23–4).

The reasons for Rome's choice to solve the question of its eastern borders diplomatically, and not by force of arms, were many and complex. One of them was the antiquity and degree of civilization reached by the Parthian Empire; another, its internal structure and the manner that the Parthians had adopted for settling internal disputes. Rome could not help but take note. Fundamentally, though, in spite of its ability to control the Mediterranean littoral and much of its hinterland (including a significant portion of Europe), imperial Rome was simply not in a position to challenge effectively the military might of a west Asian empire. Although the Parthian dynasty was itself in the third century CE overwhelmed by the increasing supremacy of the resurgent Persians under the Sassanid dynasty, neither the western Roman nor, ultimately, the eastern Byzantine empire was able (or willing) to press its military claims against a power of this calibre. Like Charlemagne centuries later, the Romans had to recognize their limits and substitute diplomacy for mastery.

CONCLUSION

In the imperfect world of human societies, peace is most often safeguarded through military and diplomatic vigilance: security measures that may involve physical fortifications, standing armies, defensive treaties, and pre-emptive strikes; and deterrence based on propaganda, posturing, and the possibility of total annihilation. The ancient custom of *andrapodismos* might be compared to today's nuclear threat; both Greeks and Romans could be ruthless in dealing with their defeated enemies, at least in part because they thought of it as a deterrent to others. When the Athenians sent a force against the little island of Melos in 416 BCE, the Melians tried to argue that they were so insignificant that surely they could just be left alone; the Athenian response was that, by leaving the Melians alone, they would be incurring harm to themselves, since they would appear weak in the eyes of others (Thuc. 5.94–7).

Much has been said in this volume about the security and peace aspects of integration and unification. Here, as things turned out, the Greeks and the Romans diverged widely from each other. In spite of various alliances, federations, and examples of outright imperial rule, the Greeks never unified, and long-lasting peace between and among the Greek city-states remained forever elusive. For the Romans, on the other hand, integration was a priority from the beginning of their expansion throughout the Italian peninsula, although it was not until the Social War of the first century BCE that they acknowledged the importance of equality of status for those integrated. Mythic stories of early Rome— the Trojan Aeneas' alliances with the Arcadian ruler Evander and the Latin King Latinus, or the amalgamation of the Romans and the Sabines through the mediation of the Sabine women—reflect this Roman penchant for peace and security through integration and unification.

CHAPTER EIGHT

Peace as Integration

PAUL BURTON

Peace achieved through integration in antiquity was less a conscious policy by statesmen than it was an occasional unintended consequence of security-seeking behavior by states. If purposes there were behind integrative structures, they were primarily aggrandizing, often defensive, and sometimes for specific purposes, such as frontier rationalization. Outside of the realm of propaganda and ideology, or as *post hoc* justification for imperial expansion, they were hardly ever for the intended goal of achieving stability or peace. Some ancient integrative systems, however, exhibited some of the same tendencies as those described by Geir Lundestad (1998) in his account of the US's encouragement of European integration after the Second World War, whereby a united western Europe under US hegemony (via the NATO alliance) would successfully contain the Soviet Union and the Warsaw Pact nations. So too the Romans, for example, successfully contained and deterred the westward expansion of Antiochos III's Seleukid empire for several years by guaranteeing the freedom of a network of Greek states in 196 BCE. This chapter explores the phenomenon of peace through such integrative strategies, regardless of whether peace was the intended goal of integration or a concrete but unintended consequence of it, across three broad areas: empires, leagues of states, and federal states.

EMPIRES

Peace achieved through empire building in the ancient world was predicated upon a superior state's control of the internal and foreign affairs of subordinate states. This conforms well to Michael Doyle's definition of empire: "a system of interaction between two political entities, one of which, the dominant metropole, exerts political control over the internal and external policy—the effective sovereignty—of the other, the subordinate periphery" (1986: 12). Metropolitan control was usually maintained through elite representatives of the metropole ("governors," "satraps") using local collaborators to keep the "provincial," subordinate populations under control. Strong metropolitan leadership, fear of the metropole or of the alternatives to it, circulation of gifts and favors between center and periphery, economic prosperity, religious toleration, and ideological cohesion all served to keep the subordinate periphery in line, and some ancient empires reasonably stable and peaceful for extended periods.

Crucial to the investigation of peace as a by-product of empire are the motives for empire. Over a century of study in the field has determined that imperialisms may be broadly classified as metrocentric, pericentric, or systemic in nature. Most ancient empires exhibit metrocentric tendencies: "the objectless disposition on the part of the state to unlimited forcible expansion" (Schumpeter 1991: 7). Occasionally, however, pericentric motivation is apparent, most frequently when chaos in the frontier zone of an empire threatens the security of that empire's peripheral possessions and/or profit, drawing the metropole's (usually military) attention to the source of the problem and resulting in the re-establishment of peace and the expansion of the imperial periphery into the former frontier zone. This dynamic, as will be seen, is most relevant to the present discussion: chaos and disorder, through such interventions, were routinely replaced by peace and order.

Imperialism theories of the systemic type argue that all states are functionally similar units predisposed to the same (security-seeking, warlike) behavior within a brutal, Hobbesian international system of states. This system is one of formal anarchy, and "because some states may at any time use force, all states must be prepared to do so—or live at the mercy of their militarily more vigorous neighbors" (Waltz 1979: 102). This theory (also called Realism) has its roots in classical antiquity in the famous formulation of the Greek historian Thucydides, whose Athenians proclaim before the people of Melos in 416 BCE that "the strong do what they can, the weak acquiesce" (5.89), the first formulation of the "might makes right" doctrine.

Ancient empires that were to all appearances established for the sake of trade or other economic purposes were at least partially motivated by maintaining peaceful conditions conducive to commerce. The earliest Aegean "empires"—if they may be labeled as such, given that they are known to us almost solely through archaeology—may have been commercial rather than annexationist. The later Greek literary-historical tradition remembered the mythical Cretan king Minos as having established a thalassocracy, a sea empire, extending throughout the Aegean (Hdt. 1.171, 3.122; Thuc. 1.4). According to these reports, Minos was the first to build a navy, with which he conquered and colonized the islands of the Aegean; he imposed tribute and military service on the inhabitants, subjected them to his sons as governors, and, most crucially, cleared the Aegean of pirates to protect his growing trade profits. The archaeologist Arthur Evans identified this maritime empire with the civilization he discovered on the island of Crete, which he duly labeled "Minoan." Whether the archaeologically visible process of widespread Minoan acculturation in the southern Aegean between ca. 1700 and 1450—"Minoanization" (Broodbank 2004; Davis 2008: 200)—was in fact accompanied by territorial conquest and colonization cannot be determined on present evidence (but see Davis 2008: 201–2; Betancourt 2008: 217).

The dominant civilization in the Aegean area that followed the Minoans was dubbed "Mycenaean" by their archaeological discoverer, Heinrich Schliemann, after the most archaeologically significant of their cultural sites. Unfortunately, the surviving Mycenaean texts (the Linear B tablets) are no more than inventory lists, and reveal almost nothing significant about Mycenaean political structures, much less the existence of a Mycenaean territorial empire. The Greek literary epic tradition, including Homer's *Iliad*, remembered a king of Mycenae, Agamemnon, as the most powerful of the Achaian (Greek) kings, and leader of an expedition against Troy to recover Helen, the kidnapped wife of his brother, the Spartan king Menelaos. If the "Ahhiya" and "Ahhiyawa" mentioned in fourteenth- to thirteenth-century BCE palace records of the Anatolian Hittite Empire may be identified with Homer's Achaians, that is, Schliemann's Mycenaeans (as Mee 2008: 374), then they too engaged in piratical kidnapping raids (Podany 2010: 262). Taken together, the evidence of the epic tradition and the Hittite documents suggests that the Mycenaeans were above all dedicated to pillage and destruction rather than to empire building. The archaeology may attest to widespread Mycenaean trade contacts, extending as far as Egypt, Cilicia, Cyprus, north Syria, and the Levant in the East, and Ischia, Malta, and Sicily in the West (Blegen 1975: 181–4; Mee 2008), but whether state-sponsored or

PEACE AS INTEGRATION

FIGURE 8.1: The ancient Near East in the Bronze Age. From Wittke et al. (eds.), *Historical Atlas of the Ancient World*, 2009. Courtesy of Brill.

independent merchants were responsible for this activity is unclear, to say nothing of whether Mycenaean Greeks colonized these places (Mee 2008: 366, 367, 382).

On the other hand, Hittite documents reveal that at some point in the late fourteenth century, the "Ahhiyawa" were part of a network of major Near Eastern territorial empires (along with New Kingdom Egypt, the Hittite Empire in Asia Minor, the kingdom of Mittani in north Syria, Kassites in Babylonia, and the Elamite kingdom beyond the Tigris) that maintained a rough balance of power between them through diplomacy (Podany 2010). Given that the Near East had always been dominated by perpetually warring regional empires of the metrocentric type since the rise of the Sumerians in the third millennium BCE, this— "history's first international system" (Cline and Graham 2011: 23)—was a remarkable achievement.

In terms of the "peace dividend" of Mycenaean power, the projection of their power outward (as may be suggested by the Achaian attack on Troy in the later Greek epic tradition, and the piratical kidnapping raids of the Ahhiya/wa mentioned in the Hittite documents) may have had the effect of limiting internecine strife among the Mycenaean states. The massive fortification walls at the major Mycenaean sites, most scholars now agree, were built for display and prestige rather than for defensive purposes (Hammond 1967: 47; Sansone 2004: 5); later Greeks marveled at the masonry, dubbing it "Cyclopean," since they thought it could only have been built by the one-eyed giants of Homer's *Odyssey*, the Cyclopes.

The temporary, loose-knit coalition of kings against Troy may indicate that Mycenaean power had always been far more diffuse and decentralized than that of its contemporary empires to the east. In any case, the Hittite records suggest that the Mycenaeans contributed as well as fell victim to the general Near Eastern and eastern Mediterranean chaos at around this time caused by the mysterious "peoples from beyond the sea," as the Egyptian documents call them. After that, a profound darkness falls across the eastern Mediterranean and the Near East, and the Mycenaean civilization was swept away along with the Near Eastern empires.

The empires that emerged from the wreckage were empires of conquest of the metrocentric type. The most important of these, for the present purposes, is that of the Persian Achaimenids. The founder of the dynasty, Cyrus "the Great" (r. 559–530 BCE),[1] seems to have been a conqueror of the "objectless dispositional" type described by Schumpeter. Always on campaign, Cyrus conquered the largest empire the world had ever seen, stretching from the shores of the Aegean Sea to the Jaxartes River (Syr Darya). He died fighting in what is today Kazakhstan against the central Asian Scythians under their formidable queen Tomyris. The biography and personality of Cyrus, the first Persian *shah-an-shah* ("king of kings"), became the archetype and paradigm for his successors. The Greek historiographical tradition thus regarded warfare and expansion as a fundamental and inescapable cultural disposition of the Persians. The Greek historian Herodotos, our main source for the Persian Empire, has the Persian king Xerxes say that the god (*theos*) compels him personally not to fall short of his predecessors in expanding the Persian Empire, which then becomes the rationale for his attack on Greece (Hdt. 7.8α1–2).

Ironically, Xerxes' defeat at the hands of a coalition of European Greek city-states marked the end of Achaimenid expansion. The management of their own far-flung empire was heavily contingent upon informal ties of loyalty between the shahs and their dependent nobles, usually of Persian stock, sometimes members of the royal family, but occasionally members of local indigenous elites. These satraps managed the twenty territorial units into which the empire was divided, usually called satrapies. Under strong

FIGURE 8.2: Bas-relief of a four-winged guardian figure representing Cyrus the Great; Pasargadae, Fars, Iran. Photo by Babak Tafreshi/National Geographic, courtesy of Getty Images.

and vigorous kings, the satraps could be relied upon to govern in the king's name, which amounted to maintaining military control, remitting taxes and tribute to the king, and, when called upon, to muster military forces for royal campaigns (Waters 2014: 100–3).

Satraps typically governed their vast holdings through local elites drawn from local populations according to local traditions of command and control (Cline and Graham 2011: 99). An inscription from Egypt commemorating a successful intervention of a local former naval commander (and defector to the Persians) named Udjahorresnet with Cyrus' successor and conqueror of Egypt, Cambyses, shows this dynamic in action: Cambyses upholds local religious and political traditions, promotes justice, and protects the weak from the strong; in return, Udjahorresnet and his family prove reliable collaborators, and are publicly and richly rewarded for their loyalty (Wiesehöfer 2009: 71; Cline and Graham 2011: 1–3; Waters 2014: 57).

Given the vast distances and slowness of communications across the empire, satrapal loyalty could be variable, and it is perhaps for this reason that a strong ideology of peace and unity emerged in Achaimenid propaganda. Multilingual royal inscriptions and tomb and palace reliefs from across the empire "emphasize the royal idea of the *pax Achaemenidica*, that is, the god-given and universal state of peace that was guaranteed by the kings and desired by their subjects. Opposition to this arrangement, in terms of the

Great Kings' announcements, would have seemed nothing short of irresponsible" (Wiesehöfer 2009: 67; cf. Wiesehöfer 2007: 124–7 and Brosius 2012). To maintain this peace, routine exploitation was necessary: a good king had to demonstrate *polydoria*, "open-handedness," in his bestowal of gifts and benefits to his satraps and dependents, and land grants to his soldiers. This was a fairly simple matter as long as the empire was expanding and the spoils of victory filled the kings' treasuries. In more settled circumstances, routine, highly centralized extraction of surplus production had to suffice. Agricultural exploitation was intensified and subject to imperial control to a greater degree than it had been under previous Near Eastern empires. Taxes and tribute in the forms of coinage, bullion, and treasure collected by the satraps' subordinates flowed into the Persian capitals, and then flowed out again to finance regal munificence (Wiesehöfer 2009: 79–83).

The overall impression created by the Persian documents is of a culturally diverse yet politically unified empire. The Persian kings compensated for the difficulties of managing their far-flung domains by taking advantage of the local knowledge of "indigenous

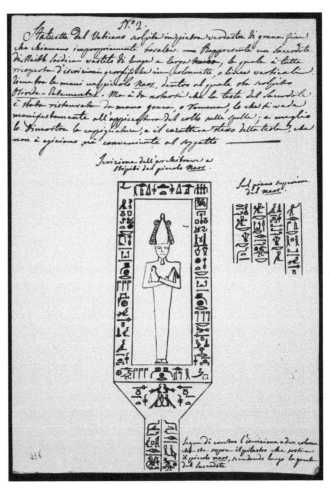

FIGURE 8.3: Naophoros statue of Udjahorresnet, showing part also of the hieroglyphic record of his deeds; from Ippolito Rosellini, *Monuments of Egypt and Nubia*, 1832–1844. Photo by DeAgostini, courtesy of Getty Images.

specialists" (Wiesehöfer 2009: 86), who in turn were compensated by the kings' open-handed generosity and, above all, the peace and stability that the empire guaranteed. The ideology of the Persian Empire "aimed at integrating the elites of the provinces within an empire-wide ruling class structure, even at integrating subjugated peoples into a kind of imperial 'symbolic universe'," in which local and imperial identities were combined in such a way that the empire's inhabitants took pride in their membership in "the most successful and prosperous political entity of [their] time" (Wiesehöfer 2009: 89–90).

It is against this backdrop that the Macedonian Alexander the Great's (r. 336–323) conquest of and method of rule over the domains of the last Achaimenid shah, Darius III, must be understood. Although Persian power yielded to the superior Macedonian military technology and daring personal tactical style of Alexander, the truly significant legacy of Persian rule—the shahs' ability "to make cultural diversity serve the needs of imperial unity" (Wiesehöfer 2009: 86)—endured under Macedonian control. Alexander largely left the satrapal system in place, as well as those Persian satraps who came over to him voluntarily. He also appears to have taken steps towards creating an integrated Persian–Macedonian elite to govern the empire over the long term. He incorporated Persian officers into his army and Persian nobles into his entourage; he began a program of training Persian youths in the Macedonian military fashion; he married the daughters of the last two Persian shahs as well as a Baktrian princess, Roxane, and arranged for ninety-two of his officers to marry Median and Persian women; at a banquet at Opis, he prayed that Persians and Macedonians might rule the empire together in harmony; and, most notoriously, he adopted elements of Persian dress and court ritual.

However, anachronistic notions that Alexander was promoting the "unity of mankind" or cultural equality between Macedonians and Persians must be resisted. After all, his adoption of Persian dress, according to Appian, was simply good policy: by doing so, he hoped not to seem completely alien to his eastern subjects (Arr. *Anab.* 7.29.4). At the banquet at Opis, Alexander's guests were carefully seated according to ethnicity, those nearest to him being the Macedonians, followed by the Persians, followed by the other peoples of the empire. The mixed Persian–Macedonian marriages, moreover, included no male Persian-female Macedonian pairings. Alexander may have trained local youths in Macedonian fashion, but when he discharged 10,000 Macedonian soldiers, he refused to allow them to take the children they fathered with local women back to Macedon for fear this might make trouble in the kingdom. Finally, shortly before he died, Alexander removed all but three Persian satraps, executing a number of them for corruption and disloyalty while he was far away on his Indian campaign, and replacing them with Macedonians.

But as the latter evidence indicates, while Alexander was off conquering the known world from the late 330s to the mid-320s, the Persian satrapal system for the most part held together the way it always had, and when a crisis of loyalty occurred (as had invariably occurred when the *shah-an-shah* was away in some remote corner of his empire), it was quickly and easily dealt with. It should also be noted that when the real threat to Alexander's personal power came, it was at the hands of his mutinous army and his own self-destructive appetites. The satrapal system was resilient. Unfortunately, the lack of a viable successor upon his death unleashed over a century and a half of almost continuous warfare across Alexander's former empire.

After a generation of fighting, Alexander's surviving associates declared themselves kings, and, according to one source, carved up his empire "as if it had been a great carcass, and took each his portion" (Plut. *Demetr.* 30). The power balance was never

FIGURE 8.4: Portrait of Alexander the Great, fourth century BCE; Archaeological Museum, Pella, Greece. Photo by DeAgostini, courtesy of Getty Images.

accepted as desirable or acknowledged as inevitable; most of the Hellenistic kings (and queens) took Alexander as their model, and regarded themselves as worthy of repeating his achievements, opportunity permitting. In the 163 years between Alexander's death and 160 BCE, there were only around five years in which none of the major kingdoms was involved in war (Eckstein 2006a: 83). The prevalence of war was in part driven by systemic pressures: this was a particularly militarized, competitive, anarchic international system (Eckstein 2006a: 94–116). But at the unit level, internally, the kingdoms were constantly on a war footing for other reasons. The successor kingdoms were technically usurper states. The dynasties had come to power through conquest of "spear-won land" (*doriktētos chōra*), not inheritance from Alexander, and so the acquisition of legitimacy through military victory became habitual—and necessary.

The other unit-level reason for constant warfare was that Hellenistic kingdoms were gift-devouring war machines. To keep his troops and his close circle of retainers happy and loyal, the king had to keep up a constant stream of gifts and donatives; the only way for that to happen (aside from taxation and internal exploitation) was to make continuous external war in the hopes of seizing enormous amounts of booty (Austin 1986). Internal peace in these circumstances was hard to come by. Two further internal problems endemic to the Egyptian and Seleukid kingdoms were intra-familial disputes over the succession and indigenous revolt. The latter was mainly caused by the imposition of an exclusive Greco-Macedonian elite on local populations (the opposite of the Persian shahs' and Alexander's approach), aggravated in the Egyptian case by ruthless economic exploitation,

PEACE AS INTEGRATION

and in the Seleukid case by the strong breakaway tendencies of a far-flung empire. Therefore, only in the direst circumstances—when population and resources were simply exhausted and had to recover for the kingdoms to remain sustainable into the next generation—did the kings allow for some respite. It was into this violent formal anarchy in the eastern Mediterranean that the Italian city-state of Rome was drawn, beginning in the late third century BCE.

It is perhaps best to begin a discussion of Roman imperialism with a few observations on how the Romans themselves regarded their imperial activity. In the poet Vergil's famous formulation, Rome's mission was "to set the force of habit upon peace, to spare those who submit and crush in war the haughty" (*Aeneid* 6.852–3).[2] Cicero believed that Rome established a "protectorate over the entire world" by defending "its allies and provinces with justice and good faith" (*De Officiis* 2.27; cf. Cic. *Rep.* 3.35). Of course, some of Rome's enemies may have seen things differently, such as the otherwise unknown Caledonian chieftain Calgacus, who, in a fictional speech attributed to him by the Roman author Tacitus, famously said "To robbery, butchery, and rapine, they give the lying name of 'empire'; they create a desolation and they call it peace." (*Agricola* 30; Mattingly translation, slightly adapted). Whichever view is closest to the truth—the evidence supports both—peace was central to Roman imperial ideology, and was perhaps a significant driver of Roman imperialism itself.

During the middle Republican period (roughly 264–150 BCE), Rome imposed an end to the perpetual cycle of Hellenistic interstate warfare not through persistent application of force but through brief, massive interventions followed by withdrawals of troops, attention, and interest. Diplomacy endured, however: the Roman senate managed its relations with Greek cities and federal Leagues as well as Hellenistic kingdoms large and small through treaties of alliance and, more commonly, informal friendships, *amicitiae* (Burton 2011). It was ultimately this network of mostly small states that was able to bring Rome, a fourth major hegemonic power, into the precariously balanced tripolar system of Hellenistic kingdoms, and thereby destabilize and disrupt it. Following the first major successful Roman intervention against Macedon in 200 BCE, Rome left behind a network of friendly Greek states whose freedom the Romans guaranteed in exchange for their loyalty and commitment to the Roman peace. Dissatisfied with the Roman arrangements, the Aitolian League provoked a Roman war with the Seleukid king Antiochos III; Roman victory in this conflict resulted in the establishment of Roman unipolar hegemony (Eckstein 2006a, 2008), and was followed by an unprecedented twenty-year period of peace among the great Hellenistic powers. Roman power was periodically challenged thereafter in the East, but never again as seriously.

The provincialization of the empire, which had been ongoing on a small scale in the West since the late third century, intensified during the late Republic and was systematized under the Roman emperors during the so-called Imperial period. With Roman troops now permanently stationed across the empire, peace and order were more easily maintained as exploitation became more routinized. After a long and bloody period of civil war (49–30 BCE), peace became the priority at home and abroad. To ensure civil war did not break out again, the state of emergency—and the new leader it created, the *princeps*, "first citizen," as the first emperor Augustus called himself—had to become permanent. According to John Rich, "the securing of peace throughout the empire ... became the emperor's permanent responsibility" (2012: 85). As astute observers noted (Tac. *Annals* 3.28), *pax et princeps*, that is, "peace and an emperor," were inextricably bound: it was impossible to have one without the other. This peace, the *pax Romana*, was simultaneously the ideological foundation of and justification for the Roman Empire.

Indeed, for the first time in world history, peace (*pax*) and empire (*imperium*) became synonymously linked. As in the Persian empire, opinion was carefully managed, dissent anathematized, and open revolt ruthlessly crushed. Altars, temples, and other monuments were built to peace, usually following periods of provincial revolt and civil war. The ideology of *pax*, therefore, concealed or at least downplayed the realities of peace, which was, in part, "a component of wider patterns of violence, a concomitant of other structures of domination" (Woolf 1993: 171). The provinces themselves were never completely pacified, but in a continual state of pacification (Woolf 1993: 185–9). The *pax Romana* "was characterized not by the absence of violence but by a carefully balanced economy of it" (Woolf 1993: 191).

By all accounts, however, the Mediterranean world enjoyed an unprecedented period of (relative) peace during the first two centuries of the Roman Imperial era. This demands explanation beyond mere skill at anticipating threats and holding subject populations down by force. Unlike most ancient states and empires, the Romans had a highly developed and sophisticated understanding of citizenship and the rights and obligations associated with it. Even more exceptionally, they realized that Roman citizenship could be extended to non-Romans. Under the emperors, local elites, governing their cities through holding local magistracies and seats in local councils, maintained peace and order on Rome's behalf in exchange for citizenship, which could enable them to migrate to Rome and become senators there once their local terms of office were complete. These policies of integration culminated in the declaration of universal citizenship for all inhabitants of the Roman Empire in 212 CE. What made the Romans exceptional, and their empire exceptionally long-lived, was not their aggressiveness as a people, the militarism of their society, the oppressiveness of their imperial rule, or the exceptional skill of their soldiers, but their capacity—and willingness, unique among ancient states—to integrate non-Romans into their empire via the mechanism of citizenship (Eckstein 2006: 310–13).

Ironically, the emperor Caracalla's universal grant of Roman citizenship came near the beginning of an existential crisis for the empire and its inhabitants. After two centuries of prosperity and relative peace, beginning in the early years of Marcus Aurelius (r. 161–180 CE), massive incursions by Germanic tribes over the Danube River profoundly disrupted the *pax Romana* in the West. Aurelius himself spent the entire last decade of his reign leading the fight in person, and thus prefigured the so-called "barracks emperors" who followed, emperors whose entire lives were spent on campaign on the frontiers. Soon, the emperor's concern for his personal security transcended his concern for the safety of the empire as a whole (Goldsworthy 2009: 414). During the "Third Century Crisis" (235–284 CE), a fifty-year period of chaos and instability, around sixty men claimed the throne and twenty officially recognized emperors rose and fell, most of them usurping power through violence at the instigation of Roman armies, and perishing in the same way (Cline and Graham 2011: 270–1; Goldsworthy 2009: 138). This permanent state of civil war tragically dovetailed with increasing incursions into the empire by Germanic tribes, and by the threat of the resurgent Persian empire under the Sassanids on the eastern frontier after 226 CE.

Traditional narratives of Roman history suggest that Diocletian (r. 284–305 CE) and Constantine (r. 306–337 CE) pulled the empire out of its death-spiral, the former through bureaucratic restructuring, provincial reorganization, and military reform, and the latter through his embrace of Christianity and relocation of the imperial capital to Constantinople. It should be stressed, however, that Diocletian's political reforms (particularly the creation

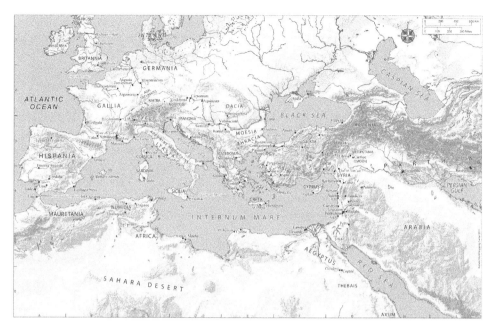

FIGURE 8.5: The Roman Empire. From Boatwright (2012) *The Romans: From Village to Empire* (2nd ed.). Courtesy of the Ancient World Mapping Center.

of the tetrarchy, an orderly system of imperial succession) failed their first tests, while Constantine ascended to the throne through the by now routine methods of usurpation and ruthless elimination of potential challengers (Goldsworthy 2009: 408). The emperor's person now became even more remote from his subjects; he was no longer *princeps*, "first citizen," but *dominus*, "master," buffered by layers of bureaucracy and hemmed in by rings of security apparatus. Peace, law, and order were maintained by a complex combination of traditional frontier garrisons (*limitanei*) and mobile strike forces (*comitatenses*) stationed well behind the frontier (Cline and Graham 2011: 283–6).

The division of the Roman Empire into eastern and western halves, begun administratively by Diocletian, started to become a geographical reality after Constantine's relocation of the empire's capital to the East. Theodosius I (r. 379–395 CE) was the last Roman emperor to rule a unified empire. The fall of the western empire, generally considered to have occurred in 476 CE when the last Roman emperor, Romulus Augustulus, was deposed by the German Odoacer, cannot be explained by any single factor. The "seepage" (Cameron 2012: 57) of Germanic tribesmen into the western provinces, the armies, and military leadership, ongoing since the German campaigns of Aurelius, combined with the retreat of visible Roman political and military authority from the provinces into the western imperial capital, Ravenna, gradually eroded the connections between emperor and subject. The long-term process of cultural and political change over the course of centuries meant that when Augustulus fell, "it is doubtful whether even the population of Italy at first noticed much difference" (Cameron 2012: 41). The change was even less pronounced since the new tribal kingdoms that emerged in the empire's place preserved Roman forms of cultural and ideological expression and political and legal systems (Cline and Graham 2011: 317).

These kingdoms—the Franks and Burgundians in Gaul, the Vandals in Africa, and the Goths in Spain and Italy—brought with them new structures of political and social organization, such as the warband (*comitatus*), feudalism and vassalage, that offered alternative sources of authority and protection, and alternative ways of achieving integration, to the long disappeared Roman political apparatus. In these kingdoms, created and maintained by force, warfare was "local . . . more frequent and less decisive" (Goldsworthy 2009: 372–3). Intra-tribal warfare among rival warbands was endemic, although complex schedules of blood-money, *wergeld*, were established to limit blood feuds, the tit-for-tat killings, amputations, and mutilations that were customary among these tribes. Peace under these new micro-imperialisms, nevertheless, would be difficult to achieve on any lasting basis. "The best that can be said [about the tribal kingdoms] was that they did not invariably have an immediate and detrimental impact" on the already less sophisticated, less prosperous, and simpler—in a word, less civilized—lifestyle of the late Roman West (Goldsworthy 2009: 378–9).

The Kingdom of the Franks emerged ahead of the pack only after centuries of consolidation. Part of the reason for this was the Merovingian Clovis' (r. 481–511 CE) early adoption of Catholic (papal) Christianity, thus tapping into already well-entrenched religious loyalties in the West. Ruthlessly eliminating all his potential rivals within his family also helped. However, because, according to Frankish custom, Clovis divided his domains among multiple heirs, perpetual civil strife soon engulfed the kingdom. Stability, and indeed expansion of Frankish power under the Merovingians' successors, the Carolingians, under Charles Martel, his son Pepin the Short (r. 741–768 CE), and grandson Charlemagne (r. 768–814 CE), reduced internecine strife to such a degree that Pepin could be credibly anointed king by a representative of the pope in 751 CE, and by Pope Stephen II himself in 754 CE, while Charlemagne was proclaimed "Emperor of the Romans" by Pope Leo III on Christmas Day, 800 CE.

In a way, this was a challenge to the eastern, Byzantine emperor, who had continued to hold that title after the fall of the West, and whose Greek-speaking subjects would continue to call themselves *Rhomaioi*, "Romans," until the Ottoman conquest of Constantinople in 1453 CE. The ability of the eastern emperors to establish relative peace within their empire during the fifth century CE is a good indication that they were far better off without the albatross of the West around their necks. Having only a single, far more defensible frontier zone than the ones in the West, shared with Sassanid Persia, certainly helped simplify Roman imperial security arrangements (Cline and Graham 2011: 304). Internal prosperity is indicated by the enormous amounts of revenue the Byzantine emperors could transform into subsidy payments to keep external tribes (Avars and Slavs) at bay, and to purchase peace with Persia. The Byzantine treasury could even sustain the prohibitively expensive (but ultimately ephemeral) reconquest of North Africa and Italy under the emperor Justinian (r. 527–565 CE).

Thereafter, a combination of factors, both internal and external, reduced the empire to a rump state in Asia Minor and the Balkans, with a few outposts in the West. Plagues and natural disasters took a significant toll on the population and prosperity of the empire. The old patterns of usurpation and civil war re-emerged after Justinian. Perhaps most significantly, a series of vigorous, expansionistic Sassanid rulers beginning in the sixth century CE gradually absorbed great chunks of Byzantine territory. Despite a significant peace treaty in 561 CE, and a brief period of a Byzantine–Persian alliance under the emperor Maurice (r. 582–602 CE), mutually exhausting and expensive wars continued. By 622 CE, much of the Middle and Near East, all of Egypt, and much of Asia Minor was

PEACE AS INTEGRATION   155

under Sassanid control. Simultaneously, the Avars and Slavs to the north were no longer content with their imperial subsidies and began invading the Balkans, the Avars combining with the Persians to besiege Byzantium itself in 626 CE. Byzantine losses were violently reversed by 628 CE. Under such circumstances, across vast swathes of the two empires, "war, not peace, was the norm, and when peace did prevail for a time it had usually been bought at a high cost" (Cameron 2012: 211). Much worse was yet to come.

The resilience of the universal empires of Byzantium and Persia—"aspirational politico-cultural world empires" in which one god, one faith, one ruler, and one empire was the predominant ideology—was overmatched by the truly politico-cultural world empire of the Islamic caliphate (Fowden 1993: 6 and *passim*). Unlike its predecessors, the Islamic religious community *was* the Islamic political community, and vice-versa: the *umma*. The entrenchment of Zoroastrianism in Sassanid Persia and Christianity in the late Roman Empire were both late, lengthy, and contested processes. By contrast, from the very outset, "what made the Islamic Empire, however briefly, into a successful world empire was the combination of imperial impetus with a universalist monotheism that was inflexible with regard to doctrinal essentials and full of missionary zeal towards polytheists but flexible, or at least prepared to exercise economy, in its dealings with other monotheisms" (Fowden 1993: 160).

The initial followers of Muhammad who swept out of the caravan cities of the Arabian peninsula shortly after the prophet's death easily overwhelmed the Sassanid and Byzantine armies, exhausted from decades of constant mutual warfare. Soon Syria-Palestine and Egypt were lost to the Byzantines, and along with them, the Byzantine state's status as a Mediterranean Roman Empire. Sassanid Persia was extinct by 651 CE. Under the Umayyad Caliphate (661–750 CE), Muslim conquests extended across north Africa and into Spain, uniting those areas to Arabia and the Middle East as far as the eastern reaches of the old empire of Alexander the Great. Consolidation accompanied conquest: the Umayyad rulers at first used local Byzantine and Persian collaborators and institutions to govern their new conquests, but within a generation or so began replacing these with Arab-speaking Muslims and Islamic legal and political institutions (Cline and Graham 2011: 332–4). Under the rule of the Abbasid dynasty (750–1258 CE), the center of gravity of the Muslim empire shifted east, to the newly built city of Baghdad, and the *umma* was gradually disaggregated into different dynasties across the Islamic world. Within the Abbasid Empire, in *dar al-Islam*, the world of peace ruled by Islam, Persian and Byzantine bureaucratic institutions persisted, more land was brought under cultivation, and tight control of the empire beyond Baghdad was kept through various means, including judges applying Sharia law and a network of intelligence-gathering spies. The Abbasid empire reached its apex of prosperity and cultural production under Harun al-Rashid (r. 786–809), whose diplomatic contacts extended as far as China in the East and Charlemagne's Roman Empire in the West.

Imperial systems, intentionally or not, could and indeed did create spaces and periods of peace in the ancient world. Within empires, the integration of diverse peoples across a broad landscape through religious tolerance, cultural pluralism, collaboration, extension of citizenship, and other such mechanisms (most of them not altruistically driven, but imposed by cultural, logistical, and technological constraints) reduced opportunities for dissent to manifest. This is not to downplay the effect of the imperial metropole's monopoly on violence in keeping the peace, or to apologize for imperialism. Whether the majority of people were better off under such circumstances, and how that is to be measured, is beyond the remit of this chapter.

LEAGUES OF STATES

Local clusters of cities, towns, and villages across the ancient Mediterranean landscape had forever been as subject to the forces of attraction as to those of repulsion. The urge to merge, both for security reasons in the face of external threats and in pursuit of closer ethno-religious ties, is apparent in both the archaeological and literary records (Beck and Funke 2015b: 25). The cities of Sparta and Rome emerged in the eighth and seventh centuries BCE from the unification of several proximate settlements—a process the Greeks called *synoikismos*, literally "a joining together of households," the standard description for the birth of a new city-state. The integration of Attica under the reforms of Kleisthenes fully realized this vision (Raaflaub 2016d: 141). In later periods, more or less formal associations of city-states (in Greek, *koina*, sing. *koinon*) emerged. These mostly took the forms of alliances or leagues (*symmachiai*, "symmachies") and, in the case of ethnically homogeneous cities in close geographic proximity to one another, federal states or confederacies.[3] Whatever their particular forms, and whatever their particular motivations for confederation, these clusterings of states were a product of the "sense of togetherness" that emerged in the age of polis formation during the Archaic period, when common ancestors, sanctuaries, cults, institutions, and ethnic identities were forming among the new city-state populations and *ethnē* (Beck and Funke 2015b: 22–6). Later, in the Hellenistic period, priorities shifted to geopolitics, with a view to balancing first the great Hellenistic powers, and then Rome.

Multilateral alliances, or "symmachies," are visible in the historical record as early as the sixth century BCE in both Italy and Greece. Not much can be reliably known about the Etruscan and Latin Leagues in Italy except that the latter was formed almost certainly in defensive response against invaders of Latium, and was often in tension with its Roman hegemon from the late sixth century until its defeat and destruction by Rome in 338 BCE. Peace was rarely a defining characteristic of central Italy during this period. Meanwhile, in Greece, in the latter half of the sixth century, Sparta united the Peloponnese (with some exceptions, including Argos) under its hegemony. The "Peloponnesian League" (called in the sources "the Lakedaimonians (Spartans) and their allies") was very loosely integrated. The allies' sovereignty was limited by treaty obligations, mostly of a military nature, but Spartan hegemony was mitigated by their lack of a navy and dependence on allied specialist military contingents. Before the Spartan victory in the Peloponnesian War (431–404 BCE), when Spartan hegemony became more oppressive to the allies, "the alliance's mere existence contributed to reducing wars in Sparta's sphere of influence [since, e]xcept for rare cases, Sparta's hegemony was uncontested" (Raaflaub 2015a: 441).

The unification of thirty-one poleis against Persia, usually called the Hellenic League (they called themselves "Hellenes" or "the Lakedaimonians, Athenians, and their allies"), had the explicit aim to "patch up their own quarrels and stop any fighting which happened to be going on among members of the confederacy" (Hdt. 7.145.1). After achieving its goal of fending off the Persians, the alliance apparently never formally broke up (Raaflaub 2015a: 442), but after the Spartans abdicated leadership, Athens assumed the role of hegemon of a new alliance system (excluding Peloponnesians) with its administrative center at the Temple of Apollo on Delos (hence the modern name of the organization, the Delian League). The League's fatal flaws were that it lacked any form of legal integration beyond what was demanded for its military purpose, and was reliant on Athenian self-restraint in its position as hegemon. In terms of the first problem, Greek cultural assumptions about citizenship and its exclusivity resulted in the Athenian failure to extend

PEACE AS INTEGRATION

Athenian citizenship to their allies, thus depriving themselves of valuable manpower and resource bases that are vital to ongoing imperial expansion (Raaflaub 2015a: 449).

In terms of the second problem, in a process vividly described by Thucydides (1.89–117), most members of the Delian League, because of their small populations relative to Athens, commuted their relatively burdensome military commitments to financial ones, and were thus rendered powerless when they tried to exit the League, and Athens used overwhelming force to compel them to remain. The alliance system, the *symmachia*, thus became an imperial system, an *archē*. The pain and suffering inflicted by Athens on its former allies was a tragic price for the peace the hegemon imposed on the Aegean: piracy, a perennial problem in the region, was virtually eliminated, and Persian power was cleared from the Aegean basin and the Ionian coast for nearly a century, while Persian meddling in Greek affairs was halted until the Peloponnesian War.

The unfortunate long-term consequences of the Spartan victory over Athens in 404 BCE included the aggrandizement of Sparta against the other Greek states, and the loss of the Greek cities in Asia Minor, the Aegean Islands, and Cyprus to Persia. A significant development in the fourth century, however, was the first attempt at a "common peace" (*koinē eirēnē*) among all Greeks, brokered by the Persian shah Artaxerxes II in 387 (and thus sometimes called the "King's Peace").[4] The treaty guaranteed peace through the domination of the Spartans, who predictably used their position as an excuse for further aggrandizement (Xen. *Hell.* 5.1.31). The peace failed and four decades of almost continuous warfare among the major mainland Greek poleis followed.

A Second Athenian League, formed in response to Spartan aggression in 378, and self-consciously designed to avoid the temptations to which the hegemon was susceptible within the framework of the Delian League, was intended, in part, to force the Spartans to allow the Greeks "to live at peace occupying their own territory in security" (*IG* II² 43, lines 9–11). The organization was also designed to be more integrated than the Delian League: the members of the *synedrion*, or council, of the League, were bound to each other as well as to Athens, and control of policy was divided between the two. Unfortunately, "changing conditions" in Greece—the rise of Thebes, for example, which united Sparta and Athens, thus removing the *raison d'être* of the League—"led to tensions, dissatisfaction, and eventually war with the allies" (Raaflaub 2015a: 447, cf. 2016d: 128–9).

The bifurcated model of *synedrion* and hegemon nevertheless survived to become the guiding principle behind Philip II of Macedon's League of Corinth in 337 (so Raaflaub 2015a: 445, 2016c: 129). In that organization, all the Greeks (except Sparta) swore an oath to abide by the peace as established by the treaty between themselves and Philip, to maintain their loyalty to Philip and his heirs, not to make war on transgressors but to leave those decisions in the hands of the hegemon, subject to the council's determination (*IG* II² 236). This amounted to a "non-aggression pact" among the League members (Smarczyk 2015: 455), guaranteed by the overwhelming power of the Macedonian hegemon. Finally, an agreeable pathway to a durable peace was discovered for the Greeks, but fear was its surety, freedom its price. Later incarnations of this framework, the Hellenic League founded by Antigonos I the One-Eyed and his son Demetrios I the Besieger, and its reformed namesake under the hegemony of Antigonos III Doson, perpetuated what "amounted to a *de facto* system of peacekeeping" (Smarczyk 2015: 465). These organizations imposed a common peace among their members, while Doson's League allowed a level of freedom and autonomy to member states unavailable to those in previous incarnations, largely due to weakness at the imperial center.

According to Kurt Raaflaub (2016d: 130), leagues of allied states (*symmachiai*),

> although motivated by a widespread desire to control endemic warfare, and proclaiming the establishment of lasting peace as a primary goal . . . tended to remain (or soon to become again) tools serving the imperial goals of the hegemonic power . . . In most cases, their failure was thus due to their inability to subordinate hegemonic ambition to alliance and integration: the dominant principle, provoking resistance rather than cooperation, remained rule through peace rather than alliance for peace.

Nevertheless, "these shortcomings . . . should not distract us from the fact that for decades international peace stood in the center of serious efforts at political experimentation." And, as Raaflaub has tried to show, societies seriously began such experiments, in thought and deed, primarily, and perhaps exclusively, after "an extraordinary experience of war [viz. the Peloponnesian War] that vastly and excruciatingly surpassed their normal expectations forced such thoughts upon them" (2016c: 17).

FEDERAL STATES[5]

The federal state model went that crucial step further towards integration. In one sense, it was a response to the failure of these models to establish durable peace in Greece (Smarczyk 2015: 452). Here was a system "in which there [was] a local citizenship in the smaller [member] communities as well as a joint or federal citizenship and in which the citizens [were] under the jurisdiction both of federal and local authorities."[6] A recent estimate puts the number of city-states in mainland Greece integrated into federal leagues in the late Classical period at roughly 40 percent (Mackil 2013: 1). This is a phenomenal amount, and it is obviously beyond the scope of this chapter to enumerate and discuss in detail the perhaps as many as twenty Greek leagues that existed at any one time in the Aegean area. In terms of structure, most leagues had a federal executive council, or *boulē* (also called a *synedrion*), consisting of elected magistrates (the chief of whom was usually designated *stratēgos*, "general," or *archon*, "leader") and their advisors, who ran the day-to-day affairs of the league; a larger representative council, which met less frequently, made up of representatives sent by each member state; and the assembly, *ekklesia*, which met only periodically.

Like the *symmachiai* before them, federated states came together for a number of reasons, but chief among them was security: "membership in a federal state brought with it a level of security unobtainable by small communities on their own" (Ager 2015: 474), especially those that were vulnerable to domination by the great Hellenistic powers (Smarczyk 2015: 452). The Achaian and Aitolian Leagues of the Hellenistic period became major second-tier powers, and the overall effect on the system of such power-balancers was to force peace on the regional hegemon (Macedon, then Rome) by increasing the costs of expansion, and by extracting security guarantees, such as peace treaties, from the expansionary state and attempting to enforce compliance. Internally, as had been the case with the *symmachiai*, integration within a federated state reduced the scope for traditional regional rivalries, and inter-city violence and warfare. For most states, the security of integration was worth giving up some measure of local autonomy (Ager 2015: 474).

Dewy-eyed optimism is out of place here, however. The same sorry litany of feuding and violence, both internal and external, dominates the chronicles of the federal states as the independent poleis, *symmachiai*, and imperial states of antiquity. Some attempts were made to litigate disputes peacefully: epigraphic and literary evidence proves that boundary disputes and quarrels over religious matters were contested by member states before federal courts. Nonetheless, violent strife persisted. Under Roman hegemony, in the 180s and 170s, we hear of violent political divisions (*staseis*) and debt crises in the Aitolian, Achaian, Thessalian, Epirote, and Boiotian confederacies, as well as in the microfederal state of Doris (Burton 2017: 89–90). Political divisions in Aitolia grew so toxic that king Perseus of Macedon installed garrisons in League territory, and later, genocidal massacres were perpetrated by the major political factions (Livy 41.25.1–4, 42.42.4). A Roman delegation sent to calm the situation failed miserably (Livy 42.2.2).

In this context, it is perhaps worth noting Polybios' observation about the first Achaian League when it was broken up by Alexander the Great's successors in the late fourth century: "they fell, chiefly thanks to the kings of Macedon, into such a state of discord and ill feeling that all the cities separated from the League and began to act against each others' interests" (Polyb. 2.41.9). The significance of his statement is ambiguous: violence and feuding remained endemic within federal states, or federal states kept a lid on those tendencies. The evidence marshaled here, unless overrepresented in our sources (because good news and status quo situations tend to be underreported, in literary texts at least), coupled with the highly competitive nature of ancient states, large and small, functioning within an anarchic international system, does not inspire confidence in the second possibility.

Nor does the behavior exhibited by some federal governments towards some of their more reluctant members. Those states that chafed under federation had to be contained by force. The most prominent examples are Sparta after 192 BCE and Messene in the late 180s, both subject to military reprisals and to forcible reincorporation into the Achaian League after their attempted secessions. The fact that the Spartans sent independent embassies to Rome to seek redress against the League, just as other poleis sought arbitrators outside the framework of their own leagues in other cases, is perhaps an indication that "our assessment of the effectiveness of the institutions and the leverage of a Greek federal state is . . . somewhat skewed in the direction of undue optimism" (Ager 2015: 483).

Finally, the extent of the contribution of at least the more dominant federal states to peace in Greece appears to have been negligible—or worse. The powerful Aitolian and Achaian Leagues were permitted (or seized the opportunity) to run riot across mainland Greece from the mid-third to the early second century. The Aitolians, for example, aggrieved by the terms of the Roman settlement ending the Second Macedonian War, invited the Seleukid king Antiochos III to "liberate" the Greeks, thus deliberately provoking a Roman war across both Greece and Asia Minor between 192 and 188. The Achaians took advantage of Rome's lack of interest in Greek affairs in the 180s to incorporate forcibly all the Peloponnese into their League. As Eckstein points out, "in the Aegean and Greece, warfare was no less constant among important city-states, and constant as well with the federal leagues" (2006: 83; cf. 90–4).

Federal states, therefore, fell short of resolving the problem of endemic violence between individual Greek communities, and indeed, as aggregations of states, increased the scale of conflict when unleashed against their peer-competitors or allied to first-tier powers in war. They nevertheless may have mitigated systemic tendencies towards inter-*polis* rivalries, moved the eastern Mediterranean system towards a less volatile power balance, and compelled first-tier states towards peaceful behavior, such as accepting mediations and honoring treaty commitments.

CONCLUSION

Peace was a precious commodity in the ancient world. The integrative structures examined in this chapter rarely, if ever, had peace as their intended goal. Most of these structures originated in, and were responses to, anarchic systems where self-help was a state's only recourse for survival. Some states may have initially coalesced around common sacred sites and places of worship, or for reasons of common regional or ethnic sentiment, but concern for security was never far behind. Common peaces and *symmachiai* were handmaidens to the growth of hegemonic power of the most powerful participating states, who did not hesitate to use their superior position to crush those trying to get out. Greek federal states used their power (and near-monopoly on coercive force) to compel reluctant member states to remain. Within federations, the usual bitter quarrels that plagued the world of the Classical city-states continued apace, including bloody *staseis* and vicious economic disputes. As for empires, some may have evolved from security-seeking behavior, but many grew out of a dispositionally expansionistic individual or people. Regardless of how or why they originated, once established, internally empires seem to have imposed an economy of violence, rather than peace *per se*. The empires behind the *paces Achaemenidica* and *Romana* relied on the usual repressive measures of militarized imperial states to crush any signs of discontent before they could evolve into open revolt. This, of course, is why the fair name of peace was so strongly put forward as a justification (and synonym) for empire by the Romans: to resist was to be an enemy of peace, and enemies of peace deserved annihilation. So too the world outside the Islamic *umma* was constructed as *dar al-harb*, "the world of war," as opposed to the community within, *dar al-Islam*, "the world of peace ruled by Islam".

While peace was never the stated goal (outside of propaganda) of these integrative structures, some mitigation of the harsh conditions of interstate anarchy—war and violence—nevertheless resulted from their existence. The relative peace and prosperity that broke out in the Roman Empire in the first and second centuries CE was not entirely illusory; the wide extension of Roman citizenship, the most important international integrative tool developed in antiquity, must have had something to do with that. The peace among the six fourteenth- and thirteenth-century BCE Near Eastern and Aegean kingdoms may indicate a preference among the kings to maintain a balance of power (with some chipping away at the edges) rather than risk destructive and expensive hegemonic war between the major powers. Even under such overtly hegemonial *symmachiai* as the Delian and Hellenic Leagues, an unprecedented number of Greek states enjoyed peace, albeit at the point of a sword, and they could be effectively marshaled against external threats, as the Delian League was against piracy and the Persian fleets. Federal states probably mitigated rivalries among their members, and balanced their peers and first-tier powers, resulting in diminutions of threats, diplomatic disputes, and treaty-violations.

In a world plagued by violence and war, which was regarded as glorious, but also a tragic waste of life and resources, it would be surprising if achieving peace, or at least containing violence, were not occasionally consciously sought. The integrative structures of empires, leagues of states, and federal states all served to mitigate the prevailing systemic tendencies towards anarchic intercommunal warfare in the ancient Mediterranean world, and the members of these entities were probably grateful to be part of them when they periodically did so.

NOTES

Introduction

1. Melko and Weigel assert that peace was the normal state of affairs in antiquity, with war being the "exceptional activity" (1981: 131); for criticism of this overly simplistic viewpoint, see Raaflaub 2007b: 9–10.

2. For the view that concepts of international law imposed some constraints in interstate relations, at least among the ancient Greeks, see Alonso 2007; Low 2007; and cf. the discussion in Giovannini 2007: 149–58.

3. The Correlates of War Project, begun by David Singer and Melvin Small, has done much to parse out and define distinctions between "war" and "militarized conflict short of war"; see http://www.correlatesofwar.org/ (accessed February 12, 2017).

4. A caveat to this claim is that some very significant deities, such as Demeter (Roman Ceres), might represent the *benefits* of peace, in her case, a plentiful harvest; see further in chapters 4 and 5 below.

5. Yates 2016: 100; Yates also points out that this first step at unification stumbled badly upon the death of the first Qin emperor, Qin Shihuangdi. See also Yates 2007.

6. On Greek concepts of just (or justified) war, see Clavadetscher-Thürlemann 1985; Giovannini 2007: 149–58; Dewald 2013; Raaflaub 2016d.

7. For a historical survey of Christianity and war, see Chilton 2013. For the argument that pre-Constantinian Christianity was not as pacifistic as is generally supposed, see Swift 2007; Gwynn 2017, and see also Wilker, Chapter 4 below.

8. On analogous developments in Buddhist thought in ancient India, see Bronkhorst 2016, and cf. Salomon 2007.

9. The speaker here is the Cretan Kleinias, who should not be taken to represent Plato's own views.

10. Some have interpreted this phenomenon as a sign of the so-called "democratic peace", the notion that democracies do not make war on each other (see, e.g., Russett and Antholis 1992; Dixon 1993; Weart 1998). The democratic peace is a subject of much discussion in contemporary scholarship, but the evidence from antiquity is too sparse and inconsistent to allow us to draw certain conclusions.

11. See, however, Raaflaub 2016d for arguments that the Greeks did develop ways and means of dealing with intrastate discord.

12. Octavian subsequently took the title Augustus and ruled as the first Roman emperor. See Champion 2004 for a variety of sources on the Roman Empire and Roman imperialism; Goldsworthy 2016; Cornwell 2017.

13. This does not mean that the peaceful segments of the Jewish population were left unaffected by the Roman victory: the monuments of Flavian Rome, such as the Arch of Titus and Vespasian's Temple of Peace, memorialized the depredations of Jewish cultural properties by the successful Roman commanders.

14. *Pacique imponere morem, parcere subiectis et debellare superbos* (Verg. *Aen.* 6.852–3; Horsfall translation); there is little support for the alternate reading *pacisque* (Horsfall 2013

162 NOTES

vol. 2: 585). The brief phrase *pacique imponere morem* is surprisingly challenging to interpret and translate, and a variety of different meanings have been suggested: "to pacify" (Fitzgerald 1983); "to put your stamp on the works and ways of peace" (Fagles 2006); "the enforcement of peace as a habit" (Ahl 2007); "peace, and then peaceful customs" (Ruden 2008).

15. *Auferre trucidare rapere falsis nominibus imperium, atque ubi solitudinem faciunt, pacem appellant* (Tac. *Agr.* 30; Mattingly translation, slightly adapted). See de Souza 2008: 95; Lavan 2017; and several of the chapters below.

16. Because of the dominant role played by the hegemons Antigonos and Demetrios, many scholars do not recognize this treaty organization as a common peace; nevertheless, its structure was clearly influenced by earlier *koinai eirēnai*. See Harter-Uibopuu 2003.

17. More successful than the *koinai eirēnai* of the fourth century at maintaining a multilateral peace among a group of allied city-states were the federal leagues of the Hellenistic period, such as the Achaian League and Aitolian League; peace within the leagues, however, did not translate to peace without, and the Greek wars of the Hellenistic age were frequent and devastating.

Chapter 1

1. For the problem of meaning in ancient Greek, see Alonso 2007. For the problem in Latin, see Barton 2007.

2. In modern peace studies, the development of cooperative international organizations that look beyond military alliance to economic union or the elimination of internal borders, such as the European Union, are usually taken as an example of positive peace (cf. Anastasiou 2007); but increasing resistance to the European Union (and particularly its domination by France and Germany) by its own members, most famously in the Brexit of June 2016, suggests that the EU may quickly become a better example of negative peace than positive peace.

3. *Spondai* indicate a truce with more permanent intent; the word *ekecheiria* was used to designate truces intended to be temporary, such as cessation of fighting to bury the dead.

4. All the examples below are literary examples from oratory or historiography. The epigraphical record largely preserves the use of *spondai* only in honorary decrees or sacred laws, in which its meaning of libation remains foremost. Only *IG* I³ 83 and II² 236 use the word in the sense of peace treaty, and both documents are fragmentary and the word has been restored (in the case of I³ 83, from the text of Thucydides 5.47, his recorded version of the treaty). Outside of the classical period, only *IG* II² 287, dating to 266/5 BCE, uses the word, in conjunction with *symmachia*, to mean "peace and alliance."

5. Schmidt 1999, esp. p. 82, takes a far more optimistic and idealistic view, going so far as to call the idea of a common peace a "new . . . philosophy of peace."

6. Most notably the Melian Dialogue (Thuc. 5.84–114) and Kleon's speech in the debate over Mytilene (3.37–40); Diodotos' speech in the same debate (3.42–48) is the rare exception.

7. For a differing point of view, see Raaflaub 2016d. For other ancient Greek authors who articulated a theory of common peace, like Gorgias or Lysias, see Kessler 1911: 8.

8. *Hēsychia* generally means tranquility; it is one of the effects of a Panhellenic peace that Isokrates posits (8.26), and it is an important concept in Hellenistic philosophy.

9. The Loeb translation of H.J. Edwards, now a century old, obscures the forcefulness implied in the verb *pacare*: "These achievements brought peace throughout Gaul."

10. See, for instance, Badian 1968 and Linderski 1984. The concept should not be confused with the modern idea of a "just war"; they are similar but not identical.

NOTES   163

11. See, for instance, Pl. *Leg.* 628e1.
12. Cf. the discussion in Chapter 8 below.
13. There is a large literature on the subject; see, for instance, Parchami 2009, Chapter 2, on the *pax Romana* as a hegemonic peace. See also chapters 6 and 7 below.
14. Cf. Barton 2007: 252, and Chapter 6 below.
15. *NH* 27.1. This is an often-overlooked positive side-effect of conquest: Alexander the Great's conquests had a similar effect on the Greek world in terms of opening up new avenues of knowledge through the discovery of previously unknown flora, fauna, or geographical features; so too did Napoleon's conquest of Egypt have a like effect on early nineteenth-century Europe.
16. Whitby 1992: 295. Other significant examples of diplomacy where the rulers were never brought face-to-face, such as the negotiation of the Byzantine-Persian treaty of 561–562 CE, suggest that much of the time it remained important that "the dignity and pre-eminence of the emperor" not be compromised (Lee 2008: 112).
17. Lee 1991 and 2008: 116; Allen 2011 on the Romanization of hostages.
18. *Pace* Whitby 2008: 123.

Chapter 2

1. Keeley 1996; Kelly 2000; Otterbein 2004; Guilaine and Zammit 2005; Myers 2005; Rosen 2005; Fry 2006, 2007, 2013; Shackelford and Weekes-Shackelford 2012 offer detailed surveys and analyzes from various perspectives.
2. https://en.wikisource.org/wiki/Seville_Statement_on_Violence (accessed April 28, 2018).
3. Book 7, Chapter 2, trans. Knoblock/Riegel 2000: 175; I thank Robin Yates for these references.
4. Most of the cited passage follows the Warner translation; I offer my own translation of the italicized phrase in order to emphasize the subtleties of the Greek text (the Warner translation reads simply "they are by nature incapable").
5. See Harris 1991: 163–6; generally on the Roman concept of just war, see Clavadetscher-Thürlemann 1985: 127–84.
6. I thank David Konstan for helpful advice on Roman sources.

Chapter 3

1. *Lys.* 520: "War is men's work" (πόλεμος δ᾽ ἄνδρεσσι μελήσει) is a direct quotation of *Iliad* 6.492.
2. This injunction by Lysistrata is part of the discourse of the "war against the barbarian" in fifth- and fourth-century Greece, which was partly about gaining retribution for the Persian wars, but also achieving unity in Greece through common cause against the "natural enemy": Mitchell 2007; see also Chapter 1 above.
3. Note, however, that Strife (*eris*, also feminine) and peace are not simple opposites. Strife (*Eris*) in Homer is the sister of Ares, god of war (*Il.* 4.441–2), and in Hesiod's *Theogony* the daughter of Night, and herself "produced burdensome Labour (*Ponos*), and the curse of Forgetfulness (*Lēthē*), Hunger, and lachrymose Pains, Conflicts of Battle and Fights and Murders and Killings of Men, Disorderly Government and her accomplice, the power of Ruin, and the oath-god Horkos . . ." (225–31). In the *Works and Days*, however, the poet acknowledges that *Eris* is of two kinds: one encourages war and battle, but the other, who is the elder daughter of dark Night, through competition with his wealthy neighbor stirs up even the helpless to pursue prosperity; "this is the Eris that benefits mortals" (11–24).

4. Early association with Dionysos and rural farmers: Smith 2011: 78–9; cf. Raaflaub 2016d: 135–6.

5. The statue group was probably not a cult-statue; although there is fourth-century testimony for the foundation of the cult, there is some modern scholarly debate about when the peace was first celebrated (either 375/4 or 371 BCE): Simon 1986: 700–5; Stafford 2001: 173–97; Smith 2011: 110–12; see also Chapter 5 and Figure 5.2 below. It is probably worth noting in passing that Athens, while it did not acquire a cult of Ares until the first century CE (Schachter 2002), was replete with images of *Nikē* (Victory), and the "collective enthusiasm for war and empire": Raaflaub 2016c: 24–5.

6. On the nudity of *Diallagē*, see Henderson 1980: 163–4.

7. See Mitchell 2007: 93–8. *Homonoia*, "harmony" or "concord", was seen as a state of "reconciliation" within a Greek city which "demanded a set of emotions, attitudes and dispositions that were distinct from those characteristic of 'ordinary' peace, whose participants usually remained quite detached from one another", and developed as a concept largely in the fourth century BCE (Gray 2017). Nevertheless, the idea that interstate war among the Greek states was in essence civil war was an idea already current in the fifth.

8. Noreña 2011: 128–9; cf. Simon 1994. See figures 1.5, 4.5, and 5.3.

9. See also, however, van Wees (2001), who notes the ties that held the Greek world together to provide a counter for war (while still recognizing the desire for power as a principal driver for war).

10. Sara Forsdyke (2008: 25 n. 72) makes the point that the story of the Athenian women is aetiological to explain why Athenian women wear Ionian dress (and so probably not historically credible).

11. Diodoros says those who sought sanctuary in the temples were not saved out of fear of sacrilege, but because the Carthaginians did not want the women to burn down the temples and so destroy the great wealth stored in them as dedications (Diod. 13.57.4).

12. Dem. 19.195–6; cf. Thuc. 5.3.4; on ransoming of captives, see Pritchett 1991: 245–83.

13. Herodotos mentions the battle of Sepeia and its aftermath (Hdt. 6.76–80), but does not make any reference to Telesilla. This would be unusual if the story were true, since he is interested in strong women whose actions go beyond the bounds of convention as social actors (see esp. Dewald 1981). Pausanias, however, claims to have seen a monument honoring her, though this may of course have been erected after the story of her deeds had become established.

14. In Herodotos the Massagetai are simply stronger than the Persians.

15. It is from Justin and Orosius that Tomyris and Semiramis are transported into medieval literature and art, where they become exemplary women. Tomyris becomes part of the medieval artistic movement called the "Power of Women" (see Wolfthal 1999: 122–4; on the "Power of Women" *topos*, see Smith 1995), although she could be represented as a temptress; nevertheless, she and Semiramis are sometimes included in the medieval lists of the Nine Worthy Women. Both of them, together with Zenobia (and other Greek and Roman heroines), are included in Boccaccio's fourteenth-century biographies of famous women, *De Mulieribus Claris* and in the early fifteenth-century *Le Livre de la Cité des Dames* of Christine de Pizan.

16. Diod. 19.11.1–8; Douris of Samos, *FGrH* 76 F 52 = *BNJ* 76 F 52; Arrian, *FGrH* 156 F 9.30–3; Carney 2000: 121–2, 132–4 and 2006: 74–5.

17. Chaniotis (2005: 103) suggests that, apart from "a few notable exceptions, women are almost absent in Hellenistic historiography in connection with war."

NOTES 165

18. Delia 1991; Bauman 1992: 83–90; Fraschetti 2001; Hallett 2015: 247–65. Spinning and working with wool was womanly work at Rome as well as in Greece: Pomeroy 1975: 199.

19. The genre was widespread: Sopater of Syrian Apamea (fourth century CE) in his *Selection of Histories* noted that there were a number of collections on the deeds of women (Photius, *Bibl.* 161).

20. Sharrock (2015), however, argues that unlike Penthesilea who in death becomes an object of erotic appeal, Vergil's Camilla, whose body is allowed in death to be returned to her home (*Aen.* 11.594–5), has her role as a warrior woman naturalized.

21. Because of the losses in the male population caused by the Peloponnesian War, the Athenians took the unusual step of legalizing marriages to more than one wife.

22. *Historia Ecclesiastica* 7.15.3; Damascius *ap. Suda* sv Hypatia; John of Nikiu, *Chronicle* 84.87–103. See Watts 2017, esp. 107–20.

23. Because of her diplomatic success, the Carthaginians rewarded her with a gold crown of one hundred talents. Diodoros says that she struck a series of coins from the crown given her by the Carthaginians, the *Demareteion*, though there are problems over claims that silver coins known from Sicily are examples: see Mitchell 2012: 13–14. Late sources, however, say she used her personal jewelry to help fund Gelon's war effort (Pollux 9.85)

24. On Livia, her connection with Hersilia, her activities as a benefactor, and the honors she received as a result, see esp. Angelova 2015: 66–107.

25. See Piccirilli 1973: no. 5. For the arguments concerning the historicity (or lack of it) of the archaic conflict between the Eleians and the Pisatans, see most recently Bourke (2018): 53–66.

26. Sommerstein (*ap.* Aristophanes 1990: 5–6) says: "It is not likely, to be sure, that we should think of Lysistrata as representing Lysimache in the sense in which Paphlagon in *Knights* represents Cleon: it is more a matter of association and reminiscence, helping to link the heroine with the power and wisdom of Athena, with the reverence and affection felt by Athenians for their patron goddess, and with the oldest religious traditions of their city, and so promoting in the audience the feeling that her cause is the cause of right, and that though women under the leadership break through the bonds of the married state and home life, the rules of conventional decency and all the norms of womanly behaviour in Athenian society, they do so in the service of the higher and divinely sanctioned principles with the object not of disrupting but of reintegrating household and communities and a Greek world disrupted by war, and fully deserve the triumph they finish by achieving."

27. Thuc. 2.45.2; translation is after Hornblower (1991–2008: 1.314).

28. It is important to distinguish between the female deity of war, Athena, and the male deity of war, Ares. The former is representative of reason and justice and statecraft, the righteous defense of the community, while the latter represents (at least in Homer) all that is violent, brutal, and despicable about war. Nevertheless, the two could be conjoined, as is evident in the cult of "Ares and Athena Areia", attested at Acharnai in Attika in the fourth century BCE (SEG 21.519).

Chapter 4

1. Cf. also *Od.* 16.284–5, 19.4–5. For Peace and Wealth see, for instance, *Od.* 24.486; Theogn. 885; Pind. *Ol.* 13.6; Eur. *Suppl.* 489–90; *Bacc.* 419–20. LaRocca 1974: 112–36.

2. For Eirēnē as Kourotrophos ("nurse of youth") see Simon 1986: 703; Smith 2011: 111.

3. *IG* I³ 1407 bis; Simon 1988: 61; Parker 1997a: 229 with n. 44; Smith 2011: 77–8.

4. The spurious reference to a cult of Eirēnē being established already after the Battle of Eurymedon in Plutarch's life of Kimon (13.6) has to be discarded as anachronistic, cf. Shapiro 1993: 45; Stafford 2001: 175–6.
5. Cf. Isokr. *Or.* 15.109–110; *schol.* Ar. *Pax* 1019; Philochoros *BNJ* 328 F 151; Paus. 1.8.2 (cf. 18.3), 9.16.2. Cf. Wycherley 1957: 65–7.
6. Paus. 1.8.2, 9.16.2; cf. Plin. *NH* 34.50. La Rocca 1974; Simon 1988: 62–4. For the statue see Figure 5.2 below.
7. The amphorae are dated to 360/59 BCE through the archonship of Kallimedes. La Rocca 1974: 124–5; Scheibler 1984: 48; Simon 1986: 702–3.
8. *IG* II² 1496 *c.* 127; *Syll³* 1029.31.64. Parker 1997a: 230; Hunt 2010: 241. Rosivach (1994: 50–3) estimated on the basis of the gains made through the skin-sale from victims sacrificed during the festival that at least a full hecatomb of oxen was sacrificed.
9. For a critical discussion of the dating and its potential revival in the 330s see Hunt 2010: 243–5; Stafford 2001: 173–5; Smith (2011: 110) argues for a connection with the peace of 371 BCE instead.
10. Kraay/Hirmer, pl. 101, 291; Scheibler 1984: 48; Simon 1986: 701–2; Simon 1988: 67–8.
11. The temple had, since the late fifth century BCE, stood in the district of Acharnai (north of the urban center of Athens); in the first century, it was dismantled and rebuilt in the Athenian Agora. Cf. *IG* II² 3250, celebrating Gaius Caesar as *neos Ares* (The New Ares). It may be significant that by now, with the Roman infiltration and control of Greece, the Roman concept of Mars was ameliorating the Greek concept of Ares. For a summary of the discussion, see Camp 2004: 116–17, 189–91; Raaflaub 2015b: 103; Stewart 2016. It should be noted, however, that the Areopagos hill in Athens had borne Ares' name from at least the Archaic period.
12. In spite of the distinction between their characters in Homer—with Athena as the rational deity of justified war and Ares as the brutal and irrational avatar of violence—there is evidence that the two could be linked in cult: a fourth-century BCE inscription from Athenian Acharnai mentions the joint dedication of an altar to Ares and to "Athena Areia" (*SEG* 21.519).
13. See in general Rüpke 1990: esp. 30–41. For the temple outside the Porta Capena in Rome (dedicated presumably in 388 BCE) see Dion. Hal. *Ant. Rom.* 6.13.4; Liv. 6.5.8, 7.23.3, 10.23.12, 12.1.2; Ov. *Fast.* 6.191. For the temple next to the Circus Flaminius by D. Iunius Brutus Callaicus (cos. 138) see Plin. *HN* 36.26; Val. Max. 8.14.2, Prop. 4.3.71.
14. The *hasta* and *ancilia* were said to have fallen from the sky, cf. Plut. *Rom.* 29.1; Gell. 4.6; Varro, *Antiquitates* frg. 18. Scott 1999, esp. 190.
15. For the respective rituals see Dion. Hal. *Ant. Rom.* 2.71–2; Ov. *Fast.* 3.365–92; Plut. *Numa* 13.1–7; Tac. *Hist.* 1.89; Serv. *Aen.* 7.188, 603, 8.3; Simon and Bauchhenss 1984, 505, 511.
16. Cicero argues in *Flac.* 67–9 that Rome's victories give proof to the superiority of the Roman gods.
17. Cf. Gordon 1999. According to Cato *Agr.* 141, Mars was evoked in an ancient agricultural prayer to secure and safeguard the fields, the cattle, and the men.
18. Liv. 10.19.17; Ov. *Fast.* 6.201–8; cf. also Livy 28.9.5–11. Viscogliosi 1993.
19. See the list of temples in Cornell 1989: 408; cf. also Harris 1991: 123–5; Ziolkowski 1992; Orlin 1997: 199–202.
20. Cf. Ov. *Fast.* 1.637–50; Plut. *Cam.* 42.3. Raaflaub 2016c: 23. For the new temple dedicated in 121 BCE and the restoration by Tiberius between 7 BCE and 10 CE see Levick 1978.
21. For the Temple of Concordia vowed by the Senate under Caesar see Dio Cass. 44.4.5; Raaflaub 2015b: 112.

NOTES

22. Cf. *RIC* I² Augustus 251 (Venus), 253 (Pax, Fortuna, or Concordia), 256 (Victoria). For a review of the discussion of the iconography and date of these emissions, see Simon 1994: 208–9; Gurval 1995: 47–65.

23. See also Burton, Chapter 8 below.

24. Cf. Hor. *Carm.* 4.15.17–20; *Epod.* 7. For the principate preventing civil war, cf. Ov. *Met.* 15.832–42; *RGDA* 3, 34; Sen. *Clem.* 1.9–11; Luc. 1.33–45; Tac. *Ann.* 3.28.3; cf. *Hist.* 1.1.1; Dion. Hal. *Ant. Rom.* 1.7.2.

25. Cf. Hor. *Carm.* 4.5.25–8, 15.21–4; Verg. *Georg.* 1.505–14 and the famous prophecy of Jupiter in Verg. *Aen.* 6.851–3. For Augustan coins, see *RIC* I² Augustus 252–3 and 476 (Ephesos); see Figure 5.4 below.

26. Liv. 1.19.3. Dio Cass. 51.20.4 lists the closure of the gates among other honorific decrees prompted by a letter by Octavian concerning the Parthians.

27. Cf. for instance, Macrob. *Sat.* 1.9.1–16. For the representation of Janus on the oldest Roman coins, *RRC* 14.

28. Liv. 1.19.2; Varro *Ling.* 5.165. Tortorici 1996.

29. Liv. 1.19.1–2 (translation T. Luce); cf. also Plut. *Numa* 20.1. Macrob. *Sat.* 1.9.16–7 presents a different aetiology and traces the ritual back to the war against the Sabines under Romulus.

30. Verg. *Aen.* 1.294–6. Hor. *Epist.* 2.1.255; Ov. *Fast.* 1.117–24, 247–55, 279–82; Liv. 1.19.2–3; cf. also Plin. *HN* 34.33; Suet. *Aug.* 22; Plut. *Numa* 20; Serv. *Aen.* 7.607; Dio Cass. 51.20, 53.27, 89.13. Simon 1994: 205.

31. For the discussion see, inter alia, Rüpke 1990: 30 and esp. 136–41; Simon 1990: 618; Gurval 1995: 19–36; DeBrohun 2007: 257–60. In general Turcan 1981; Simon 1988: 72–3.

32. An alternative inscription reads PACE PR VBIQ PARTA IANVM CLVSIT ("After he [Nero] had established the Peace of the Roman People everywhere, he closed (the gates) of Janus."); *RIC* I² Nero 263–71, 283–91, 300–11, 323–8, 337–42, 347–50, 353–5. Simon 1990: 619. However, it is noteworthy that after Augustus the ritual closure of the gates is confirmed only for Nero (Suet. *Nero* 13.2); Vespasian (Oros. 3.7.3), and another, unknown emperor (Oros. 7.19.4); yet see also Amm. Marc. 16.10.1.

33. *RGDA* 13. Cf. in general Rich 2003; Raaflaub 2011a: 323–4.

34. Cf. Ov. *Fast.* 5.545–98; Vell. Pat. 2.100.2; Dio Cass. 55.10.2–6.

35. See also already Ov. *Ars Am.* 1.171–8; Suet. *Div. Aug.* 29; Dio Cass. 55.10.2–3. Beard, North, and Price 1996, I 199; cf. in general Croon 1981.

36. Cf. Ov. *Fast.* 5.549–70; *RGDA* 21.29, Vell. Pat. 2.39.2; Suet. *Aug.* 29.2, 31.5, Dio Cass. 55.10.2–4. Croon 1981; Zanker 1988: 194–205, 210–15; Herbert-Brown 1994: 95–108; Galinsky 1996: 197–213; Beard, North, and Price 1996: I 199–200; Rich 1998; Spannagel 1999; Barchiesi 2000; Ganzert 2000: 54–76. 97–110; Woolf 2015: 219–21. The relief of the Ara Pietatis Augustae (the so-called Villa Medici Relief) is believed to represent the front of the temple. The Pantheon was dedicated to all major gods and goddesses, but Mars and Venus were attributed a central role, Dio Cass. 53.27.2; Simon and Bauchhenss 1984: 511.

37. Augustus accordingly used the money allocated by the Senate and the people to dedicate statues of Concordia, Pax, and Salus Publica; Dio Cass. 54.35.1. Cf. also, for instance Ov. *Fast.* 1.709–11 (Apollo celebrates Pax adorned with Actian laurel), 4.407–8 (Pax and Ceres). For more examples, see Simon 1994: 209–11.

38. *RGDA* 12.2 for Augustus' return from Spain; Ov. *Fast.* 1.709–22 stresses the connection with Actium instead.

39. See *RGDA* 12.2; Ov. *Fast.* 1.709–10. Elsner 1991; Simon 1994: 204; Raaflaub 2015b: 108–9. In general see Zanker 1988: 120–3,179–83, 203–4; Billows 1993.

40. The obelisk and the Ara Pacis were erected in conjunction to one another and presumably even dedicated on the same day. Simon 1988: 73–4; Zanker 1988: 144–5; Elsner 1991: 52–4; Henslin 1997; Raaflaub 2011a: 331–3; Haselberger 2011 (with responses, 74–98); Raaflaub 2015b: 107.
41. For the visual program of the Ara Pacis see Judith Fletcher's contribution in Chapter 5. Cf., inter alia, Zanker 1988: 120–2, 158–9, 172–9; Elsner 1991: 54–8; Billows 1993.
42. See, for instance, Rüpke 1990: 21; Raaflaub 2015b: 109. The close connection between the reverence of Pax and the imperial cult also becomes evident in the inscription of the *koinon* of Asia (9 BCE) that celebrated Augustus as a god who had brought an end to war and would impose peace. (*OGIS* 458, ll.35–6).
43. Raaflaub 2015b: 111. See, for instance, Otho's coins featuring Pax, *RIC* I², Otho nos. 3–6 (*pax orbis terrarum*).
44. Plin. *HN* 36.102; Stat. *Silv.* 4.3.17; Jos. *BJ* 7.159–62; Herodian 1.14.2; Anderson 1984: 101–18; Raaflaub 2015b: 106.
45. For Pax on Vespasian's coins see *RIC* II Vespasian 10, 18, 39, 90, 104, 185, 193, 200, 212 (seated), *RIC* II Vespasian 9, 47, 56, 63, 156, 161, 168, 258, 263 (standing). For the coin imagery see Stevenson 2010: 189–90. Cf. also the altar to the Pax Augusta from 71 CE by members of the *tribus Sucusana*, *CIL* VI 199.
46. Jos. *BJ* 7.159–62; Plin. *HN* 12.94, 34.84, 35.102–3, 109, 36.27, 58; Paus. 6.9.3; cf. Suet. *Vesp.* 9; Dio Cass. 65.15.1; Aur. Vict. 9.7; all stating that the temple was erected *ex manubiis* (from the spoils (of war)). See, inter alia, Darwall-Smith 1996: 58–65; Noreña 2003; Packer 2003: 170–2; Millar 2005: 111–13; Taraporewalla 2010.
47. Cf. Raaflaub 2015b: 106. For *pax* in the representation of Vespasian in general, see Noreña 2003: esp. 29–35.
48. Among the more famous cases of *prodigia* are Thuc. 1.118.3, 2.8.3, 54.2–5; Xen. *Anab.* 3.1.5–7, *Hell.* 6.4.7; Diod. 15.52.3–6. For the notion that the gods support a just war, see Thuc. 2.74.1–2; Xen. *Cyr.* 1.5. 13–14; Dion. Hal. *Ant. Rom.* 2.72.3.
49. See, for example, *Il.* 2.284–332. 339–43, 3.276–91; Xen. *Anab.* 2.5.7–8; 3.1.21–2; *Ages.* 1.13; *Hell.* 5.4.1; Diod. 17.84.2. See in general Scharff 2016.
50. Burkert 1985: 251, 445 n. 8; Bayliss 2013: 160–1. See the list in Scharff 2016: 317–21 and the database of the Nottingham project "The Oath in Archaic and Classical Greece" (http://www.nottingham.ac.uk/greatdatabase/brzoaths/public_html/index.php (accessed October 10, 2018)).
51. Polyb. 7.9.2–3; cf. 3.25.4–9. See Scharff 2016: 326–7.
52. *Il.* 3.298–301; Thuc. 1.118.3, 7.18.2; Xen. *Anab.* 2.5.7–8; 3.1.21–2; *Ages.* 1.13; *Hell.* 5.4.1. Bayliss 2013: 167–75; Scharff 2016: 46–64.
53. For the agreement between the two parties to make the duel happen, see Baltrusch 1994: 104–9.
54. Cf., for instance, Onasandros *Strat.* 37.2–5.
55. Rich 1976: 56–7. For the history, and in particular the origin of these rituals see, inter alia, Saulnier 1980: 174–5; Wiedemann 1986; Rüpke 1990: esp. 97–117; Watson 1993; Rich 2011.
56. See, for instance the debate about Caesar's actions in Germany: Plut. *Caes.* 22.3.
57. Cf. Cic. *Rep.* 3.35; *Off.* 1.35, 80–1. For the religious and ritual context, see Rüpke 1990: 117–22.
58. The famous Olympian Peace, the *ekecheiria*, only guaranteed that athletes and spectators were able to travel unharmed to and from the site of major competitions, cf. Plut. *Lyc.* 1.2; Paus. 5.20.1.
59. For peace as a central message of Jesus' teachings, see Matthew 5.38–42; 26.52; Mark 14.46–9; Luke 6.29, 22.49–51. Cf. also Justin Martyr, *First Apology* 15–16, 39; *Dial.* 109–10, drawing on the prophecy of swords into plowshares in *Isaiah* 2:40.

NOTES   169

60. Tert. *Apol.* 30.4, 37.4, 42.3; *On Idolatry* 19.1–3. Swift 2007: 283–4.
61. Cf. also Orig. *Cels.* 6.1, 8.73. Swift 2007: 281–2 (with more examples), 285.
62. See, most explicitly, Euseb. *Paneg.* 2.3; *Vita Const.*1.6. Swift 2007: 286.
63. Aug. *Civ.* 3.10. Swift 2007: 291; Schulz 2008, esp. 99–107.

Chapter 5

1. Raaflaub (2009: 238) notes how the texts of Homer and Hesiod "reflect a strong interest in problems of war and peace and make interesting conceptual use of the contrast between them."
2. The connection between Peace and Wealth in Greek literature is exhaustively surveyed by Stafford (2001: 182–4).
3. Plutarch (*Kimon* 16) records that she was a cult figure in the mid-fifth century, but in all likelihood he has misunderstood his sources (Shapiro 1993: 45).
4. The calyx krater is attributed to the Dinos Painter. The Beazley archive gives a possible date between 450 and 410 for this vessel: http://www.beazley.ox.ac.uk/record/25B6D2A8-F9D3-4904-8E72-1162D5AF05B1 (accessed October 10, 2018). Stafford's suggestion that the representation of Eirēnē might have been influenced by Aristophanes' *Peace* depends on a later date, and is very speculative.
5. The fragment may also be part of a statue base. Smith (2003) speculates that the other two figures are perhaps Eunomia, or Theoria (Festival) and Opora (Harvest).
6. The first-century CE biographer Cornelius reports that the Athenians celebrated their victory over Sparta by establishing the first altars of peace, along with a *pulvinar*, which is a couch used at banquets. Stafford (2001: 175) discusses the possibility that Eirēnē's cult included a *theoxenia*, a ritual feast, which the divinity would putatively attend.
7. For differing views on the creation of the statue see Stafford 2001: 175–6 and Smith 2011: 110–11.
8. As Herodotos (7.149.1) explains, thirty years is long enough for a new generation to be produced. Olson 2002: 131 suggests that Aristophanes may be thinking specifically of a recent thirty-year peace treaty between Athens and Sparta in 446 after Athens captured Euboia. That treaty was broken with the onset of the Peloponnesian War in 431.
9. For further discussion of the wine imagery in *Acharnians* see Newiger 1996: 148, and cf. Chapter 1 above.
10. Newiger (1996: 150) asserts that the goddess is represented by a statue here.
11. As Dillon (1987: 99) observes, the fragments of lost plays by Aristophanes similarly use agricultural metaphors for peace, for example his *Farmers* (probably produced sometime in the 420s) features a wish for the war to end so that the farmers can work in the fields again, and enjoy the pleasures of wine (fr. 111 *PCG*).
12. Lewis (1955) bases this conjecture on inscriptional evidence; as Henderson notes (1987: 208), Lysimache is mentioned by name at *Peace* 991–2.
13. Bowie (1993: 182) notes that the reference to sacrifices suggests an opening of hostilities, while the wine sacrifice evokes the *spondai* that ended them. Thus "their actions are both a declaration of war and an attempt to make peace."

Chapter 6

1. For third-party arbitration in ancient Greece, see Piccirilli 1973; Ager 1996; Magnetto 1997.
2. Homer, *Odyssey* 24.486. In the Athenian agora, Kephisodotos' statue depicting *Eirēnē* with

Ploutos as a boy on her arm was on display after the peace of 375 BCE (Philochoros in *FGrH* 328 F 151 = *BNJ* 328 F 151; Cornelius Nepos *Timotheus* 2; Pausanias 1.8.2). See chapters 3 and 4 above, and Figure 5.2.

3. Dreher 2013, citing Bravo 1980 and Gräber 1992.
4. For the ubiquity of warfare in the Hellenistic period also among Greek cities, see Ma 2000, Chaniotis 2005.
5. See Austin 1986. Examples: Seleukos I Nikator ("Victor", 305–281 BCE), Antiochos IV Theos Epiphanes Nikēphoros ("God Manifest Bringer of Victory", 175–164 BCE), Ptolemy Keraunos ("Lightning Bolt", 281–279 BCE), Demetrios I Poliorketes ("Besieger", 306–285 BCE); see Muccioli 2013.
6. For these key issues, two works are of lasting and fundamental importance: Brunt 1971 and Sherwin-White 1973. For the Roman consolidation of Italy, see Bispham 2007.
7. Cf. Chapter 3 above. Other chapters in this volume have drawn attention to the famous lines in Vergil's *Aeneid*, in which the shade of Anchises, the father of Aeneas, foretells the future history of the Roman state as conqueror and pacifier (*Aen.* 6. 852–3).
8. For moral wrangling in the senatorial debates, see Polyb. 1.10–11; and for Polybios' representation of the events and his authorial motivations, see Champion 2013: 148–56.
9. On slogans and propaganda concerning the "freedom of the Greeks," see Gruen 1984 1: 132–57 and Dmitriev 2011; for the career of Flamininus, see Badian 1973.
10. For Antiochos' public image as invincible conqueror and his diplomatic relations with the Greek cities of Asia Minor, see Ma 1999.
11. For an excellent overview of this period in Roman history and its manifold aspects, see Garnsey and Saller 2014; see also de Souza 2008.
12. By 641 CE, the Arabs had overthrown the Persians and had conquered much of the Byzantine empire's Asian holdings, such as Syria and Palestine (Gregory 2010: 176–81).

Chapter 7

1. *Andrapodismos* refers to a brutal treatment meted out to a conquered people, consisting of the enslavement of the entire populace, often accompanied by the execution of all males of military age.
2. See for example *IG* II² 43, the "charter" of the Second Athenian Sea League, with Adcock and Mosley 1975: 71–8; Hunt 2010: 104–5.
3. For the phenomenon of the common peace (*koine eirēnē*) in the fourth century BCE, see chapters 1 and 8. Although it could be argued that the common peaces provided mechanisms for collectivized security, in reality they were exploited by the dominant powers of the time as a means to controlling others.
4. See Polyb. 15.20 and Plut. *Pyrr.* 14, with Billows 2007; Chaniotis 2005: 57–77; Serrati 2007.
5. An "Italian" people *per se* did not exist; rather, Rome used the fictitious ethnonym to simplify the characteristics and differences of the many peoples who lived in Central Italy. The same term, *Italici*, would be proudly claimed by the rebels in the Social War at the beginning of the first century BCE.
6. The Principate refers to the period of imperial rule from Augustus until towards the end of the third century CE.
7. Peace is one of the recurring themes of Augustan communication from the cistophoric coins of Ephesos to the Ara Pacis (Zanker 1988); see Chapter 5 above.

NOTES 171

8. *Maiestas* ("dignity, majesty", literally "greaterness") was a concept core to the Roman state's perception of itself vis-à-vis others in the ancient Mediterranean, and alliances often bound the other party to respect the *maiestas* of the Roman people. *Crimen minutae/laesae maiestatis*—the crime of diminishing or harming by whatever means the reputation and standing of Rome—was treason, and by a process of metonymy and shorthand, the term *maiestas* alone came often to mean "treason".

Chapter 8

1. Although not technically part of the Achaimenid dynasty (Waters 2014: 8, 148–50), he is conventionally considered as such (Wiesehöfer 2009: 94 n. 1) and will be so considered here.
2. Horsfall translation; on the translation of *pacique imponere morem*, "to set the force of habit on peace," i.e., to make peace (as opposed to war) habitual, see Ullman 1945.
3. Variously referred to as *koina*, *ethnē*, and *sympoliteiai* in the Greek sources; Larsen 1968: xiv–xv; Beck and Funke 2015b: 14–15.
4. Unless, that is, we are to believe Plut. *Per.* 17, who mentions an initiative of Perikles *ca.* 450 for a common peace of the Greeks against Sparta. See Raaflaub 2016d: 127–8 for discussion, and cf. Chapter 1 above.
5. See Larsen 1968 (still indispensable), and now Beck and Funke 2015a (a "New Larsen": 28), upon both of which much of this section is based.
6. Larsen 1968: xv, but see the caveats at Beck and Funke 2015b: 18–19.

ABBREVIATIONS AND BIBLIOGRAPHY

Unless otherwise stated, translations of ancient literary works employed in this volume are common English translations included in the bibliography below under the ancient author's name; some slight adaptations have been made in order to suit syntactic context and maintain consistency of orthography throughout the volume.

ABBREVIATIONS

Abbreviations of ancient literary works generally conform to the system employed by the *Oxford Classical Dictionary*, 4th edition (available online: http://classics.oxfordre.com/staticfiles/images/ORECLA/OCD.ABBREVIATIONS.pdf (accessed October 10, 2018)).

ANET   Pritchard, James B. (1955), *Ancient Near Eastern Texts Relating to the Old Testament*, 2nd edn, Princeton NJ: Princeton University Press.

ANRW   *Aufstieg und Niedergang der römischen Welt* (1972–), Berlin: De Gruyter.

BMC Attica Head, Barclay (1888), *Catalogue of Greek Coins in the British Museum, Attica—Megaris—Aegina*, London: British Museum.

BNJ   Worthington, Ian, ed. (2006–), *Brill's New Jacoby*, Brill Online.

BNP   Cancik, Hubert, and Helmuth Schneider, eds. (1996–), *Brill's New Pauly*, Brill Online.

CIL   *Corpus Inscriptionum Latinarum* (1863–), Berlin: Berlin-Brandenburgische Akademie der Wissenschaften.

DK   Diels, Hermann, and Walther Kranz (1952–), *Die Fragmente der Vorsokratiker*, 6th edn., Berlin: Weidmann.

DNP   Cancik, Hubert, and Helmuth Schneider, eds. (1996–), *Der neue Pauly*, Stuttgart: J.B. Metzler; also Brill Online.

FGrH   Felix Jacoby (1923–), *Die Fragmente der griechischen Historiker*, Berlin: Weidmann.

FRH   Hans Beck and Uwe Walter, eds. (2001), *Die frühen römischen Historiker*, Darmstadt: WBG.

GW   Gagarin, Michael, and Paul Woodruff, eds. (1995), *Early Greek Political Thoughts from Homer to the Sophists*, Cambridge: Cambridge University Press.

IEleus.   K. Clinton, ed. (2005–2008), *Eleusis. The Inscriptions on Stone*, Athens: Greek Archaeological Society.

IG	*Inscriptiones Graecae* (1873–), Berlin: Berlin-Brandenburgische Akademie der Wissenschaften.
LIMC	*Lexicon Iconographicum Mythologiae Classicae* (1981–2009), Zurich et al.: Artemis and Winkler.
LTUR	E.M. Steinby, ed. (1993–2000), *Lexicon Topographicum Urbis Romae*, 6 vols., Rome: Edizioni Quasar.
OGIS	Dittenberger, Wilhelm (1903), *Orientis Graecae Inscriptiones Selectae*, 2 vols., Leipzig.
PCG	Kassel, Rudolf, and Colin Austin, eds. (1983–), *Poetae Comici Graeci*, Berlin: De Gruyter.
PMG	Page, Denys L. (1962), *Poetae Melici Graeci*, Oxford: Clarendon Press.
RE	Pauly, August, and Georg Wissowa et al., eds. (1839–1980), *Realenzyklopädie der klassischen Altertumswissenschaft*, Stuttgart: J.B. Metzler.
RGDA	*Res Gestae Divi Augusti* (*The Achievements of the Divine Augustus*). For translation, see Sherk 1988.
RRC	Crawford, Michael H. (1975), *Roman Republican Coinage*, Cambridge: Cambridge University Press.
RIC	Mattingly, Harold, et al., eds. (1923–1994), *Roman Imperial Coinage*, London: Spink.
SEG	*Supplementum Epigraphicum Graecum* (1923–), Brill Online.
Syll[3]	Dittenberger, Wilhelm, ed. (1915), *Sylloge Inscriptionum Graecarum*, 4 vols., Leipzig.
SVA I–III	Von Scala, Rudolf, Hermann Bengtson, and Hatto Schmidt, eds. (1898–1975), *Die Staatsverträge des Altertums I–III*, Leipzig and Munich: Teubner and Beck.
TGrF	Bruno Snell et al., eds. (1971–), *Tragicorum Graecorum Fragmenta*, 5 vols., Göttingen: Vandenhoek and Ruprecht.

BIBLIOGRAPHY

Adcock, Frank, and Derek J. Mosley (1975), *Diplomacy in Ancient Greece*, London: Thames and Hudson.

Ager, Sheila L. (1993), "Why War? Some Views on International Arbitration in Ancient Greece," *Echos du monde classique/Classical Views* 37: 1–13.

Ager, Sheila L. (1996), *Interstate Arbitrations in the Greek World, 337–90 BC*, Berkeley: University of California Press.

Ager, Sheila L. (2005), "Sacred Settlements: The Role of the Gods in the Resolution of Interstate Disputes," in J.-M. Bertrand (ed.), *La violence dans les mondes grec et romain*, 413–29, Paris: Publications de la Sorbonne.

ABBREVIATIONS AND BIBLIOGRAPHY

Ager, Sheila L. (2009), "Roman Perspectives on Greek Diplomacy," in Claude Eilers (ed.), *Diplomats and Diplomacy in the Roman World*, 15–43, Leiden: Brill.

Ager, Sheila L. (2015) "Peaceful Conflict Resolution in the World of the Federal States," in Beck and Funke 2015a, 471–86.

Allen, Joel (2011), *Hostages and Hostage-Taking in the Roman Empire*. Cambridge: Cambridge University Press.

Alonso, Victor (2007), "War, Peace, and International Law in Ancient Greece," in Raaflaub 2007a, 206–25.

Anastasiou, Harry (2007), "The EU as a Peace Building System: Deconstructing Nationalism in an Era of Globalization," *International Journal of Peace Studies* 12: 31–50.

Anderson, James C. (1984), *The Historical Topography of the Imperial Fora*, Bruxelles: Collection Latomus.

Angelova, Diliana N. (2015), *Sacred Founders: Women, Men and Gods in the Discourse of Imperial Founding, Rome through Early Byzantium*, Oakland: University of California Press.

Anson, Edward M. (2013), *Alexander the Great: Themes and Issues*, London: Bloomsbury.

Ardrey, Robert (1961), *African Genesis. A Personal Investigation into the Animal Origins and Nature of Man*, New York.

Aristophanes (1990), *Lysistrata*, trans. Alan H. Sommerstein, Warminster: Aris and Phillips.

Aristotle (1932), *Politics*, trans. H. Rackham, Cambridge MA: Harvard University Press.

Augustine. See under Swift 1983.

Austin, Michel (1986), "Hellenistic Kings, War, and the Economy," *Classical Quarterly* 36: 450–66.

Austin, Michel (2006), *The Hellenistic World from Alexander to the Roman Conquest. A Selection of Ancient Sources in Translation*, 2nd edn, Cambridge: Cambridge University Press.

Bacchylides (1992), *Greek Lyric IV: Bacchylides, Corinna, and Others*, trans. David A. Campbell, Cambridge MA: Harvard University Press.

Badian, Ernst (1958), *Foreign Clientelae, 264–70 B.C.*, Oxford: Clarendon Press.

Badian, Ernst (1959), "Rome and Antiochus the Great: A Study in Cold War," *Classical Philology* 54: 81–99.

Badian, Ernst (1965), "The Administration of the Empire," *Greece and Rome* 12, 166–82.

Badian, Ernst (1968), *Roman Imperialism in the Late Republic*. Ithaca.

Badian, Ernst (1973), *Titus Quinctius Flamininus: Philhellenism and Realpolitik*, Cincinnati: Norman University of Cincinnati.

Baltrusch, Ernst (1994), *Symmachie und Spondai. Untersuchungen zum griechischen Völkerrecht der archaischen und klassischen Zeit (8.-5. Jahrhundert v.Chr.)*, Berlin: De Gruyter.

Baltrusch, Ernst (2008), *Außenpolitik, Bünde und Reichsbildung in der Antike*, Munich: R. Oldenbourg.

Barash, David P. (2000), *Approaches to Peace. A Reader in Peace Studies*, Oxford: Oxford University Press.

Barchiesi, Allesandro (2000), "Martial Arts. Mars Ultor in the Forum Augustum. A Verbal Monument with Vengeance," in Geraldine Herbert-Brown (ed.), *Ovid's Fasti. Historical Readings at its Bimillenium*, 1–22, Oxford: Oxford University Press.

Barfield, Thomas J. (1993), *The Nomadic Alternative*, Prentice Hall: Englewood Cliffs, NJ.

Barton, Carlin A. (2007), "The Price of Peace in Ancient Rome," in Raaflaub 2007a, 245–55.

Bauman, Richard A. (1992), *Women and Politics in Ancient Rome*, London and New York: Routledge.

Bauslaugh, Robert A. (1990), *The Concept of Neutrality in Classical Greece,* Berkeley and Los Angeles: University of California Press.

Bayliss, Andrew J. (2013), "Oaths and Interstate Relations," in Alan H. Sommerstein and Andrew J. Bayliss (eds.), *Oath and State in Ancient Greece,* 147–306, Berlin: De Gruyter.

Beard, Mary (2009), *The Roman Triumph,* Cambridge MA: Harvard University Press.

Beard, Mary, John North, and Simon Price (1996), *Religions of Rome,* Cambridge: Cambridge University Press.

Beck, Hans, and Peter Funke, eds. (2015a), *Federalism in Greek Antiquity,* Cambridge: Cambridge University Press.

Beck, Hans, and Peter Funke, eds. (2015b), "Introduction to Federalism in Greek Antiquity," in Beck and Funke 2015a, 1–29.

Bederman, David J. (2001), *International Law in Antiquity,* Cambridge: Cambridge University Press.

Bell, Lanny (2007), "Conflict and Reconciliation in the Ancient Middle East. The Clash of Egyptian and Hittite Chariots in Syria, and the World's First Peace Treaty between 'Superpowers'," in Raaflaub 2007a, 98–120.

Best, Jan G. P. (1969), *Thracian Peltasts and their Influence on Greek Warfare,* Groningen: Wolters-Noordhoff.

Betancourt, Philip P. (2008), "Minoan Trade," in Cynthia W. Shelmerdine (ed), *The Cambridge Companion to the Aegean Bronze Age,* 209–29, Cambridge: Cambridge University Press.

Bickel, Susanne (2016), "Concepts of Peace in Ancient Egypt," in Raaflaub 2016a, 43–66.

Billows, Richard (1993), "The Religious Procession of the Ara Pacis Augustae. Augustus' *Supplicatio* in 13 B.C.," *Journal of Roman Archaeology* 6: 80–92.

Billows, Richard (2007), "International Relations," in Sabin, van Wees, and Whitby (eds.), 303–24.

Bispham, Edward (2007), *From Asculum to Actium: The Municipalization of Italy from the Social War to Augustus,* Oxford: Oxford University Press.

Blegen Carl W. (1975), "The Expansion of Mycenaean Civilization," in Iorwerth E.S. Edwards et al. (eds.), *The Cambridge Ancient History Volume 2, Part 2: The Middle East and the Aegean Region, c.1380–1000 BC,* 3rd edn, 165–87, Cambridge: Cambridge University Press.

Blockley, R. C. (1992), *East Roman Foreign Policy: Formation and Conduct from Diocletian to Anastasius,* Leeds: Cairns.

Boatwright, Mary T. (2012), *The Romans: From Village to Empire,* New York: Oxford University Press.

Boedeker, Deborah, and Kurt Raaflaub, eds. (1998), *Democracy, Empire, and the Arts in Fifth-Century Athens,* Cambridge MA: Harvard University Press.

Bourke, Graeme. (2018), *Elis: Internal Politics and External Policy in Ancient Greece,* Abingdon and New York: Routledge.

Bowie, A. M. (1994), *Aristophanes: Myth, Ritual and Comedy,* Cambridge: Cambridge University Press.

Bravo, B. (1980), "*Sylân*: représsailles et justice privée contre des étrangers dans les cités grecques," *Annali della Scuola Normale Superiore di Pisa, Cl. di Lettere e Filosofia* 3.10: 675–987.

Briant, Pierre (1996), *Histoire de l'empire perse de Cyrus à Alexandre,* Paris: Fayard.

Brizzi, Giovanni (2005), "Cartagine e Roma: dall'intesa al confronto," in Cinzia Bearzot, Franca Landucci Gattinoni, and Giuseppe Zecchini (eds.), *L'equilibrio internazionale dagli antichi ai moderni,* 29–44, Milan: Vita e Pensiero.

Bronkhorst, Johannes (2016), "Thinking about Peace in Ancient India," in Raaflaub 2016a, 67–97.

ABBREVIATIONS AND BIBLIOGRAPHY

Broodbank, Cyprian (2004), "Minoanisation," *Proceedings of the Cambridge Philological Society* 50, 46–91.

Brosius, Maria (2012), "Persian Diplomacy between 'Pax Persica' and 'Zero-Tolerance'," in Wilker 2012a, 150–64.

Brown, Robert (1995), "Livy's Sabine Women and the Ideal of *Concordia*," *Transactions of the American Philological Association* 125: 291–319.

Brunt, P.A. (1971), *Italian Manpower, 225 B.C.–A.D. 14*, Oxford: Oxford University Press.

Bugh, Glenn R. (1988), *The Horsemen of Athens*. Princeton NJ: Princeton University Press.

Burkert, Walter (1985), *Greek Religion*. Cambridge MA: Harvard University Press.

Burton, Paul. J. (2013), *Friendship and Empire. Roman Diplomacy and Imperialism in the Middle Republic (353–146 BC)*, Cambridge: Cambridge University Press.

Burton, Paul. J. (2017), *Rome and the Third Macedonian War*, Cambridge: Cambridge University Press.

Caesar (1917), *The Gallic War*, trans. H.J. Edwards, Cambridge MA: Harvard University Press.

Cameron, Averil (2012), *The Mediterranean World in Late Antiquity AD 395–700*, 2nd edn, Oxford and New York: Routledge.

Camp, John M. (2004), *The Archaeology of Athens*, New Haven: Yale University Press.

Carman, John, and Anthony Harding, eds. (1999), *Ancient Warfare: Archaeological Perspectives*, Stroud: Sutton Publishing.

Carney, Elizabeth (2000), *Women and Monarchy in Macedonia*, Norman OK: University of Oklahoma Press.

Carney, Elizabeth (2006), *Olympias: Mother of Alexander the Great*, New York/Abingdon: Routledge.

Carney, Elizabeth (2013), *Arsinoë of Egypt and Macedon: A Royal Life*, Oxford: Oxford University Press.

Carter, Nicholas P. (2014), "Sources and Scales of Classic Maya History," in Raaflaub 2014a, 340–71.

Cassola, Filippo (1983), "Tendenze filopuniche e antipuniche in Roma," in *Atti del I Congresso Internazionale di Studi Fenici e Punici*, 35–59, Roma: CNR.

Chadwick, John (1976), *The Mycenaean World*, Cambridge: Cambridge University Press.

Champion, Craige B. ed. (2004), *Roman Imperialism. Readings and Sources*, Malden: Blackwell Publishing.

Champion, Craige B. ed. (2013), "Historiographic Patterns and Historical Obstacles in Polybius' *Histories*: Marcellus, Flaminius, and the Mamertine Crisis," in Bruce Gibson and Thomas Harrison (eds.), *Polybius and His World: Essays in Memory of F.W. Walbank*, 143–57, Oxford: Oxford University Press.

Champion, Craige B., and Arthur M. Eckstein (2004), "The Study of Roman Imperialism," in Champion 2004, 1–10.

Chaniotis, Angelos (2005), *War in the Hellenistic World. A Social and Cultural History*, Malden: Blackwell Publishing.

Cicero (1913), *On Duties*, trans. Walter Miller, Cambridge MA: Harvard University Press.

Cicero (1928), *On the Republic; On the Laws*, trans. Clinton W. Keyes, Cambridge MA: Harvard University Press.

Cicero (1958), *Pro Caelio; De Provinciis Consularibus; Pro Balbo*, trans. R. Gardner, Cambridge MA: Harvard University Press.

Clavadetscher-Thürlemann, Silvia (1985), *ΠΟΛΕΜΟΣ ΔΙΚΑΙΟΣ und Bellum Iustum: Versuch einer Ideengeschichte*, Zurich.

Clayman, Dee L. (2014), *Berenice II and the Golden Age of Ptolemaic Egypt*, Oxford: Oxford University Press.

Clement of Alexandria. See under Swift 1983.

Cline, Eric H., and Mark W. Graham (2008), *Ancient Empires: from Mesopotamia to the Rise of Islam*, New York: Cambridge University Press.

Coltrain, Joan B., Joel Janetski, and Michael D. Lewis (2012), "A Re-assessment of Basketmaker II Cave 7: Massacre Site or Cemetery Context," *Journal of Archaeological Science* 39: 2220–30.

Connolly, Joan B. (2007), *Portrait of a Priestess: Women and Ritual in Ancient Greece*, Princeton and Oxford: Princeton University Press.

Cook, John M. (1983), *The Persian Empire*, New York: Schocken.

Cornell, Tim J. (1989), "The Conquest of Italy," in Frank W. Walbank et al. (eds.), *Cambridge Ancient History VII.2: The Rise of Rome to 220 BC*, 351–419, 2nd edn, Cambridge: Cambridge University Press.

Cornwell, Hannah (2017), *Pax and the Politics of Peace: Republic to Principate*, Oxford: Oxford University Press.

Coşkun, Altay, and Alex McAuley, eds. (2016), *Seleukid Royal Women: Creation, Representation and Distortion of Hellenistic Queenship in the Seleukid Empire*, Stuttgart: Franz Steiner.

Croally, N. T. (2007), *Euripidean Polemic. The Trojan Women and the Function of Tragedy*, Cambridge: Cambridge University Press.

Crocker, Chester A., Fen Osler Hampson, and Pamela Aall (2005), "Mapping the Nettle Field," in Chester A. Crocker, Fen Osler Hampson, and Pamela Aall (eds.), *Grasping the Nettle: Analyzing Cases of Intractable Conflict*, 3–30, Washington DC: US Institute of Peace.

Croon, Johan H. (1981), "Die Ideologie des Marskultes unter dem Prinzipal und ihre Vorgeschichte," *ANRW* II.17.1: 246–71.

Crowley, Jason (2012), *The Psychology of the Athenian Hoplite: The Culture of Combat in Classical Athens*, Cambridge: Cambridge University Press.

Cunliffe, Richard J. (1977), *A Lexicon of the Homeric Dialect*, Norman OK: University of Oklahoma Press.

D'Altroy, Terence N. (2014), *The Incas*, Malden: Wiley Blackwell.

Dart, Christopher J. (2016), "Frontiers, Security and Military Policy," in Andrew Zissos (ed.), *A Companion to the Flavian Age of Imperial Rome*: 207–22, Oxford: Wiley Blackwell.

Darwall-Smith, Robin H. (1996), *Emperors and Architecture. A Study of Flavian Rome*, Brussels: Collection Latomus.

Davis, Jack L. (2008), "Minoan Crete and the Aegean Islands," in Shelmerdine (2008), 186–208.

DeBrohun, Jeri B. (2007), "The Gates of War (and Peace): Roman Literary Perspectives," in Raaflaub 2007a, 256–78.

De Grummond, Nancy Thomson (1990), "Pax Augusta and the Horae on the Ara Pacis Augustae," *American Journal of Archaeology* 94: 663–77.

Delia, Diana (1991), "Fulvia Reconsidered," in Sarah B. Pomeroy (ed.), *Women's History and Ancient History*, 197–217, Chapel Hill and London: University of North Carolina Press.

De Romilly, Jacqueline (1972), "Vocabulaire et propagande ou les premiers emplois du mot homonoia," in Françoise Bader (ed.), *Mélanges de linguistique et de philologie grecques offerts à Pierre Chantraine*, 199–209, Paris: Klincksieck.

De Souza, Philip (2008), "*Parta Victoriis Pax*: Roman Emperors as Peacemakers," in de Souza and France 2008, 76–106.

De Souza, Philip, and John France, eds. (2008), *War and Peace in Ancient and Medieval History*, Cambridge: Cambridge University Press.

ABBREVIATIONS AND BIBLIOGRAPHY

De Ste. Croix, Geoffrey E.M. (1972), *The Origins of the Peloponnesian War*, London: Duckworth.

Dewald, Carolyn (1980), "Biology and Politics: Women in Herodotus' *Histories*," *Pacific Coast Philology*, 15: 11–18.

Dewald, Carolyn (1981), "Women and Culture in Herodotus' *Histories*," in Helene Foley (ed.), *Reflections of Women in Antiquity*, 91–125, London and New York: Routledge.

Dewald, Carolyn (2013), "Justice and Justifications: War Theory among the Ancient Greeks," in Jacob Neusner, Bruce D. Chilton, and R.E. Tully (eds.), *Just War in Religion and Politics*, 27–50, Lanham MD.

Dillon, Matthew (1987), "The *Lysistrata* as a Post-Deceleian Peace Play," *Transactions of the American Philological Association* 117: 97–104.

Dixon, William J. (1993), "Democracy and the Management of International Conflict," *Journal of Conflict Resolution* 37.1: 42–68.

Dmitriev, Sviatoslav (2011), *The Greek Slogan of Freedom and Early Roman Politics in Greece*, Oxford: Oxford University Press.

Dobbs, Darrell (1994), "Natural Right and the Problem of Aristotle's Defense of Slavery," *The Journal of Politics* 56.1: 60–94.

Donnan, Christopher B., and Donna McClelland (1999), *Moche Fineline Painting*, Los Angeles: University of California at Los Angeles.

Doyle, Michael (1986), *Empires*, Ithaca: Cornell University Press.

Dreher, Martin (2013), "Peace," in *The Encyclopedia of Ancient History*, Wiley. DOI: 10.1002/9781444338386.wbeah09181.

Ducat, Jean (2006), *Spartan Education: Youth and Society in the Classical Period*, Swansea: Classical Press of Wales.

Eckstein, Arthur M. (2005), "The Pact between the Kings, Polybius 15.20.6, and Polybius' View of the Outbreak of the Second Macedonian War," *Classical Philology* 100: 228–42.

Eckstein, Arthur M. (2006a), *Mediterranean Anarchy, Interstate War, and the Rise of Rome*, Berkeley: University of California.

Eckstein, Arthur M. (2006b), "Conceptualizing Roman Imperial Expansion under the Republic: An Introduction," in Nathan Rosenstein and Robert Morstein-Marx (eds.), *A Companion to the Roman Republic*, 567–89, Malden: Blackwell.

Eckstein, Arthur M. (2008), *Rome Enters the Greek East. From Anarchy to Hierarchy in the Hellenistic Mediterranean, 230–170 BC*, Malden: Blackwell.

Einhard (2008), *The Life of Charlemagne (Vita Karoli Magni/VKM)*, in David Ganz (trans.), *Einhard and Notker the Stammerer: Two Lives of Charlemagne*, London: Penguin Books. VKM.

Einstein, Albert (1949), *The World as I See It*, trans. Alan Harris, New York: Philosophical Library.

Elsner, John (1991), "Cult and Sacrifice: Sacrifice in the Ara Pacis Augustae," *Journal of Roman Studies* 81: 50–61.

Eph'al, Israel (forthcoming), "Ancient Israel," in Meissner, Raaflaub, and Yates (forthcoming).

Euripides (2008), *Fragments: Aegeus—Meleager*, trans. Christopher Collard and Martin Cropp, Cambridge MA: Cambridge University Press.

Fabre-Serris, Jacqueline, and Alison Keith, eds. (2015), *Women and War in Antiquity*, Baltimore: Johns Hopkins University Press.

Fales, Frederick M. (2010), *Guerre et paix en Assyrie: Religion et impérialisme*, Paris.

Ferguson, R.B. (2008), "War Before History," in Philip de Souza (ed.), *The Ancient World at War: A Global History*, 15–27, London: Thames and Hudson.

Ferrill, Arther (1997), *The Origins of War from the Stone Age to Alexander the Great*, Boulder CO.

Figueira, Thomas (2010), "Gynecocracy: How Women Policed Masculine Behaviour in Archaic and Classical Sparta," in Anton Powell and Stephen Hodkinson (eds.), *Sparta: The Body Politic*, 265–96, Swansea: The Classical Press of Wales.

Finley, Moses I. (2002), "The Silent Women of Rome," in Laura K. McClure (ed.), *Sexuality and Gender in the Classical World*, 147–56, Blackwell: Oxford. Originally published Moses I. Finley (1968), *Aspects of Antiquity: Discoveries and Controversies*, London: Chatto and Windus.

Forni, Giovanni (1987), "*Limes*: nozioni e nomenclature," in Marta Sordi (ed.), *Il confine nel mondo classico*, 272–94, Milan: Vita e Pensiero.

Forsdyke, Sara (2008), "Street Theatre and Popular Justice in Ancient Greece: Shaming, Stoning and Starving Offenders Inside and Outside the Courts," *Past and Present* 201: 3–50.

Foster, Benjamin (2007), "Water under the Straw: Peace in Mesopotamia," in Raaflaub 2007a, 66–80.

Fowden, Garth (1993), *Empire to Commonwealth: Consequences of Monotheism in Late Antiquity*, Princeton, NJ: Princeton University Press.

Fraschetti, Augusto (1990), *Roma e il principe*, Bari-Roma: Laterza.

Fraschetti, Augusto (2001), *Roman Women*, trans. Linda Lappin, Chicago: University of Chicago Press.

Fry, Douglas P. (2006), *The Human Potential for Peace: An Anthropological Challenge to Assumptions about War and Violence*, Oxford: Oxford University Press.

Fry, Douglas P. (2007), *Beyond War: The Human Potential for Peace*, Oxford: Oxford University Press.

Fry, Douglas P. ed. (2013), *War, Peace, and Human Nature: The Convergence of Evolutionary and Cultural Views*, Oxford: Oxford University Press.

Gabba, Emilio (1989), "Le strategie militari, le frontiere imperiali," in Emilio Gabba and Aldo Schiavone (eds.), *Storia di Roma* 4. *Caratteri e morfologie*: 487–513. Turin: Einaudi.

Gabba, Emilio (1990), "Roma e l'Italia," in Carmine Ampolo (ed.), *Roma e l'Italia*, radices Imperii, Milan: Garzanti, 41–87.

Galinsky, Karl (1996), *Augustan Culture. An Interpretive Introduction*, Princeton: Princeton University Press.

Galsterer, Hartmut (2006), "Rom und Italien vom Bundesgenossenkrieg bis zu Augustus," in Martin Jehne and René Pfeilschifter (eds.), *Herrschaft ohne Integration? Rom und Italien in republikanischer Zeit*, Frankfurt am Main: Verlag Antike, 293–308.

Ganzert, Joachim (2000), *Im Allerheiligsten des Augustusforums. Fokus "Oikoumenischer Akkulturation,"* Mainz: Philipp von Zabern.

Garnsey, Peter, and Richard P. Saller (2014), *The Roman Empire: Economy, Society, and Culture*, 2nd edn, Berkeley and Los Angeles: University of California Press.

Geib, Phil R., and Winston B. Hurst (2013), "Should Dates Trump Context? Evaluation of the Cave 7 Assemblage Radiocarbon Dates," *Journal of Archaeological Science* 40: 2054–70.

Gera, Deborah L. (1997), *Warrior Women: The Anonymous* Tractatus De Mulieribus, Leiden, New York, Köln: Brill.

Gimbutas, Marija (1991), *The Civilization of the Goddess: The World of Old Europe*, San Francisco: Harper.

Giovannini, Adalberto (2007), *Les relations entre états dans la Grèce antique*, Stuttgart: Franz Steiner Verlag.

Glover, Jonathan (1999), *Humanity: A Moral History of the Twentieth Century*, New Haven and London: Yale University Press.

Gnirs, Andrea (1999), "Ancient Egypt," in Raaflaub and Rosenstein 1999, 71–104.

ABBREVIATIONS AND BIBLIOGRAPHY

Goldsworthy, Adrian (2009), *The Fall of the West: The Death of the Roman Superpower*, London: Weidenfeld and Nicholson.

Goldsworthy, Adrian (2016), *Pax Romana. War, Peace and Conquest in the Roman World*, New Haven: Yale University Press.

Gomme, Arnold W. (1945), *A Historical Commentary on Thucydides 1*, Oxford: Oxford University Press.

Gordimer, Nadine (2008), *Beethoven was One-Sixteenth Black*, New York: Penguin.

Gordon, Richard L. (1999), "Mars," *DNP* VII: 946–50.

Gräber, A. (1992), "Friedensvorstellung und Friedensbegriff bei den Griechen bis zum Peloponnesischen Krieg," *Zeitschrift der Savigny-Stiftung für Rechtsgeschichte, Romanistische Abteilung* 109: 116–61.

Gray, Benjamin (2017), "Reconciliation in Later Classical and Post-Classical Cities: A Question of Peace and Peacefulness?" in Moloney and Williams 2017, 66–85.

Gregory, Justina (1997), *Euripides and the Instruction of the Athenians*, Ann Arbor: University of Michigan Press.

Gregory, Timothy E. (2010), *A History of Byzantium*, 2nd edn, Malden: Wiley-Blackwell.

Gruen, Erich S. (1984), *The Hellenistic World and the Coming of Rome*, Berkeley, Los Angeles, and London: University of California Press.

Grundy, George B. (1911), *Thucydides and the History of his Age*, London: John Murray.

Guilaine, Jean, and Jean Zammit (2005), *The Origins of War: Violence in Prehistory*, trans. Melanie Hersey, Malden: Blackwell.

Gurval, Robert A. (1995), *Actium and Augustus. The Politics and Emotions of Civil War*, Ann Arbor: University of Michigan Press.

Gwynn, David M. (2017), "Blessed are the Peacemakers: Visions of Christian Peace from Christ to Constantine," in Moloney and Williams 2017a, 115–29.

Haas, Jonathan, ed. (1990), *The Anthropology of War*, Cambridge: Cambridge University Press.

Habermas, Jürgen (2003), *The Future of Human Nature*, Cambridge: Cambridge University Press.

Hall, Jonathan M. (2007), "International Relations," in Sabin, van Wees, and Whitby 2007, 85–107.

Hallett, Judith (2015), "Fulvia: the Representation of an Elite Roman Woman Warrior," in Fabre-Serris and Keith 2015, 247–65.

Hammond, Nicholas G.L. (1967), *History of Greece to 322 BC*, 2nd edn, Oxford: Clarendon Press.

Hansen, Mogens Herman (1999), *The Athenian Democracy in the Age of Demosthenes*, Norman OK: University of Oklahoma Press.

Hanson, Victor D. (1991), 'Hoplite Technology in Phalanx Battle', in Victor D. Hanson (ed), *Hoplites: The Classical Greek Battle Experience*, London: Routledge, 63–84.

Hanson, Victor D. (2000), *The Western Way of War: Infantry Battle in Classical Greece*, London: University of California Press.

Harders, Ann-Cathrin (2016), "The Making of a Queen: Seleukos Nikator and His Wives," in Coşkun and McAuley 2016, 25–38.

Harris, William V., ed. (1984a), *The Imperialism of Mid-Republican Rome*, Rome: American Academy.

Harris, William V., ed. (1984b), "The Italians and the Empire," in Harris 1984a, 89–109.

Harris, William V. (1991), *War and Imperialism in Republican Rome 327–70 BC*, 2nd edn (slight revisions), Oxford: Clarendon Press.

Harter-Uibopuu, Kaja (2003), "Der Hellenenbund des Antigonos I Monophthalmos und des Demetrios Poliorketes, 302/1 v. Chr.," in G. Thür and F. J. Fernandez Nieto (eds.), *Symposion 1999, Akten der Gesellschaft für griechische und hellenistische Rechtsgeschichte*, 315–37. Vienna.

Haselberger, Lothar (2011), "A Debate on the Horologium of Augustus," *Journal of Roman Archaeology* 24: 47–73.

Hassig, Ross (1988), *Aztec Warfare: Imperial Expansion and Political Control*, Norman OK: University of Oklahoma Press.

Hassig, Ross (1992), *War and Society in Ancient Mesoamerica*, Berkeley: University of California Press.

Hassig, Ross (2007), "Peace, Reconciliation, and Alliance in Aztec Mexico," in Raaflaub 2007a, 312–28.

Heather, Peter (1997), "*Foedera* and *Foederati* in the Fourth Century," in Walter Pohl (ed), *Kingdoms of the Empire: The Integration of Barbarians in Late Antiquity*, 57–74. Leiden: Brill.

Henderson, Jeffrey (1980), "*Lysistrate*: the Play and its Themes," *Yale Classical Studies* 26: 153–218.

Henderson, Jeffrey (1987), *Aristophanes Lysistrata*, Oxford: Oxford University Press.

Henderson, Jeffrey (1990), "The Demos and Comic Competition," in John J. Winkler and Froma I. Zeitlin (eds.), *Nothing to Do with Dionysus*, 271–313, Princeton: Princeton University Press.

Henslin, Peter (2007), "Augustus, Domitian and the So-called Horologium Augusti," *Journal of Roman Studies* 97: 1–20.

Herbert-Brown, Geraldine (1994), *Ovid and the Fasti. An Historical Study*, Oxford: Oxford University Press.

Hermann, Peter (1965), "Antiochos der Grosse und Teos," *Anadolu* 9: 29–159 and plates 1–5.

Herodotus (Herodotos) (1954), *The Histories*, trans. Aubrey de Sélincourt, London: Penguin Books.

Hesiod (1983), *The Poems of Hesiod*, trans. R.M. Frazer, Norman OK: University of Oklahoma Press.

Hodkinson, Stephen (2006), "Was Classical Sparta a Military Society?" in Stephen Hodkinson and Anton Powell (eds.), *Sparta and War*, 111–62, Swansea: Classical Press of Wales.

Homer (1951), *The Iliad*, trans. Richmond Lattimore, Chicago: University of Chicago Press.

Homer (1967), *The Odyssey*, trans. Richmond Lattimore, New York et al.: HarperCollins.

Horace (2004), *Odes and Epodes*, trans. Niall Rudd, Cambridge MA: Harvard University Press.

Hornblower, Simon (1991–2008), *A Commentary on Thucydides*, 3 volumes, Oxford: Oxford University Press.

Hume, David (1739–1740), *A Treatise of Human Nature*, London. Republished London 1988, Mineola NY 2003.

Hunt, Peter (1998), *Slaves, Warfare, and Ideology in the Greek Historians*, Cambridge: Cambridge University Press.

Hunt, Peter (2007), "Military Force," in Sabin, van Wees, and Whitby 2007, 108–46.

Hunt, Peter (2010), *War, Peace, and Alliance in Demosthenes' Athens*, New York: Cambridge University Press.

Hunt, Peter (2012), "Legalism and Peace in Classical Greece," in Wilker 2012a, 135–49.

Hyland, Ann (2013), "The Development and Training of Cavalry in Greece and Rome," in Brian Campbell and Lawrence Tritle (eds.), *The Oxford Handbook of Warfare in the Classical World*, 512–26, Oxford: Oxford University Press.

ABBREVIATIONS AND BIBLIOGRAPHY

Isaac, Benjamin (1993), *The Limits of Empire: The Roman Army in the East*, Oxford: Oxford University Press.

Isocrates (Isokrates) (1928–1945), *Isocrates I–III*, trans. George Norlin and La Rue Van Hook, Cambridge MA: Harvard University Press.

James, William (1910), "The Moral Equivalent of War." Available online: www.consitution.org/wj/meow.htm (accessed July 20, 2018).

James, Sharon L., and Sheila Dillon, eds. (2012), *A Companion to Women in the Ancient World*, Malden, Oxford, and Chichester: Wiley-Blackwell.

Jehne, Martin (1994), *Koine Eirene: Untersuchungen zu den Befriedungs- und Stabilisierungsbemühungen in der griechischen Poliswelt des 4. Jahrhunderts v. Chr*, Stuttgart: Steiner.

Jones, D. (2008), "Killer Instincts: what can evolution say about why humans kill—and about why we do so less than we used to?" *Nature* 451: 512–15.

Jones, David M. (2012), *The Complete Illustrated History of the Inca Empire*, London: Lorenz Books.

Julien, Catherine (2007), "War and Peace in the Inca Heartland," in Raaflaub 2007a, 329–47.

Kallet-Marx, Lisa (1993), *Money, Expense and Naval Power in Thucydides' History 1–5.24*, Berkeley: University of California Press.

Karavites, Peter (1982), "*Eleutheria* and *Autonomia* in Greek Interstate Relations," *Revue international des droits de l'antiquité* 29: 145–62.

Keegan, John (1976), *The Face of Battle*, London: J. Cape.

Keeley, Lawrence H. (1996), *War Before Civilization: The Myth of the Peaceful Savage*, Oxford: Oxford University Press.

Kelly, Raymond Case (2000), *Warless Societies and the Origin of War*, Ann Arbor: University of Michigan Press.

Kent, J.P.C. (1978), *Roman Coins*, London: H.N. Abrams.

Kerferd, G.B. (1981), *The Sophistic Movement*, Cambridge: Cambridge University Press.

Kessler, Josef (1911), *Isokrates und die panhellenische Idee*, Berlin: F. Schöningh.

Kirk, Geoffrey S., John E. Raven, and Malcolm Schofield (1983), *The Presocratic Philosophers*, 2nd edn, Cambridge: Cambridge University Press.

Knoblock, John (1990), *Xunzi: A Translation of the Complete Works* II, Stanford: Stanford University Press.

Knoblock, John, and Jeffrey K. Riegel, trans. (2000), *The Annals of Lü Buwei*, Stanford: Stanford University Press.

Kostial, Michaela (1995), *Kriegerisches Rom? Zur Frage von Unvermeidbarkeit und Normalität militärischer Konflikte in der römischen Politik*. Stuttgart: Franz Steiner.

Krentz, Peter (2007), "War," in Sabin, van Wees, and Whitby 2007, 147–85.

Krüger, Thomas (2007), "'They Shall Beat their Swords into Plowshares': A Vision of Peace through Justice and its Background in the Hebrew Bible," in Raaflaub 2007a, 161–71.

Kuhrt, Amélie (1995), *The Ancient Near East*, 2 volumes, London: Routledge.

Lambert, Patricia M. (2002), "The Archaeology of War: A North American Perspective," *Journal of Archaeological Research* 10: 207–41.

Lambert, Patricia M. (2007), "The Osteological Evidence for Indigenous Warfare in North America," in R.J. Chacon and R.G. Mendoza (eds.), *North American Indigenous Warfare and Ritual Violence*, 202–21, Tucson: University of Arizona Press.

Lambert, Patricia M. (2012), "War Histories in Evolutionary Perspective: Insights from Prehistoric North America," in Shackelford and Weekes-Shackelford 2012, 324–38.

Lambert, Patricia M. (forthcoming), "North American Native Peoples," in Meissner, Raaflaub, and Yates (forthcoming).

La Rocca, Cristina (2012), "*Consors Regni*: A Problem of Gender? The *Consortium* between Amalasuntha and Theodahad in 534," in Janet L. Nelson, Susan Reynolds, and Susan M. Johns (eds.), *Gender and Historiography: Studies in the Earlier Middle Ages in Honour of Pauline Stafford*, 127–43, London: Institute of Historical Research.

La Rocca, Eugenio (1974), "Eirēnē e Ploutos," *Jahrbuch des Deutschen Archäologischen Instituts* 89: 112–36.

Larsen, Jakob A.O. (1968), *Greek Federal States: Their Institutions and History*, Oxford: Clarendon Press.

Lavan, Myles (2017), "Peace and Empire: *Pacare*, *Pacatus*, and the Language of Roman Imperialism," in Moloney and Williams 2017a, 102–14.

Lawrence, Arnold W. (1979), *Greek Aims in Fortification*, Oxford: Clarendon Press.

Lazenby, John F. (1993), *The Defence of Greece 490–479 BC*, Warminster: Aris and Phillips.

Lazenby, John F., and David Whitehead (1996), "The Myth of the Hoplite's *Hoplon*," *Classical Quarterly* 46: 27–33.

Lee, A.D. (1991), "The Role of Hostages in Roman Diplomacy with Sasanian Persia," *Historia* 40: 366–74.

Lee, A.D. (2008), "Treaty-Making in Late Antiquity," in de Souza and France 2008: 107–19.

Leiber, Laura S. (2012), "Jewish Women: Texts and Contexts," in James and Dillon 2012: 329–42.

Le Roux, Patrick (2011), "Armées et ordre public dans le monde romain à l'époque impériale," in Patrick Le Roux (ed.), *La toge et les armes*: 217–37. Rennes: Presse Universitaire.

Levi, Marco Attilio (1969), "*Maiestas* e *crimen maiestatis*," *Parola del passato* 24: 81–96.

Levick, Barbara (1978), "Concordia at Rome," in R.A.G. Carson and Colin M. Kraay (eds.), *Scripta Nummaria Romana. Essays Presented to Humphrey Sutherland*, I: 223–33, London: Spink and Son.

Lewis, David (1955), "Notes on Attic Inscriptions (II). XXIII: Who Was Lysistrata?" *Annual of the British School at Athens* 50: 1–36.

Lewis, Sian (2002), *The Athenian Woman: An Iconographic Handbook*, London and New York: Routledge.

Linderski, Jerzy (1984), "*Si vis pacem, para bellum*: Concepts of Defensive Imperialism," in Harris 1984a, 133–64.

Lintott, Andrew W. (2008), "How High a Priority did Public Order and Public Security have under the Republic?" in Cédric Brélaz and Paul Ducrey (eds.), *Sécurité collective et ordre public dans les sociétés anciennes*: 205–20. Vandoeuvres-Genève: Presse Fondation Hardt.

Lissarrague, François (1989), "The World of the Warrior," in Claude Bérard and Christiane Bron (eds.), *A City of Images: Iconography and Society in Ancient Greece*, 39–51, trans. Deborah Lyons, Princeton: Princeton University Press.

Livy (1919–2018), *History of Rome*, various translators, Cambridge MA: Harvard University Press.

Lloyd, Geoffrey E.R., ed. (1978), *Hippocratic Writings*, trans. J. Chadwick and W.N. Mann, Harmondsworth: Penguin Classics.

Long, Jacqueline (1996), *Claudian's In Eutropium: Or, How, When, and Why to Slander a Eunuch*, Chapel Hill and London: University of North Carolina Press.

Loraux, Nicole (2006), *The Invention of Athens: The Funeral Oration in the Classical City*, Cambridge MA: The MIT Press.

Lorenz, Konrad Z. (1966), *On Aggression*, trans. M.K. Wilson, New York: Harcourt, Brace, and World.

ABBREVIATIONS AND BIBLIOGRAPHY

Low, Polly (2007), *Interstate Relations in Classical Greece. Morality and Power*, Cambridge: Cambridge University Press.

Low, Polly (2012), "Peace, Common Peace, and War in Mid-Fourth-Century Greece," in Wilker 2012a, 118–34.

Lundestad, Geir (1998), *Empire by Integration: The United States and European Integration, 1945–1997*, New York and Oxford: Oxford University Press.

Luttwak, Edward N. (1976), *The Grand Strategy of the Roman Empire from the First Century AD to the Third*, Baltimore: Johns Hopkins University Press.

Ma, John (1999), *Antiochos III and the Cities of Western Asia Minor*, Oxford: Oxford University Press.

Ma, John (2000), "Fighting *Poleis* of the Hellenistic World," in van Wees 2000, 337–76.

Mackil, Emily (2013), *Creating a Common Polity: Religion, Economy, and Politics in the Making of the Greek* Koinon, Berkeley, Los Angeles, and London: University of California Press.

Magnetto, Anna (1997), *Gli arbitrati interstatali greci II: dal 337 al 196 a.C.* Pisa.

Magnetto, Anna (2016), "Interstate Arbitration and Foreign Judges," in Edward V. Harris and Mirko Canevaro, eds., *The Oxford Handbook of Ancient Greek Law*, Oxford. Available online: http://www.oxfordhandbooks.com/view/10.1093/oxfordhb/9780199599257.001.0001/oxfordhb-9780199599257 (accessed July 12, 2017).

Maidment, K.A. (trans.) (1941), *Minor Attic Orators I: Antiphon and Andocides*, Cambridge MA: Harvard University Press.

Marquardt, Patricia A. (1982), "Hesiod's Ambiguous View of Women," *Classical Philology* 77: 283–91.

Martin, Simon (2001), "Under a Deadly Star: Warfare among the Classic Maya," in Nikolai Grube (ed.), *Maya: Divine Kings of the Rain Forest*, 175–85, Köln: Könemann.

Martin, Simon, and Nikolai Grube (2000), *Chronicle of the Maya Kings and Queens: Deciphering the Dynasties of the Ancient Maya*, London: Thames and Hudson.

Mattern, Susan (2002). *Rome and the Enemy: Imperial Strategy in the Principate*, Berkeley: University of California Press.

Mazzarino, Santo (1983), "Il tema della terra Italia da Polibio a Dionisio e ai gromatici," in Santo Mazzarino (ed.), *Il pensiero storico classico*, vol. 2: 212–32. Bari, Roma: Laterza.

McCabe, Donald F. (1985), *Didyma Inscriptions. Texts and List*. The Princeton Project on the Inscriptions of Anatolia, Princeton: The Institute for Advanced Study.

McDonald, Melissa, Carlos Navarrete, and Mark Van Vugt (2012), "Evolution and the Psychology of Intergroup Conflict: The Male Warrior Hypothesis," *Philosophical Transactions of the Royal Society B* 367: 670–9.

McRaven, William H. (1995), *Spec Ops: Case Studies in Special Operations Warfare: Theory and Practice*, Novato, CA: Presidio Press.

Mead, Margaret (1940), "Warfare is only an Invention—Not a Biological Necessity," *Asia* 40: 402–5.

Mee, Christopher (2008), "Mycenaean Greece, the Aegean and Beyond," in Shelmerdine 2008, 362–86.

Meissner, Burkhard, Kurt A. Raaflaub, and Robin D.S. Yates (forthcoming), *The Cambridge History of War* I, Cambridge: Cambridge University Press.

Melko, Matthew, and Richard D. Weigel (1981), *Peace in the Ancient World*, Jefferson NC: McFarland and Company, Inc.

Michalowski, Piotr (2014), "The Presence of the Past in Early Mesopotamian Writings," in Raaflaub 2014a, 144–68.

Millar, Fergus (1982), "Emperors, Frontiers and Foreign Relations 31 BC to AD 378," *Britannia* 13: 1–23.

Millar, Fergus (2005), "Last Year in Jerusalem. Monuments of the Jewish War in Rome," in Jonathan Edmondson, Steve Mason, and James Rives (eds.), *Flavius Josephus and Flavian Rome*, 101–28, Oxford: Oxford University Press.

Mitchell, Barbara (2000), "Cyrene: Typical or Atypical?" in Roger Brock and Stephen Hodkinson (eds.), *Alternatives to Athens. Varieties of Political Organization and Community in Ancient Greece*, 82–102, Oxford: Oxford University Press.

Mitchell, Lynette (1997), "*Philia, Eunoia,* and Greek Interstate Relations," *Antichthon* 31: 28–44.

Mitchell, Lynette (2007), *Panhellenism and the Barbarian in Archaic and Classical Greece*, Swansea: Classical Press of Wales.

Mitchell, Lynette (2012), "The Women of Ruling Families in Archaic and Classical Greece," *Classical Quarterly* 62: 1–21.

Moloney, E.P., and Michael Stuart Williams, eds. (2017a), *Peace and Reconciliation in the Classical World*, London and New York: Routledge.

Moloney, E.P., and Michael Stuart Williams (2017b), "Imagining, Establishing, and Instituting Peace," in Moloney and Williams 2017a, 1–12.

Morrison, John S., and R.T. Williams (1968), *Greek Oared Ships, 900–322 BC*, Cambridge: Cambridge University Press.

Moses, Jeremy (2018), "Peace without Perfection: the Intersections of Realist and Pacifist Thought," *Cooperation and Conflict* 53: 42–60.

Muccioli, Federicomaria (2013), *Gli epiteti ufficiali dei re ellenistici*, Stuttgart: Franz Steiner Verlag.

Musti, Domenico (1986), "Italia (Storia del nome)," in *Enciclopedia Virgiliana*, vol. III, 34–40. Roma: Istituto dell'Enciclopedia italiana.

Münzer, F. (1910), "Fulvius", *RE* 7.

Myers, Darryl (2005), *War Before History: A Critical Survey*, MA Diss., Florida State University.

Nathan, Geoffrey (2015), "The Ideal Male in Late Antiquity: Claudian's Example of Flavius Stilicho," *Gender and History* 27: 10–27.

Newiger, Hans-Joachim (1996), "War and Peace in the Comedy of Aristophanes," in Erich Segal (ed.), *Oxford Readings in Aristophanes*, 143–61, Oxford: Oxford University Press.

Niditch, Susan (1993), *War in the Hebrew Bible: A Study in the Ethics of Violence*, Oxford: Oxford University Press.

Niditch, Susan (2007), "War and Reconciliation in the Traditions of Ancient Israel: Historical, Literary, and Ideological Considerations," in Raaflaub 2007a, 141–60.

Nippel, Wilfried (1995), *Public Order in Ancient Rome*, Cambridge: Cambridge University Press.

Noreña, Carlos F. (2003), "Medium and Message in Vespasian's Templum Pacis," *Memoirs of the American Academy in Rome* 48: 25–43.

Noreña, Carlos F. (2011), *Imperial Ideals in the Roman West: Representation, Circulation, Power*, Cambridge: Cambridge University Press.

Oates, Whitney J., and Eugene O'Neill Jr. (1971), *The Complete Greek Drama: All the Extant Tragedies of Aeschylus, Sophocles and Euripides, and the Comedies of Aristophanes and Menander in a Variety of Translations*, New York: Random House.

Olson, S. Douglas (1998), *Aristophanes: Peace, edited with introduction and commentary*, Oxford: Oxford University Press.

Olson, S. Douglas (2002), *Aristophanes: Acharnians, edited with introduction and commentary*, Oxford: Oxford University Press.

ABBREVIATIONS AND BIBLIOGRAPHY

Orlin, Eric M. (1997), *Temples, Religion, and Politics in the Roman Republic*, Leiden: Brill.

Ostwald, Martin (1996), "Peace and War in Plato and Aristotle," *Scripta Classica Israelica* 15: 102–18.

Otterbein, Keith F. (2004), *How War Began*, College Station TX: Texas A & M University Consortium Press.

Otterbein, Keith F. (2009), *The Anthropology of War*, Long Grove IL: Waveland Press.

Packer, James E. (2003), "*Plurima et Amplissima Opera*. Parsing Flavian Rome," in Anthony J. Boyle and William J. Dominik (eds.), *Flavian Rome. Culture, Image, Text*, 167–98, Leiden: Brill.

Palmer, Robert E.A. (1997), *Rome and Carthage at Peace*, Stuttgart: F. Steiner Verlag.

Parchami, Ali (2009), *Hegemonic Peace and Empire: The* Pax Romana, Britannica *and* Americana. London and New York: Routledge.

Parker, Robert (1997a), *Athenian Religion: A History*, Oxford: Oxford University Press.

Parker, Robert (1997b), *Cleomenes on the Acropolis. An Inaugural Lecture delivered before the University of Oxford on 12 May 1997*, Oxford: Oxford University Press.

Parker, Robert (2016), "War and Religion in Ancient Greece," in Krysztof Ulanowski (ed.), *The Religious Aspects of War in the Ancient Near East, Greece, and Rome*, 123–32, Leiden: Brill.

Pausanias (1918–1935), *Description of Greece*, 5 vols., trans. W.H.S. Jones and H.A. Ormerod, Cambridge MA: Harvard University Press.

Piccirilli, Luigi (1973), *Gli arbitrati interstatali greci I: dalle origini al 338 a.C.*, Pisa.

Pindar (1997), *Olympian Odes. Pythian Odes*, trans. William H. Race, Cambridge MA: Harvard University Press.

Pinker, Steven (2011), *The Better Angels of Our Nature: Why Violence Has Declined*, New York: Viking Penguin.

Plato (1975), *The Laws (Leges)*, trans. Trevor J. Saunders, revised edn, Harmondsworth: Penguin Books.

Plutarch (1920), *Lives IX. Demetrius and Antony. Pyrrhus and Gaius Marius*, trans. Bernadotte Perrin, Cambridge MA: Harvard University Press.

Podany, Amanda H. (2010), *Brotherhood of Kings. How International Relations Shaped the Ancient Near East*. Oxford: Oxford University Press.

Polybius (Polybios) (2010–2012), *The Histories*, trans. W.R. Paton, revised by Frank W. Walbank and Christian Habicht, Cambridge MA: Harvard University Press.

Pomeroy, Sarah B. (1975), *Goddesses, Whores, Wives and Slaves: Women in Classical Antiquity*, New York: Dorcas Press.

Pomeroy, Sarah B. (1984), *Women in Hellenistic Egypt: From Alexander to* Cleopatra, New York: Schocken Books.

Pritchett, William Kendrick (1974), *The Greek State at War 2*, Berkeley and Los Angeles: University of California Press.

Pritchett, William Kendrick (1991), *The Greek State at War 5*, Berkeley and Los Angeles: University of California Press.

Quass, Friedemann (1991), "Der Königsfriede aus dem Jahre 387/6 v. Chr.," *Historische Zeitschrift* 252: 33–56.

Raaflaub, Kurt A., ed. (2007a), *War and Peace in the Ancient World*, Malden: Blackwell.

Raaflaub, Kurt A., (2007b), "Searching for Peace in the Ancient World," in Raaflaub 2007a, 1–33.

Raaflaub, Kurt A., (2008), "Homeric Warriors and Battles: Trying to Resolve Old Problems," *Classical World* 101: 469–83.

Raaflaub, Kurt A., (2009), "Conceptualizing and Theorizing Peace in Ancient Greece," *Transactions of the American Philological Association* 139: 250–9.

Raaflaub, Kurt A., (2011), "Peace as the Highest Good? The Role of Peace in Roman Thought," in Günther Moosbauer and Rainer Wiegels (eds.), *Fines imperii—imperium sine fine: Römische Okkupations- und Grenzpolitik im frühen Prinzipat*, 323–38, Rahden Westfalen: Marie Leidorf.

Raaflaub, Kurt A., (2011b), "Riding on Homer's Chariot: The Search for a Historical 'Epic Society'," *Antichthon* 45:1–34.

Raaflaub, Kurt A., (2013), "*Ktema es aiei*: Thucydides' Concept of 'Learning Through History' and its Realization in his Work," in Antonis Tsakmakis and Melina Tamiolaki (eds.), *Thucydides between History and Literature*, 3–21, Berlin: De Gruyter.

Raaflaub, Kurt A., ed. (2014a), *Thinking, Recording, and Writing History in the Ancient World*, Malden MA: Wiley Blackwell.

Raaflaub, Kurt A., (2014b), "War and the City: The Brutality of War and its Impact on the Community," in Peter Meineck and David Konstan (eds.), *Combat Trauma and the Ancient Greeks*, 15–46, New York: Palgrave Macmillan.

Raaflaub, Kurt A., (2015a), "Forerunners of Federal States: Collaboration and Integration through Alliance in Archaic and Classical Greece," in Beck and Funke 2015a, 434–51.

Raaflaub, Kurt A., (2015b), "The Politics of Peace Cults in Greece and Rome," in Thomas R. Kämmerer and Mait Kõiv (eds.), *Cultures in Comparison. Religion and Politics in Ancient Mediterranean Regions*, 103–29, Münster: Ugarit-Verlag.

Raaflaub, Kurt A., (2016a), *Peace in the Ancient World. Concepts and Theories*, Malden: Wiley Blackwell.

Raaflaub, Kurt A., (2016b), "Introduction", in Raaflaub 2016a, 1–11.

Raaflaub, Kurt A., (2016c), "Abhorring War, Yearning for Peace: The Quest for Peace in the Ancient World," in Raaflaub 2016a, 12–42.

Raaflaub, Kurt A., (2016d), "Greek Concepts and Theories of Peace," in Raaflaub 2016a, 122–57.

Raaflaub, Kurt A., (2016e), "*Lysistrata* and War's Impact on the Home Front," in Victor Caston and Silke-Maria Weineck (eds.), *Our Ancient Wars: Rethinking War through the Classics*, 38–74, Ann Arbor: University of Michigan Press.

Raaflaub, Kurt A., and Nathan Rosenstein, eds. (1999), *War and Society in the Ancient and Medieval Worlds*, Cambridge MA: Harvard University Press.

Radner, Karen (forthcoming), "Warfare in Mesopotamia: Case Study Assyria," in Meissner, Raaflaub, and Yates (forthcoming).

Ramsey, Gillian (2016), "The Diplomacy of Seleukid Women: Apama and Stratonike," in Coşkun and McAuley 2016, 87–104.

Reese, Roger (1993), "Images and Image: A Re-examination of Tetrarchic Iconography," *Greece and Rome* 40: 181–200.

Ricci, Cecilia (2011), "*In custodiam urbis*. Notes on the *cohortes urbanae* (1968–2010)," *Historia* 60: 484–508.

Rich, John (1976), *Declaring War in the Roman Republic in the Period of Transmarine Expansion*, Bruxelles: Latomus.

Rich, John (1998), "Augustus's Parthian Honours, the Temple of Mars Ultor and the Arch in the Forum Romanum," *Papers of the British School at Rome* 1998: 71–128.

Rich, John (2003), "Augustus, War and Peace," in Lukas De Blois et al. (eds.), *The Representations and Perception of Roman Imperial Power*: 329–57. Amsterdam: Gieben.

Rich, John (2011), "The Fetiales and Roman International Relations," in James Richardson and Federico Santangelo (eds.), *Priests and State in the Roman World*, 187–242, Stuttgart: Franz Steiner Verlag.

ABBREVIATIONS AND BIBLIOGRAPHY

Rich, John (2012), "Making the Emergency Permanent: *Auctoritas*, *Potestas* and the Evolution of the Principate of Augustus," in Yann Rivière (ed), *Des réformes augustéennes*, 37–121, Rome: École Française de Rome.

Rich, John, and Graham Shipley, eds. (1993), *War and Society in the Roman World*, London and New York: Routledge.

Richardson, John S. (2008), *The Language of Empire: Rome and the Idea of Empire from the Third Century BC to the Second Century AD*, Cambridge: Cambridge University Press.

Rigsby, Kent (1996), *Asylia. Territorial Inviolability in the Hellenistic World*, Berkeley: University of California Press.

Rivière, Yann (2004), "Les batailles de Rome. Présence militaire et guérilla urbaine à l'époque impériale," *Histoire urbaine* 10: 63–87.

Roisman, Joseph (2005), *The Rhetoric of Manhood: Masculinity in the Attic Orators*, London: University of California Press.

Rosen, Stephen P. (2005), *War and Human Nature*, Princeton NJ: Princeton University Press.

Rosenstein, Nathan (2007), "War and Peace, Fear and Reconciliation at Rome," in Raaflaub 2007a, 226–44.

Roser, Max, *Our World in Data*. Available online: https://ourworldindata.org (accessed October 10, 2018).

Rosivach, Vincent J. (1994), *The System of Public Sacrifice in Fourth-Century Athens*, Atlanta: Scholars Press.

Roth, Jonathan (2007), "War," in Sabin, van Wees, and Whitby 2007, 368–98.

Roy, James (1998), "The Masculinity of the Hellenistic King," in Lin Foxhall and John Salmon (eds.), *When Men Were Men: Masculinity, Power and Identity in Classical Antiquity*, 111–35, London: Routledge.

Roy, James (2003), "The Achaian League," in Kostas Buraselis and Kleanthis Zoumboulakis (eds), *The Idea of the European Community in History 2: Aspects of Connecting Poleis and Ethne in Ancient Greece*, 81–95, Athens: National and Capodistrian University of Athens.

Ruffell, Ian (2017), "(What's so Funny 'bout) Peace, Love, and Understanding? Imagining Peace in Greek Comedy," in Moloney and Williams 2017a, 44–65.

Rung, Eduard (2008), "War, Peace and Diplomacy in Graeco-Persian Relations from the Sixth to the Fourth Century BC," in de Souza and France 2008, 28–50.

Rüpke, Jörg (1990), *Domi Militiae. Die religiöse Konstruktion des Krieges in Rom*, Stuttgart: Franz Steiner Verlag.

Russett, Bruce, and William Antholis (1992), "Do Democracies Fight Each Other? Evidence from the Peloponnesian War," *Journal of Peace Research* 29.4: 415–34.

Ryder, T.T.B. (1957), "The Supposed Common Peace of 366/5 BC," *Classical Quarterly* 7: 199–205.

Ryder, T.T.B. (1965), *Koine Eirene: General Peace and Local Independence in Ancient Greece*. Oxford: Oxford University Press.

Sabin, Philip, Hans van Wees, and Michael Whitby, eds. (2007), *The Cambridge History of Greek and Roman Warfare 1: Greece, the Hellenistic World, and the Rise of Rome*, Cambridge: Cambridge University Press.

Sabin, Philip, and Philip de Souza (2007), "Battle," in Sabin, van Wees, and Whitby 2007, 399–460.

Sablayrolles, Robert (2001), "La rue, le soldat et le pouvoir: la garnison de Rome de César à Pertinax," *Pallas* 55: 127–58.

Sallust (2013), *The War with Catiline; The War with Jugurtha*, trans. J.C. Rolfe, revised by John T. Ramsey, Cambridge MA : Harvard University Press.

Salomon, Richard (2007), "Ancient India: Peace Within and War Without," in Raaflaub 2007a, 53–65.

Sansone, David (2004), *Ancient Greek Civilization*, Malden, MA, and Oxford: Wiley-Blackwell.

Saulnier, Christiane (1980), "Le rôle des prêtres et l'application du ius fetiale à Rome," *Revue historique de droit français et étranger* 58: 171–99.

Schachter, Albert (2002), "Ares," *BNP* 1: 1047–51.

Schaps, David (1982), "The Women of Greece in Wartime," *Classical Philology* 77: 195–6.

Scharff, Sebastian (2016), *Eid und Außenpolitik: Studien zur religiösen Fundierung der Akzeptanz zwischenstaatlicher Vereinbarungen im vorrömischen Griechenland*, Stuttgart: Franz Steiner Verlag.

Scheibler, Ingeborg (1984), "Götter des Friedens in Hellas und Rome," *Antike Welt* 15: 39–57.

Schmidt, Katrin (1999), "The Peace of Antalcidas and the Idea of the *Koine Eirene*," *Revue international des droits de l'antiquité* 46: 81–98.

Schulz, Raimund (2008), "Augustinus und der Krieg," *Millennium* 5: 93–110.

Schumpeter, Joseph A. (1991), "The Sociology of Imperialisms," in *Imperialism and Social Classes*, 3–130, reprint, trans. Heinz Norden, Philadelphia: Orion.

Schwartz, Adam (2009), *Reinstating the Hoplite: Arms, Armour and Phalanx Fighting in Archaic and Classical Greece*, Stuttgart: Franz Steiner.

Scott, Kenneth (1925), "The Identification of Augustus with Romulus-Quirinus," *Transactions of the American Philological Association* 56: 82–105.

Scott, Russell T. (1999), "Regia," *LTUR* IV: 189–92.

Scullard, H.H. (1981), *Festivals and Ceremonies of the Roman Republic*, London: Thames and Hudson.

Scully, Stephen (2003), "Reading the Shield of Achilles: Terror, Anger, Delight," *Harvard Studies in Classical Philology* 101: 29–47.

Sebillotte Cuchet, Violaine (2015), "The Warrior Queens of Caria (Fifth to Fourth Centuries BCE): Archeology, History and Historiography," in Fabre-Serris and Keith (2015), 228–46.

Sekunda, Nicholas, and Philip de Souza (2007), "Military Forces," in Sabin, van Wees, and Whitby 2007, 325–67.

Serrati, John (2007), "Warfare and the State," in Sabin, van Wees, and Whitby 2007, 461–97.

Shackelford, Todd K., and Viviana A. Weekes-Shackelford, eds. (2012), *The Oxford Handbook of Evolutionary Perspectives on Violence, Homicide, and War*, Oxford: Oxford University Press.

Shannon, Richard S. (1975), *The Arms of Achilles and Homeric Compositional Technique*, Leiden: Brill.

Shapiro, Harvey Alan (1993), *Personifications in Greek Art: The Representation of Abstract Concepts, 600–400 BC*, Ann Arbor: University of Michigan Press.

Sharrock, A. (2015), "Warrior Women in Roman Epic," in Fabre-Serris and Keith (2015), 157–78.

Shay, Jonathan (1994), *Achilles in Vietnam: Combat Trauma and the Undoing of Character*, New York: Touchstone.

Sheets, George A. (1994), "Conceptualizing International Law in Thucydides," *American Journal of Philology* 115: 51–73.

Shelmerdine, Cynthia W., ed. (2008), *The Cambridge Companion to the Aegean Bronze Age*, Cambridge: Cambridge University Press.

Sherk, Robert K. (1988), *The Roman Empire: Augustus to Hadrian*, Cambridge: Cambridge University Press.

Sherwin-White, Adrian N. (1973), *The Roman Citizenship*, 2nd edn, Oxford: Oxford University Press.

ABBREVIATIONS AND BIBLIOGRAPHY

Simon, Erika (1986), "*Eirene*," *LIMC* 3: 700–5.

Simon, Erika (1988), *Eirene und Pax: Friedensgottin in der Antike*, Stuttgart: Franz Steiner.

Simon, Erika (1990), "Ianus," *LIMC* V.1: 618–23.

Simon, Erika (1994), "*Pax*," *LIMC* 7: 204–12.

Simon, Erika, and Dieter Bauchhenss (1984), "Mars," *LIMC* II.1: 505–80.

Skinner, Marilyn (2005), *Sexuality in Greek and Roman Culture*, Oxford: Blackwell.

Smith, Amy C. (2003), "Athenian Political Art from the Fifth and Fourth Centuries BCE: Images of Political Personifications," in Christopher W. Blackwell (ed), *Dēmos: Classical Athenian Democracy*, The Stoa: a Consortium for Electronic Publication in the Humanities (www.stoa.org); edition of 18 January 18 2003.

Smith, Amy C. (2011), *Polis and Personification in Classical Athenian Art*, Leiden: Brill.

Smith, David L. (2012), "War, Evolution, and the Nature of Human Nature," in Shackelford and Weekes-Shackelford 2012, 339–50.

Smith, Michael E. (2003), *The Aztecs*, 2nd edn, Malden MA: Wiley Blackwell.

Smith, Nicholas D. (1983), "Aristotle's Theory of Natural Slavery," *Phoenix* 37: 109–22.

Smith, Susan L. (1995), *The Power of Women. A* Topos *in Medieval Art and Literature*, Philadelphia: University of Pennsylvania Press.

Spaeth, Barbette Stanley (1994), "The Goddess Ceres in the Ara Pacis Augustae and the Carthage Relief," *American Journal of Archaeology* 98: 65–100.

Spalinger, Anthony J. (2005), *War in Ancient Egypt*, Malden MA: Wiley Blackwell.

Spannagel, Martin (1999), *Exemplaria Princeps. Untersuchungen zur Entstehung und Ausstattung des Augustusforums*, Heidelberg: Verlag Archäologie und Geschichte.

Stafford, Emma (2001), *Worshipping Virtues: Personification and Divine in Ancient Greece*, London and Swansea: Duckworth and the Classical Press of Wales.

Stehle, E. (2012), "Women and Religion in Greece," in James and Dillon 2012: 191–203.

Stevenson, T.R. (2010), "Personifications on the Coinage of Vespasian (AD 69–79)," *Acta Classica* 53: 181–205.

Stewart, Andrew (2016), "The Borghese Ares Revisited: New Evidence from the Agora and a Reconstruction of the Augustan Cult Group in the Temple of Ares," *Hesperia* 85: 577–625.

Stillman, Nigel, and Nigel Tallis (1984), *Armies of the Ancient Near East, 3000–539 BC*, Devizes: Wargames Research Group.

Strassler, Robert B., ed. (2007), *The Landmark Herodotus: The Histories*, New York: Free Press.

Strassler, Robert B. (2008), *The Landmark Thucydides: A Comprehensive Guide to the Peloponnesian War*, New York: Free Press.

Strauss, Barry S. (1991), "Of Balances, Bandwagons, and Ancient Greeks," in Richard Ned Lebow and Barry S. Strauss (eds.), *Hegemonic Rivalry: From Thucydides to the Nuclear Age*, Boulder: Westview Press, 189–210.

Swift, Louis J. (1970), "St. Ambrose on Violence and War," *Transactions of the American Philological Association* 101: 533–43.

Swift, Louis J. (1983), *The Early Fathers on War and Military Service*, Wilmington DE: Michael Glazier.

Swift, Louis J. (2007), "Early Christian Views on Violence, War, and Peace," in Raaflaub 2007a, 279–96.

Tacitus (1970), *The Agricola and the Germania*, trans. H. Mattingly, revised by S.A. Handford, Harmondsworth: Penguin Books.

Taraporewalla, Rashna (2010), "The Templum Pacis: Construction of Memory under Vespasian," *Acta Classica* 53: 145–63.

Tertullian. See under Swift 1983.

Thomas, Rosalind (2000), *Herodotus in Context: Ethnography, Science, and the Art of Persuasion*, Cambridge: Cambridge University Press.

Thucydides (1954), *History of the Peloponnesian War*, trans. Rex Warner, London: Penguin Books.

Tibullus (2012), *Elegies*, trans. A.M. Juster, Oxford: Oxford University Press.

Tortorici, Edoardo (1996), "Ianus Geminus," *LTUR* III: 92–3.

Toynbee, Arnold J. (1965), *Hannibal's Legacy*, London: Oxford University Press.

Trimm, Charlie (2017), *Fighting for the King and the Gods: A Survey of Warfare in the Ancient Near East*, Atlanta: Society of Biblical Literature.

Tritle, Lawrence R. (2007), "'Laughing for Joy': War and Peace among the Greeks," in Raaflaub 2007a, 172–90.

Trundle, Matthew (2004), *Greek Mercenaries from the Late Archaic Period to Alexander*, London: Routledge.

Turcan, Robert (1981), "Janus à l'époque imperiale," *ANRW* II.17.1: 374–402.

Turney-High, Harry Holbert (1971), *Primitive War: Its Practice and Concepts*, Columbia SC: University of South Carolina Press.

Ullman, Berthold L. (1945), "We Want a Virgilian Peace," *Classical Journal* 41, 1–3.

Van de Mieroop, Marc (2007), *A History of the Ancient Near East, ca. 3000–323 BC*, Malden MA: Wiley Blackwell.

Van Vugt, Mark (2012), "The Male Warrior Hypothesis: The Evolutionary Psychology of Intergroup Conflict, Tribal Aggression, and Warfare," in Shackelford and Weekes-Shackelford 2012, 291–300.

Van Wees, Hans, ed. (2000), *War and Violence in the Greek World*, London: Duckworth and the Classical Press of Wales.

Van Wees, Hans (2001), "War and Peace in Ancient Greece," in Anja V. Hartmann and Beatrice Heuser (eds.), *War, Peace, and World Orders in European History*, 33–47, London and New York: Routledge.

Van Wees, Hans (2004), *Greek Warfare: Myths and Realities*, London: Bloomsbury.

Van Wees, Hans (2006), "Defeat and Destruction: the Ethics of Ancient Greek Warfare," in Margit Linder and Sabine Tausend, *"Böser Krieg": excessive Gewalt in der antiken Kriegsführung und Strategien zu deren Vermeidung*, Graz: Karl-Franzens-Universität, 69–110.

Van Wees, Hans (2007), "War and Society," in Sabin, van Wees, and Whitby 2007, 273–99.

Van Wees, Hans (2016), "Broadening the Scope: Thinking about Peace in the Pre-Modern World," in Raaflaub 2016a, 158–80.

Vencl, Slavomil (1999), "Stone Age Warfare," in Carman and Harding 1999, 57–72.

Virgil (Vergil) (2006), *The Aeneid*, trans. Robert Fagles, New York: Viking.

Virgil (Vergil) (2013), *Aeneid 6*, translation and commentary by Nicholas Horsfall, 2 vols., Berlin: De Gruyter.

Viscogliosi, Alessandro (1993), "Bellona, Aedes in Circo," *LTUR* I: 190–3.

Vitiello, Massimiliano (2017), *Amalasuintha: The Transformation of Queenship in the Post-Roman World*, Philadelphia: University of Pennsylvania Press.

Von Beseler, Gerhard (1929), "Bindung und Lösung," *Zeitschrift der Savigny-Stiftung für Rechtsgeschichte. Romanistische Abteilung* 49: 404–60.

Walden, Catherine (1990), "The Tetrarchic Image," *Oxford Journal of Archaeology* 9: 221–35.

Walt, Stephen M. (1987), *The Origins of Alliances*, Ithaca: Cornell University Press.

Waltz, Kenneth N. (1979), *Theory of International Politics*, Reading, MA: Addison-Wesley.

Walzer, Michael (2000), *Just and Unjust Wars: a Moral Argument with Historical Illustrations*, 3rd edn, New York: Basic Books.

ABBREVIATIONS AND BIBLIOGRAPHY

Waters, Matt (2014), *Ancient Persia: A Concise History of the Achaemenid Empire, 550–330 BCE*, New York: Cambridge University Press.

Watson, Alan (1993), *International Law in Archaic Rome; War and Religion*, Johns Hopkins University Press, Baltimore MD.

Watts, Edward J. (2017), *Hypatia: The Life and Legend of an Ancient Philosopher*, Oxford: Oxford University Press.

Weart, Spencer R. (1998), *Never at War. Why Democracies Will Not Fight One Another*. New Haven/London.

Webster, David L. (1999), "Ancient Maya Warfare," in Raaflaub and Rosenstein 1999, 333–60.

Webster, David L. (2000), "The Not So Peaceful Civilization: A Review of Maya War," *Journal of World Prehistory* 14(1): 65–119.

Weigall, David (2003), *International Relations. A Concise Companion*, London: Arnold.

Weinstock, Stephan (1960), "Pax and the 'Ara Pacis'," *Journal of Roman Studies* 50: 44–58.

Welwei, Karl-Wilhelm (1974–1988), *Unfreie im antiken Kriegsdienst*, 3 vols., Wiesbaden: Steiner.

West, Martin L. (1971), *Iambi et Elegi Graeci I*, Oxford: Oxford University Press.

West, Martin L. (1997), *The East Face of Helicon: West Asiatic Elements in Greek Poetry and Myth*, Oxford: Oxford University Press.

Wheeler, Everett L. (1982), "*Hoplomachia* and Greek Dances in Arms," *Greek, Roman, and Byzantine Studies* 23: 223–33.

Wheeler, Everett L. (2007), "The Army and the Limes in the East," in Paul Erdkamp (ed.), *A Companion to the Roman Army*: 235–66. Oxford: Wiley-Blackwell.

Whitby, Michael (1992), "From Frontier to Palace: The Personal Role of the Emperor in Diplomacy," in Jonathan Shepard and Simon Franklin (eds), *Byzantine Diplomacy*, 295–303. Aldershot: Variorum.

Whitby, Michael (2008), "Byzantine Diplomacy: Good Faith, Trust and Co-operation in International Relations in Late Antiquity," in de Souza and France, 120–40.

Whittaker, Charles R. (1983), "Trade and Frontiers in the Roman Empire," in Peter Garnsey and Charles R. Whittaker (eds.), *Trade and Famine in Classical Antiquity*: 110–27. London: Chatto & Windus; Hogarth Press.

Whittaker, Charles R. (1994), *Frontiers of the Roman Empire. A Social and Economic Study*. Baltimore: The Johns Hopkins University Press.

Wiedemann, Thomas (1986), "The *Fetiales*: a Reconsideration," *Classical Quarterly* 36: 478–90.

Wiesehöfer, Josef (2007), "From Achaemenid Imperial Order to Sasanian Diplomacy: War, Peace, and Reconciliation in Pre-Islamic Iran," in Raaflaub 2007a, 121–40.

Wiesehöfer, Josef (2009), *Ancient Persia from 550 BC to 650 AD*, trans. Azizeh Azodi, London and New York: I.B. Tauris.

Wilcken, Ulrich (1942), *Über Entstehung und Zweck des Königsfriedens*, Berlin: Akademie der Wissenschaften.

Wilker, Julia, ed. (2012a), *Maintaining Peace and Interstate Stability in Archaic and Classical Greece*, Mainz: Verlag Antike.

Wilker, Julia (2012b), "War and Peace at the Beginning of the Fourth Century. The Emergence of the *Koine Eirene*," in Wilker 2012a, 92–117.

Williams, Jennifer M., et al. (2004), "Why do Male Chimpanzees Defend a Group Range?" *Animal Behaviour* 68(3): 523–32.

Winter, Frederick E. (1971), *Greek Fortifications*, London: Routledge.

Wittke, Anne-Maria, et al., eds. (2009), *Historical Atlas of the Ancient World: Brill's New Pauly Supplements, Volume 3*, Leiden: Brill.

Wolfthal, Diane (1999), *Images of Rape: The "Heroic Tradition" and its Alternatives*, Cambridge: Cambridge University Press.

Woolf, Greg (1993), "Roman Peace," in Rich and Shipley 1993: 171–94.

Woolf, Greg (2015), "Mars and Memory," in Karl Galinsky and Kenneth Lapatin (eds.), *Cultural Memories in the Roman Empire*, 206–24, Los Angeles: J. Paul Getty Museum.

Woolf, Greg (2016), "Conquering with Efficiency." *Wall Street Journal*, September 9. Available online: http://www.wsj.com/articles/conquering-with-efficiency-1473456506 (accessed January 22, 2017).

Worley, Leslie J. (1994), *Hippeis: the Cavalry of Ancient Greece*, Boulder: Westview Press.

Worthington, Ian, ed. (2012), *Alexander the Great: A Reader*, 2nd edn, London and New York: Routledge.

Wycherley, Richard E. (1957), *The Athenian Agora III: Literary and Epigraphical Testimonia*, Princeton: The American School of Classical Studies at Athens.

Xenophon (1966), *A History of My Times (Hellenica/Hellenika)*, trans. Rex Warner, London: Penguin Books.

Yates, Robin D.S. (1999), "Early China," in Raaflaub and Rosenstein 1999: 7–45.

Yates, Robin D.S (2007), "Making War and Making Peace in Early China," in Raaflaub 2007a, 34–52.

Yates, Robin D.S (2016), "Searching for Peace in the Warring States: Philosophical Debates and the Management of Violence in Early China," in Raaflaub 2016a, 98–121.

Yates, Robin D.S (forthcoming), "China before the Unification," in Meissner, Raaflaub, and Yates (forthcoming).

Zanker, Paul (1988), *The Power of Images in the Age of Augustus*, Ann Arbor: University of Michigan Press.

Ziolkowski, Adam (1992), *The Temples of Mid-Republican Rome and their Historical and Topographical Context*, Rome: L'Erma di Bretschneider.

CONTRIBUTORS

Sheila L. Ager is Professor of Classical Studies at the University of Waterloo and Research Associate with the Waterloo Institute for Hellenistic Studies in Waterloo, Canada. She is the author of *Interstate Arbitrations in the Greek World, 337–90 BC* (Berkeley, 1996) and co-editor (with Riemer Faber) of *Belonging and Isolation in the Hellenistic World* (Toronto, 2013); she has published numerous articles, book chapters, and encyclopedia entries on ancient Greek and Roman diplomacy, peaceful conflict resolution, and Hellenistic history. She is also an Area Editor (Hellenistic World) for Wiley-Blackwell's *Encyclopedia of Ancient History*.

Sarah Bolmarcich is a multi-year lecturer in the School of International Letters and Cultures at Arizona State University and has previously taught at the University of Michigan and the University of Texas at Austin. She works on international relations in the ancient Greek world, and has published numerous articles, book chapters, and encyclopedia entries on the topic in such venues as Wiley-Blackwell's *Encyclopedia of Ancient History*, *The Oxford Encyclopedia of Ancient Greece and Rome*, and the journals *Greek, Roman, and Byzantine Studies*, *Historia*, *Chiron*, and *Classical Quarterly*.

Paul Burton is Senior Lecturer in the Centre for Classical Studies at the Australian National University in Canberra, Australia, and Research Associate with the Waterloo Institute for Hellenistic Studies in Waterloo, Canada. He is the author of *Friendship and Empire: Roman Diplomacy and Imperialism in the Middle Republic (353–146 BC)* (Cambridge, 2011) and *Rome and the Third Macedonian War* (Cambridge, 2017). He has published numerous articles on topics ranging from George Orwell and the Classics to the reception of Classics in film and political and popular culture. He is also a contributing editor to Wiley's *Encyclopedia of Diplomacy*.

Craige B. Champion is Professor of Ancient History in the Maxwell School of Citizenship and Public Affairs at Syracuse University in Syracuse, NY, USA. His research focuses on cultural and political interactions, particularly the interplay between the Greek and Roman worlds. He is the author of *Cultural Politics in Polybius's Histories* (Berkeley, 2004) and *The Peace of the Gods: Elite Religious Practices in the Middle Roman Republic* (Princeton, 2017); editor of *Roman Imperialism: Readings and Sources* (Wiley, 2004); and one of the General Editors of Wiley-Blackwell's *Encyclopedia of Ancient History* (2013).

Jason Crowley is Senior Lecturer in Ancient History at the Manchester Metropolitan University in Manchester, UK. His main area of research is the psychology of combat, particularly the close-quarters combat favored by the classical Greeks. His book, *The Psychology of the Athenian Hoplite: The Culture of Combat at Classical Athens* (Cambridge, 2012), applies modern theories of combat motivation to the ancient world;

subsequent publications have explored both the human experience of war and the way it is portrayed in the ancient historian Thucydides.

Judith Fletcher is Professor of History and Ancient Studies at Wilfrid Laurier University and Research Associate with the Waterloo Institute for Hellenistic Studies in Waterloo, Canada. In addition to numerous articles on Greek poetry and drama, she is the author of *Performing Oaths in Classical Greek Drama* (Cambridge, 2011), *Myths of the Underworld in Contemporary Culture* (Oxford, 2019) and co-editor (with Alan Sommerstein) of *Horkos: The Oath in Greek Society* (Liverpool, 2007) and (with Bonnie MacLachlan) *Virginity Revisited* (Toronto, 2007).

Lynette Mitchell is the Professor of Greek History and Politics at Exeter University in Exeter, UK. She is the author of three monographs—*Greeks Bearing Gifts: The Public Use of Private Relationships in the Greek World, 435–323 BC* (Cambridge, 1997); *Panhellenism and the Barbarian in Archaic and Classical Greece* (Swansea, 2007), and *The Heroic Rulers of Archaic and Classical Greece* (Bloomsbury, 2013)—and editor or co-editor of three more volumes. She has written about women in the ancient world, as well as a number of articles on ancient Greek history and Greek politics.

Kurt A. Raaflaub is David Herlihy University Professor and Professor of Classics and History Emeritus at Brown University in Providence, RI, USA. His research focuses on both ancient Greece and Rome, in particular on the subjects of warfare and peace. Publications include *The Discovery of Freedom in Ancient Greece* (Chicago, 2004), *Origins of Democracy in Ancient Greece* (co-authored, Berkeley, 2007), and, among (co-)edited volumes, *War and Society in the Ancient and Medieval Worlds* (Harvard, 1999), *War and Peace in the Ancient World* (Wiley, 2007), *Peace in the Ancient World: Concepts and Theories* (Wiley, 2016), and *The Landmark Julius Caesar* (Pantheon, 2017).

Cecilia Ricci is Associate Professor of Roman History and Latin Epigraphy at the University of Molise in Campobasso, Italy, and President of the Course of Literature and Cultural Heritage and Director of her University Language Centre. She is the author of numerous publications on the history and culture of ancient Rome: *Il Monumentum familiae Statiliorum. Un riesame* (co-authored with M. Letizia Caldelli; Quasar, 1999); *Qui non riposa. Cenotafi antichi e moderni fra memoria e rappresentazione* (Quasar, 2006); *Soldati, ex soldati e vita cittadina: l'Italia romana* (Rome, 2010); and *Security in Roman Times. Rome, Italy and the Emperors* (Routledge, 2018).

Julia Wilker is Associate Professor of Classical Studies at the University of Pennsylvania in Philadelphia, PA, USA. Her main research interests include the history of Hellenistic-Roman Judaea and interstate relations in late classical and Hellenistic times. She has published monographs on the Herodians and the province of Judaea (*Für Rom und Jerusalem: Die herodianische Dynastie im 1. Jahrhundert n. Chr.*, Verlag Antike, 2007) and the role of women in the Judaean dynasties. Her edited and co-edited volumes include *Maintaining Peace and Stability in Archaic and Classical Greece* (Verlag Antike, 2013) and *Amici—Socii—Clientes? Abhängige Herrschaft im Imperium Romanum* (2015).

INDEX

Abbasid Caliphate 155
Achaian League 23, 133, 158, 159, 162
Achaimenid dynasty (Persia) 8, 85, 113, 141, 146, 147, 149, 171
Achilles (Homeric warrior and prince) 4, 6, 89
    shield of 53, 71, 89–91, 92, 96, 97, 104
Adea Eurydike (granddaughter of Philip II) 64
Aeneas (Trojan prince, founder of the Roman people) 13, 28–9, 75, 101, 142, 170
Aeneas Tacticus 10
Agamemnon (Homeric ruler of Mycenae) 4, 84, 144
ager publicus (public land) 135
Ahhiya(wa) 144–6
Aigina 59
Aischines (Athenian politician) 20, 62
Aitolian League 115–16, 151, 158, 159, 162
Alcibiades (Athenian politician) 45–6, 112
Alexander III ("the Great") of Macedon 6, 52, 54, 64, 68, 85, 113, 116, 132, 141, 149, 150, 155, 159, 163
Alexander IV of Macedon 64
Alkidamas (Greek philosopher) 44
alliance(s) 4, 12, 14, 16, 24, 28, 52, 53, 59, 67, 83, 84, 85, 99, 109, 111, 112, 113, 116, 119, 131–2, 134, 135, 136, 137, 142, 143, 151, 154, 156–8, 162, 171
Amalasuintha (Gothic queen) 66
Amazons 60, 64, 65
amicitia. See friendship, international
anarchy 8–9, 52, 108, 109, 119, 123, 125, 144, 150, 151, 159, 160
Anchises (father of Aeneas) 13, 28–30, 120, 170
Andokides (Athenian orator) 21, 113
andrapodismos (mass enslavement) 128, 142, 170
andreia (masculine courage) 58, 64
Andromache (wife of Hektor) 9, 53, 55, 56, 69
Antigonos I Monophthalmos 14, 157, 162
Antigonos III Doson of Macedon 157

Antiochos III ("the Great"; Seleukid king) 11–12, 32–3, 116–19, 143, 151, 159, 170
Antiochos IV (Seleukid king) 170
Antonine dynasty (Rome) 121, 141
Antonius, M. (Marc Antony) 12, 64, 77, 78, 99, 141
Apama, wife of Seleukos I 65
Apameia, Peace (Treaty) of 32–3
Aphrodite 92. *See also* Venus
Apollo 4, 52, 73, 80, 93, 156
Appian (Greco-Roman historian) 134, 149
apragmōn, apragmosynē (passivity) 24, 45–6
Ara Pacis Augustae (Altar of Augustan Peace) 57, 80–1, 101–2, 138, 168, 170
Arabs 34, 155, 170
arbitration 7, 12, 15, 22, 23, 52, 90, 91, 107, 126–7, 158–9, 169
archē. See empire(s)
Archidamos (king of Sparta) 111
Ares 4, 57, 74, 84, 92, 163, 164, 165, 166. *See also* Mars
aretē (valour, excellence) 43, 59
Arete (Homeric queen of the Phaiakians) 69
Argos 15, 20, 21, 60, 61, 62, 112, 126, 128, 156
Aristagoras (tyrant of Miletos) 1
Aristophanes 4, 10, 53, 55, 57, 58, 68, 70, 72, 95–9, 107, 108, 110, 112, 119, 165, 169
    Acharnians 10, 53, 72, 96
    Birds 108
    Lysistrata 10, 53, 55, 57, 58, 65, 68–9, 70, 72, 97–9, 112, 163, 165
    Peace (*Eirēnē*) 4, 10, 53, 57, 72, 97, 107, 112, 169
Aristotle 44, 46, 54
    Politics 44, 46
Arkadia, Arkadian League 7, 23
Armenia, ancient 33, 141
Arsinoë II (member of Ptolemaic dynasty) 64, 65
Artaphernes (Persian satrap) 12
Artaxerxes II of Persia 22, 112, 113, 157

198 INDEX

Artemisia I of Karia 64
Asia Minor 1, 12, 21, 32, 112, 117, 146, 154, 157, 159, 170
Assyria 6
asylia (inviolability) 8
Athalaric (Gothic ruler) 66
Athena 4, 68, 69–70, 74–5, 84, 126, 165, 166. *See also* Minerva
Athens 1, 4, 6–7, 9, 10, 14, 15, 20, 21, 22, 24, 34, 43, 44, 45, 46, 51, 53–4, 59, 61–2, 65, 68, 72–5, 93–9, 107–8, 111–13, 125, 126, 128, 129, 131, 132, 144, 156–7, 164, 166, 169
Attalos I of Pergamon 12
Audata of Illyria (wife of Philip II) 64
Augustine, Saint 7, 87
    City of God 7, 87
Augustus 12, 30, 31, 67, 76–83, 85, 88, 99–102, 119–21, 138–9, 141, 151, 161, 167, 168, 170
Aurelius Antoninus, M. (Marcus Aurelius) 119, 152, 153
autonomia ("having one's own laws", internal sovereignty) 14, 15, 22, 113, 116, 128, 134, 157, 158
Avars 7, 34, 123, 154–5
Aztecs 40, 41, 42, 49, 50

Babylonia 15, 62, 146
Bacchylides (Greek poet) 71–2, 73, 92–3
Baghdad 155
balancing 127, 132, 156
bandwagoning 128, 132
Battle of
    Actium (31 BCE) 12, 99, 115, 138, 167
    Aigospotamoi (405 BCE) 112
    Cannae (216 BCE) 116
    Carrhae (53 BCE) 120, 141
    Chaironeia (338 BCE) 52, 113, 132
    Himera (480 BCE) 66
    Kadesh (1274 BCE) 48
    Kynoskephalai (197 BCE) 116
    Lake Regillus (c. 493 BCE) 26, 114, 133–4
    Magnesia (189 BCE) 117
    the Margus River (285 CE) 103
    the Milvian Bridge (312 CE) 7
    Philippi (42 BCE) 79
    Plataia (479 BCE) 1
    Salamis (Cyprus) (306 BCE) 133
    Salamis (Greece) (480 BCE) 1, 64, 129
    Thermopylai (480 BCE) 1, 128
    Zama (202 BCE) 116

Bellona 76, 85
bellum iustum. See war, just
Berenike (sister of Agrippa I) 66
Berenike II (wife of Ptolemy III of Egypt) 66
Boiotia, Boiotian League 23, 98, 159
Brasidas (Spartan military commander) 97, 111
Byzantium (Byzantion) and Byzantine Empire 3, 16, 17, 23, 33, 34, 103, 122, 142, 152, 154–5, 163, 170

caduceus (herald's staff) 57, 100–1, 102
Caesar, C. Julius 16, 26, 32, 76, 77, 80, 100, 101, 141, 166, 168
Calgacus (Caledonian warleader) 14, 27–8, 121, 122, 151
Calpurnius Piso Frugi, L. (Roman historian) 78
Cambyses II of Persia 147
Camilla (mythic female warrior in Vergil's *Aeneid*) 65, 165
Caracalla (Roman emperor) 121, 141, 152
Carthage 28, 60, 66, 84, 115–16, 136–7, 138, 164, 165
Cassiodorus (late Roman historian) 66
Çatal Hüyük 40
cavalry 130–1
Celsus (Greek philosopher) 87
Celts (Italy) 136
Ceres 80, 101–2. *See also* Demeter
Charlemagne 2–3, 7, 16, 154, 155
Charles Martel (Carolingian ruler) 154
Chamberlain, Neville 19
China, ancient 6, 40, 42, 48–9, 155
Chios 23
Chremonides decree 65
Christianity 7, 8, 86–8, 122–3, 152, 154, 155, 161
Cicero 26, 27, 31, 46–7, 85, 151
    On Duties 47, 151
    On the Consular Provinces 27
    On the Laws 46–7
    On the Republic 46, 151
    Second Catilinarian Oration 26
civitas (citizenship) 134, 135, 136, 138, 152, 160
Claudius Caecus, Ap. (Roman politician) 76
Clement of Alexandria 87
Cleopatra VII of Egypt 12, 78, 85, 99
clientela 33, 116, 140–1. *See also* friendship, international
Clovis (Merovingian ruler) 154

INDEX

collective security 9, 11, 14, 15, 128
Commodus (Roman emperor) 121
common peace 14–15, 22–3, 24, 52, 112–13, 123, 157, 160, 162, 170, 171
concordia (harmony) 11, 41, 57, 66–7, 76–7, 80, 103–5, 138
Concordia (personification/goddess of harmony) 41, 57, 67, 68, 76, 77, 80, 103, 166, 167
Confucius (Chinese philosopher) 42
Constantine I ("the Great") 7, 87, 103, 122–3, 152–3, 161
Constantinople. *See* Byzantium (Byzantion)
Constantius Chlorus (Roman emperor) 103
constitutio Antoniniana 120, 152
Constructivism 108–11, 112, 123
Corcyra 10, 24, 53, 61, 62, 111, 127, 131
Corinth 15, 24–5, 45, 54, 86, 92, 98, 111, 112, 113, 116, 126, 127, 131, 157
Cornelius Scipio Barbatus, L. (Roman politician) 115
cornucopia 57, 95, 101, 103
Cortés, Hernán 51
Crassus, M. Licinius (Roman politician and commander) 141
Cyprus 22, 133, 144, 157
Cyrus II ("the Great") of Persia 9, 43, 57, 62–3, 146, 147, 171

Damarete (wife of Sicilian tyrant Gelon) 66, 70
Darius I ("the Great") of Persia 1, 12
Darius III of Persia 149
deditio (unconditional surrender) 13, 26
Delian League 14, 156–7, 160
Delphi 22, 52
Demeter 72, 95, 97, 102, 161. *See also* Ceres
Demetrios I Poliorketes 14, 73–4, 133, 157, 162, 170
democracy 10–11, 42, 51, 53, 93, 96, 128, 161
Demosthenes (Athenian politician) 59, 62, 112–13,
Diadochoi (Successors of Alexander the Great) 116, 132, 141, 149–50, 159
diallagē (reconciliation) 57, 98, 164
dicio (power, dominion) 26
Dido (queen of Carthage in Vergil's *Aeneid*) 28
Dikaiopolis (comic hero of Aristophanes' *Acharnians*) 96
Dikē (goddess of justice) 53, 57, 71, 92, 107

Diocletian (Roman emperor) 7, 103, 122, 152–3
Diodoros (Greek historian) 165
Dionysios II of Syracuse 136
Dionysios of Halikarnassos (Greco-Roman historian) 7
Dionysos 93, 95, 96, 99, 164
diplomacy 4, 15–16, 20, 21, 23, 26, 33, 34, 35, 52, 65–6, 68, 108, 109, 110, 113, 115, 116, 117, 118, 120, 123, 127, 133, 136, 138, 140–2, 146, 151, 155, 160, 163
Domitian (Roman emperor) 27

Egypt, ancient 4–6, 12, 15, 40, 42, 47–8, 62, 63, 64, 66, 78, 81, 118, 144, 146, 147, 150, 154, 155
Einhard (Frankish historian) 3, 7
eirēnē (peace) 9, 10, 11, 20, 21–3, 57, 89
Eirēnē (personification/goddess of peace) 53, 57, 71–5, 77, 86, 89, 92–9, 102, 104, 107, 164, 165, 166, 169
ekecheiria (truce) 162, 168
Eleusinian Mysteries 20, 95. *See also* Demeter; Persephone
eleutheria (freedom) 128
Elis 7, 20, 68, 165
empire(s) and imperialism 1, 2, 6, 12–14, 16, 21, 23, 27–8, 31–2, 33–4, 35, 48–51, 77–83, 87–8, 89, 99–100, 119–23, 137, 143–55, 157, 160, 161, 163. *See also* Byzantium (Byzantion) and Byzantine Empire; Persian Empire; Roman Empire
Ephesos 100, 170
epimachia (defensive alliance) 131
Epiros 61, 85, 159
Eris (goddess of strife) 163
Esther (wife of Ahasuerus (Xerxes I)) 66
Etruscans 137, 156
Eumenes II of Pergamon 32–3
Eunomia (goddess of good laws) 53, 57, 71, 92, 93, 104, 107, 169
Euripides 9, 43, 53, 58, 62, 65, 72, 107–8, 112
  Iphigeneia in Aulis 43
  Medea 58
  Orestes 53
  Suppliants 53, 65
  Trojan Women 9, 53, 62, 107, 112
European Union 23, 162

200 INDEX

Eutropius (late Roman consul) 65
Evander (ally of Aeneas in Vergil's *Aeneid*) 28–9

Felicitas (personification of blessedness, happiness) 80
fetiales (fetial priests) 7, 46, 76, 85
feuding 39, 154, 158, 159
fides (good faith) 13, 77, 109
Flamininus, T. Quinctius (Roman politician and commander) 116–17, 170
foedus. *See* alliance(s); treaties.
foedus Cassianum 26, 114, 133
Franks 3, 7, 16–17, 154
freedom of the Greeks 116, 159, 170
friendship, international 4, 15–17, 28–9, 109, 127, 131, 151
Frontinus (Roman politician and author) 10
Fulvia (wife of M. Antony) 64

Gaia 83. *See also* Tellus
Galerius (Roman emperor) 103
Gallienus (Roman emperor) 32
Gaul 26, 27, 31, 162
Germans 3, 12, 16, 33, 34, 99, 140, 152, 153, 168
Geta (Roman emperor) 121
Gorgias (Greek philosopher) 54, 162
Gorgo (daughter of Kleomenes I, queen of Sparta) 66
Goths 66, 122, 154
Gracchus, C. Sempronius (Roman tribune) 135, 138
Gracchus, T. Sempronius (Roman tribune) 135, 138

Hannibal (Carthaginian military commander) 115–16, 119, 134, 137
Harun al-Rashid (Abbasid Caliph) 3, 155
Hattusili III (Hittite ruler) 48
hegemon, hegemony 24, 73, 109, 112, 113, 114, 115, 119, 120, 128, 151, 156–8, 159, 160, 162
hegemonic peace 28, 163
Hektor (Homeric warrior and prince of Troy) 9, 53, 55, 56, 69, 91
Hekuba (Homeric queen of Troy) 62
Helen (Homeric queen of Sparta, lover of Paris of Troy) 20, 89, 144
Helios 83
Hellenic League(s) 14, 126, 156, 157, 160
Hephaistos 89, 90, 91, 92
Hera 57, 68, 84. *See also* Juno

Herakleitos (Greek philosopher) 53, 59
Herakles (Hercules) 6
Hermes 57, 97
Herodotos (Greek historian) 1, 6, 9, 12, 20, 21, 34, 43, 46, 53, 57, 59, 125, 146, 164
Hersilia (Sabine woman) 66–7, 70, 165
Hesiod (Greek poet) 53, 57, 71, 72, 91–2, 163, 169
  Works and Days 53, 91–2, 163
  Theogony 53, 57, 71, 92, 163
hēsychia (peace, tranquility) 20, 24–5, 46, 162
Hiero II of Syracuse 115
Hippocrates, Hippocratic corpus 42–3
Hitler, Adolf 19
Hittites 15, 48, 144–6
Holy Roman Empire 33
Homer (Greek poet) 1, 9, 20, 21, 51, 53, 55, 57, 59, 69, 89, 99, 104, 107, 144, 163, 169
  Iliad 4, 6, 9, 20, 51, 52, 53, 55, 71, 74, 84, 89–91, 104, 144
  Odyssey 69, 91, 99, 146
homonoia (concord) 11, 53, 71, 164
hoplite (Greek infantryman) 51, 58, 97, 129–30
Horace (Roman poet) 77, 100
Horai (Eirēnē, Dikē, Eunomia) 71, 72, 92, 107
hostages 19, 32, 33, 115, 163
Huns 6, 7, 65, 122, 123
Hypatia (Greek female philosopher) 66

Imbros 22
imperialism. *See* empire(s)
imperium. *See* empire(s)
Incas 40, 42, 50
India, ancient 42, 92, 117, 161
Indians, American 39, 40, 41, 42
Institutionalism 14, 52
international law 3, 7, 109, 126–7, 161
International Relations theory 8–9, 14, 107–11, 114, 119, 123, 143–4
Ionian Revolt 1, 6, 12, 66
Islam 8, 123, 155, 160
Isokrates (Greek speechwriter and philosopher) 10, 23–5, 34, 46, 54, 73, 93, 113, 162
Israel, ancient 42, 48
Isthmian proclamation 116–17

Janus, Temple of 29, 78–9, 100, 115, 138
Jason (mythic Greek warrior) 58

INDEX

201

Jericho 40
Jesus Christ 7, 86, 168
Jews, Judaism 8, 12–13, 66, 81, 120, 161
Josephus (Jewish historian) 13, 66
Juno 76. *See also* Hera
Jupiter 76, 167. *See also* Zeus
Justinian I (Byzantine emperor) 16, 66, 154

Kallimachos (Greek poet) 66
Kalypso 91
Kassandreia 64
Kavadh I (Sassanid ruler) 16
Kephisodotos (Greek sculptor) 57, 72, 77,
    94–5, 99, 102, 169, 170
Kimon (Athenian politician and general) 107
King's Peace 14, 22, 34, 112, 113, 157
kings, Hellenistic 4, 11–12, 14, 15, 16, 23, 52,
    64–6, 73–4, 114, 117–19, 133, 149–51.
    See also marriage, diplomatic
kinship, international 4, 15–16, 109, 125. *See
    also* marriage, diplomatic
Klazomenai 22
Kleisthenes (Athenian politician) 156
Kleomenes I of Sparta 62, 66, 68
Kleon (Athenian politician and general) 10,
    96–7, 111, 162, 165
koinē eirēnē. See common peace
koinon (pl. *koina*). *See* alliance(s); leagues,
    federal; Achaian League; Aitolian League
Kos 23
Kroisos (ruler of Lydia) 9, 57
Kronos 91
Kynnane (daughter of Philip II) 64

Lamachos (Athenian general) 10
Latins, Latin League 26, 28, 114, 156
Latinus (ruler of the Latins in Vergil's *Aeneid*)
    28
law, international. *See* international law
League of Corinth 24, 54, 113, 157
League of Nations 14, 52
leagues, federal 23, 114, 133, 137, 151, 156,
    158–9, 162, 170
Lemnos 22
Leo III (Pope) 3, 154
Licinius I (Roman emperor) 122
limes (border, frontier) 140–1, 153
Livia (wife of Augustus) 67, 70, 165
Livy (Roman historian) 7, 26, 66, 78, 104
Lokroi Epizephyroi 73, 100
Lucius Verus (Roman emperor) 141
Lucretius (Roman poet) 47

Lykourgos (Athenian politician) 59
Lysander (Spartan military commander) 112
Lysimache (Athenian priestess of Athena
    Polias) 68, 98
Lysimachos (ruler of Thrace, Macedon, and
    Asia Minor) 64, 65

Macedon, ancient 6, 23, 64, 113, 115, 132,
    133, 137, 138, 151, 158
maiestas 30, 138–9, 142, 171
Mamertines 115
Mantinea 20
Marathon (Attica) 1–2, 6
Mardonios (Persian military commander) 59
marriage, diplomatic 65–6
Mars 4, 75–6, 79–80, 81, 114, 115, 166, 167.
    See also Ares
    Mars Ultor 76, 79–80
masculinity 4, 39, 52, 58, 115, 127
Massagetai 62, 164
Maurice (Byzantine emperor) 34, 154
Maxentius (Roman emperor) 7, 87
Maximian (Roman emperor) 103
Mayans 40, 42, 50
Medea (sorceress and wife of Jason in Greek
    myth) 58
mediation 15, 142, 159
Melos 9, 44, 45, 61–2, 107, 128, 142, 144,
    162
Mencius (Mengzi; Chinese philosopher) 42
Menelaos (Homeric king of Sparta; husband
    of Helen) 20, 84, 144
Mesopotamia 40, 42, 48, 144–6
Messana (Sicily) 115
Messene (Greece) 159
Miletos 1, 65
militarism 4, 52, 109–10, 114, 115, 117–18,
    121, 127, 133, 150,
Minerva 80. *See also* Athena
Minoans 144
Minos (mythical king of Crete) 144
Mittani 146
Moche 40, 50
Mongols 6
monotheism 7–8, 86–8, 122–3, 155, 160
Muhammad 155
Mussolini, Benito 101
Mycenae, Mycenaeans 51, 144–6

Napoléon Bonaparte 163
Nero (Roman emperor) 33, 78–9, 81, 100–1,
    139, 141–2, 167

Nestor (Homeric king of Pylos) 20
neutrality 4, 22, 24–5, 111, 127–8, 132
Nikē (goddess of victory) 74, 164
Nikias (Athenian politician and general) 45–6, 107
Nikias, Peace of 20, 21, 23, 34, 96, 107, 111
nomos (law, custom) 43, 44
North Atlantic Treaty Organization 14, 143
Numa (early king of Rome) 78

oaths 12, 20, 21, 23, 31, 33, 83–4, 85, 98, 127
Octavian. *See* Augustus
Odoacer (Germanic (?) commander, first King of Italy) 122, 153
Odysseus (Homeric ruler of Ithaka) 91
oikos (home, household) 58, 59, 69
oligarchy 10–11, 53, 54, 128
Olympia 7, 22
Olympias (wife of Philip II and mother of Alexander the Great) 64, 68
Olympic Games 7
Olympic truce 7, 20, 168
Opora (Harvest) 93–4, 95, 97, 169
Origen (early Christian writer) 86–7
Ovid (Roman poet) 100

Pallas (ally of Aeneas in Vergil's *Aeneid*) 28–9
Palmyra 63
Panhellenism 22, 23–5, 34, 109, 125, 162
Paris (Homeric prince of Troy; lover of Helen) 20, 84, 89
Parthia and Parthians 6, 12, 32–3, 120, 140–2, 167
pax (peace) 25–8, 32, 41, 57, 66–7, 89, 105, 151
Pax (personification/goddess of peace) 32, 41, 57, 71, 76, 77–83, 86, 99, 100, 102, 103, 168
pax Romana/pax Augusta 12, 28, 30–1, 77–83, 99, 120, 123, 138, 151–2, 160, 163, 168
Peace of Antalkidas. *See* King's Peace
Peace, Temple of (Vespasian) 57, 81–3, 161, 168
Peloponnesian League 128, 156
peltast (light-armed Greek infantryman) 130
Pepin the Short (Carolingian ruler) 154
Perdikkas II of Macedon 65
Perikles (Athenian politician and general) 45, 53, 58, 111, 125, 170, 171
Persephone 97
Perseus of Macedon 159

Persian Empire 1, 6, 8, 10, 12, 21–2, 23–4, 34, 43, 45, 46, 54, 85, 132, 141, 146–9, 154–5, 156, 157, 163, 170
Phaiakians 69, 91, 99
phalanx (hoplite formation) 129–30
Pharaoh. *See* Egypt
Pharnabazos (Persian satrap) 21–2
Pheretime of Cyrene 62, 69
philia. See friendship, international
Philip II of Macedon 23–5, 35, 51–2, 54, 62, 64, 65, 85, 112–13, 132, 157
Philip III Arrhidaios of Macedon 64
Philip V of Macedon 84, 115–16, 118–19, 137
Phraates IV of Parthia 141
physis (nature) 42–3, 44, 46
Pindar (Greek poet) 92
Pisa (Greece) 68, 165
Plataia 60
Plato 9, 10, 11, 46, 54, 161
    Laws 9, 10, 11, 161
    Republic 10
Pliny the Elder (Roman writer) 30
Pliny the Younger (Roman writer) 13, 31
Ploutos (god of wealth) 57, 71–2, 94–5, 102, 107, 165, 169, 170
Plutarch (Greco-Roman essayist) 59, 64
    Antony 64
    Sayings of Spartan Women 59
polemos (war) 9, 11, 57, 59
Polemos (personification/god of war) 57, 59, 72, 97
Polyainos (Greek writer) 10
Polybios (Greek historian) 4, 108, 114, 115, 118, 134, 136, 159, 170
polypragmosynē (meddlesomeness) 46
pomerium (sacred boundary of the city of Rome) 76, 139
Poseidon 84
Praetorian Guard 139
Procopius (Byzantine historian) 66, 78
provinces, Roman 12, 13, 139–40, 151–3
Ptolemy II of Egypt 65
Ptolemy V of Egypt 118
Ptolemy Keraunos 64, 65, 114, 170
Pylos 96
Pyrrhos of Epiros 60, 85, 135, 136

Qin Shihuangdi (Chinese emperor) 49, 161

Ramesses II (Egyptian pharaoh) 48
Ramesses III (Egyptian pharaoh) 4–6
Ravenna 153

INDEX

Realism and (Neo)-Realism 9, 14, 107, 107, 108–11, 114, 123, 144,
Red Cross 52
Remus (mythic founding hero of Rome) 75, 102, 114
Rhandeia, Treaty of 32–3
Rhea Silvia (mother of Romulus and Remus) 101–2
Rhodes 23, 137
Roman Empire 8, 12, 27–8, 77–83, 119–23, 140–2, 151–53, 161
Roman Republic 7, 10, 78, 99, 109, 114, 115–19, 133, 136, 137, 151
Romulus (mythic founding hero of Rome) 66–7, 75, 102, 114, 167
Romulus Augustulus (Roman emperor) 122, 153
Roxane of Baktria (wife of Alexander the Great) 149

Sabine women 66–7, 115
Sallust (Roman historian) 47
Salus (personification/goddess of health and well-being) 76, 80
Samnites 26, 27, 76, 114
Sassanid dynasty (Persia) 12, 16, 33, 123, 140–2, 152, 154–5
satrap, satrapy 12, 21, 143, 146–9
Sea Peoples 4–6, 146
Second Athenian Sea League 112, 157, 170
securitas 80, 138
Seleukos I (Seleukid ruler) 65, 114, 170
Selinous 60
Semiramis (Shammuramat, Assyrian queen) 62–4, 164
Severus, L. Septimius (Roman emperor) 121, 141
Sicarii 13
Sicilian Expedition, 45–6, 62, 97, 108
Sidicini 27
siege warfare 131, 133
Skyros 22
slaves, slavery 9, 39, 43, 44, 46, 61–2
Slavs 123, 154–5
socius and *societas. See* alliance(s).
Sparethe (Sakian woman) 62
Sparta 1, 6–7, 10, 14–15, 20–5, 34, 45, 51, 53, 59, 65, 66, 73, 83, 93–9, 111–12, 113, 126, 127, 128, 130, 132, 144, 156–7, 159, 169, 171
spondai (libations; treaties) 20–2, 23, 83, 96, 162, 169

stasis. See war, civil
Stephen II (Pope) 154
Sulla, L. Cornelius (Roman politician and commander) 100
Sulpicius Galba, P. (Roman politician and commander) 116
Sumeria 15, 146
Sunzi (Sun Wu, Sun Tzu; Chinese writer) 10
The Art of War 10
symmachia (defensive/offensive alliance) 131, 136, 156–8, 160, 162
syngeneia. See kinship, international
synoikismos ("living together", political amalgamation) 72, 93–4, 156
synthēkai 23
Syracuse 115, 137

Tacitus (Roman historian) 13–14, 27–8, 33, 100, 104, 121, 151, 162
Agricola 13–14, 27–8, 121, 151, 162
Telesilla (Argive female poet) 62, 164
Tellus (Roman Mother Earth) 101–2
Teos 11–12
Tertullian (early Christian writer) 86–7
tetrarchy (four-emperor rule) 7, 103–5, 122, 152–3
Thebes (Greece) 51, 112–13, 126, 132, 157
Themis (mythic mother of the Horai) 57, 71, 92, 107
Theodahad (Gothic ruler) 66
Theodora (Byzantine empress, wife of Justinian I) 66
Theodosius I (Roman emperor) 153
Thessalian League 159
Thetis (mythic mother of Achilles) 89
Thirty Years' Peace 15, 20, 21, 23, 111
Thucydides (Greek historian) 6–7, 10–11, 20, 21, 44–6, 53, 57, 62, 96, 104, 108, 109, 111–12, 125, 128, 131, 144, 162
Tiberius (Roman emperor) 120, 166
Tiberius II Constantine (Byzantine emperor) 34
Tibullus (Roman poet) 77
Timotheos (Athenian general) 73, 94–5
Timotheos of Miletos 93
Tiridates I of Armenia 141
Tomyris (queen of the Massagetai) 62–4, 146, 164
Trajan (Roman emperor) 13, 31, 140
tranquillitas 138
treaty, treaties 4, 14, 15, 19, 20–1, 22, 26, 27, 31, 32, 33, 34, 46, 48, 65, 83, 84, 85, 93, 95, 96, 97, 98, 99, 100, 109, 111,

112, 113, 116, 119, 123, 127, 131, 133,
134, 136, 137, 138, 142, 151, 154, 156,
157, 158, 159, 160, 162, 163, 169
trireme 52, 131
Troy, Trojans 9, 20, 28, 53, 55, 62, 69, 84, 89,
91, 107, 112, 142, 144, 146
Trygaios (comic hero of Aristophanes' *Peace*)
4, 57, 72, 97
Turnus (Rutulian warrior, enemy of Aeneas in
Vergil's *Aeneid*) 28
Tyche (Fortune) 118

Udjahorresnet of Egypt 147–8
Umayyad Caliphate 155
United Nations 14, 15, 38, 52
United States 6, 143
Union of Soviet Socialist Republics 6, 143

Vandals 122, 154
Vegetius (late Roman writer) 27
Venus 75, 76, 80, 101–2, 167. *See also*
Aphrodite
Vergil (Roman poet) 10, 13, 27–8, 31, 65, 99,
104, 121, 151, 161–2, 170
Aeneid 13, 27–8, 65, 99, 104, 121, 151,
161–2, 170
Eclogues 10
Georgics 10
Versailles, Treaty of 19
Vespasian (Roman emperor) 81–2, 168
Victoria (goddess of victory) 76, 101
Vologeses I of Parthia 33

war
civil 10–11, 12, 44, 53–4, 76–8, 81, 99,
151, 152, 154, 159, 160, 164, 167

defensive/offensive 6, 10, 27
just 6–7, 10, 15, 46, 47, 85, 87, 99, 137,
161, 162, 163, 168
War(s)
Archidamian 20, 111
Corinthian 112, 132
First Macedonian 115
First Peloponnesian 20
First Punic 78, 115, 136, 137
First World 19
Peloponnesian 6–7, 10–11, 14, 15,
20–1, 42, 51, 53, 72, 93–9, 107,
111–12, 125, 127, 132, 156–7, 164,
169
Persian 1, 6, 24, 42, 51, 56, 107, 125, 128,
129, 132
Perusine 64
Roman-Parthian 33
Samnite 26, 76
Second Macedonian 116, 119, 159
Second Punic (Hannibalic) 115–16, 134–5,
137
Second World 19, 107, 143
Social (Greece) 115–16
Social (Italy) 135, 170
Vietnam 110
Warsaw Pact 143

Xenophon 21–2, 65
Xerxes I of Persia 1, 6, 43, 64, 125, 146
Xunzi 42

Zenobia (queen of Palmyra) 63–4, 164
Zeus 4, 52, 53, 55, 57, 71, 74, 83–4, 92, 97.
See also Jupiter
Zoroastrianism 8, 155